The Supreme Court

Second Edition

The Supreme Court

Second Edition

Lawrence Baum
Ohio State University

A division of Congressional Quarterly Inc.
1414 22nd Street N.W. Washington D.C. 20037

Printed in the United States of America

Library of Congress Cataloging in Publication Data

Baum, Lawrence.
  The Supreme Court.

  Bibliography: p. 251.
  Includes indexes.
  1. United States.   Supreme Court.   I. Title.
KF8742.B35   1985   347.73'26   84-23864
ISBN 0-87187-343-5   347.30735
ISBN 0-87187-327-3 (pbk.)

To my parents
Ruth Klein Baum and Irving Baum

Preface

I began the preface to the first edition of *The Supreme Court,* published in 1981, by asserting that the Supreme Court stands at the center of American life. Since then, the Court certainly has not declined in importance. It continues to play a major role in resolving policy issues, issues as diverse as the rights of criminal defendants and government policy toward corporate mergers. And the Court in recent years has been a focus of national attention, even an issue in presidential contests.

The Supreme Court, second edition, attempts to provide an understanding of that important political institution. The book is intended to serve students as a short but comprehensive source on the Supreme Court. It also is meant both to serve the needs of other people who would like to learn more about the Court and to provide a general reference source on the Court. I have intended this book to be useful to people with a wide range of backgrounds, from readers with little prior knowledge of the Supreme Court to experts on the Court. The book describes the basics of the Court's workings, but it also offers explanations for the behavior of the Court and of people and institutions that affect the Court. In addition, the book addresses issues about the Court that have concerned and divided scholars.

The basic approach and organization of the second edition are similar to those of the first. Throughout this edition, however, I have taken into account events and developments of the 1980s. While there have been no fundamental changes in the Supreme Court in the past five years, the Court has not remained exactly as it was. For instance, conflict among the justices over policy and procedure has become more open, and in a more conservative Congress efforts to overturn Court decisions of the 1960s and 1970s have accelerated. Perhaps most important, there are hints that the Court is beginning to take a more strongly conservative position in its own policies. These changes are reflected in my descriptions and explanations of processes involving the Court. I also have made use of new material on the Court from scholarly and other sources, material that offers additional insights into this institution.

The first chapter of the book, "The Court," serves as an introduction. It discusses the Court's role in general, examines the place of the Court in the judicial system, and takes a first look at the Court as an institution and at its history.

Each of the remaining five chapters deals with one important set of topics. Chapter 2 examines the justices: their selection, their personal characteristics, and under what circumstances they leave the Court. Chapter 3 discusses the process by which cases reach the Court and are chosen for full decision; the chapter's final section addresses the Court's caseload and efforts to deal with the problem of too many cases.

In Chapter 4, "Decision Making," I look at the Court's process of decision in the cases that it decides fully. After outlining the decision-making procedures, I turn to the primary concern of the chapter, the factors that influence the Court's choices among alternative decisions and policies. Chapter 5, "Policy Outputs," has several concerns: the kinds of issues on which the Court concentrates, the policies that it supports, and the extent of its activism in policy making. I examine all of these subjects as they stand today and as they have changed over time, and I seek to explain important patterns in Supreme Court policy. The final chapter, "The Court's Impact," deals with how the Court's decisions are treated by other government policy makers and with the decisions' impact on American society. The chapter is a fitting conclusion to the book, because the Court's ultimate significance depends on the effects of its decisions.

In the first edition I offered my thanks to a great many people who helped me in writing the book. This edition continues to reflect their help. I remain especially grateful to Jean L. Woy for initiating the project and for her work as editor.

I have benefited from a good deal of additional help in revising the book for this edition. Bradley Canon of the University of Kentucky and my colleague Elliot Slotnick at Ohio State University offered a great many helpful suggestions for the revision and improvement of the book. Amy Nolan and Brian Prokop provided research assistance that facilitated my efforts. As always, the political science department at Ohio State University made my work easier in a variety of ways; for that help I should thank Randall B. Ripley, chair of the department, and William Lydon, its administrative associate.

I owe more specific thanks to those who provided me with information that I needed for the book's revision. Toni House, the Supreme Court's Public Information Officer, verified several pieces of information about the Court for Chapter 1. Karen O'Connor and Lee Epstein of Emory University shared with me and allowed me to use the insights gained from their current research on interest groups and the Court for Chapter 3. Richard Pacelle of Indiana University was particularly generous in allowing me to make extensive use of his research findings on the Court's agenda for Chapter 5.

I appreciate the considerable help that I have received from CQ Press in the development of this second edition. Susan Joseph was primarily responsible for the book's editing, and Mary Ames Booker supervised its final production. Nola Healy Lynch played a crucial and very helpful role in both the editing and the production processes. Joanne D. Daniels provided the continuing direction and encouragement that were needed to see this project through.

All of these people have my thanks for making this book possible and for making it better than it would have been without their help.

Contents

The Supreme Court

Second Edition

The Court 1

In recent years a good deal of political discussion and activity has focused on the United States Supreme Court. Opponents of its rulings on abortion and school prayer have undertaken major campaigns to overturn those decisions. Newspapers have given headline treatment to the Court's decisions on home videotaping and on congressional vetoes of administrative rules. One important issue in the 1984 presidential election was what types of justices each candidate could be expected to appoint to the Supreme Court over the next four years and what the effects of those appointments would be on the direction taken by the Court.

In a sense, it is striking that a court should be of such interest in the political arena. Yet recent interest in the Supreme Court is nothing new; throughout most of American history since the adoption of the Constitution, the Court has been a major topic of political concern. Nor should this interest be surprising, in light of the critical role that the Court plays through its decisions. The Supreme Court helps to resolve many of the most important and controversial issues in the United States, and in doing so it shapes government policy in areas as diverse as civil rights and environmental protection.

The role that the Supreme Court plays makes it important to understand this institution. Who are the people that serve on the Court, and how do they get there? How is it determined which cases and issues the Court decides? In resolving the cases before it, on what bases does the Court choose between alternative decisions? In what policy areas is it active, and what kinds of policies does it make in those areas? Finally, what happens to the Court's decisions after they are handed down, and what effects do those decisions actually have?

This book is an effort to provide an understanding of the Supreme Court by answering these questions. Each question will be the subject of one of the chapters that follow. This chapter introduces the book by taking a general look at the Court, supplying the necessary background for the more detailed discussions that constitute the remainder of the book.

A Perspective on the Court

The Court in Law and Politics

The Supreme Court as a Political Body. People often speak of courts as if they are, or at least ought to be, "nonpolitical." In a literal sense, of course, this is impossible. Courts are an integral part of government, so they are political institutions by definition. But many people believe that courts are not political in the way that we generally speak of politics: they are removed from the mainstream of the political process, and they are not influenced by partisanship and other presumably petty considerations.

Popular though this view of the courts may be, it is simply inaccurate. The Supreme Court is "political" in a variety of ways. Most of the people appointed to the Court have been active participants in politics, and appointments frequently are the subject of considerable political contention. Interest groups often help to bring cases to the Court. The justices' perceptions of public and congressional opinion affect the Court's decisions. Those decisions themselves often lead to major controversies in government and the nation at large, and the justices may be attacked by members of Congress and other political leaders who disagree with their policies.

Thus it is impossible to understand the Supreme Court except in the context of the political process, a perspective I will take throughout this book.

The Court as a Legal Institution. As a political body, the Supreme Court is similar to other government institutions, such as Congress and administrative agencies. Yet it would be a mistake to view the Court as identical to those other, nonjudicial policy makers. The Court's behavior and its position in the political system are affected in fundamental ways by the fact that it is a *court*.

First of all, the Supreme Court makes decisions within the framework of the law. The policy choices that the Court faces are framed as matters of legal interpretation. In this respect the Court's task differs from that of Congress and of some administrative agencies, and the legal context in which the justices work provides a constraint from which legislators are free.

Furthermore, the widespread belief that the Court should be nonpolitical leads to a certain degree of actual insulation from the political process. Supreme Court justices are given lifetime appointments that allow some freedom from concerns about public approval. Most justices remain fairly aloof from partisan politics; open involvement in partisan activity is perceived as illegitimate. Because most people view direct contact between lobbyists and justices as unacceptable, interest group activity in the Court is restricted primarily to formal channels of legal argument.

For these reasons, the Supreme Court should be viewed as a legal institution as well as a political one. What it does and how it operates are influenced both by the political process and by the legal system. Such an ambiguous position makes the Court more complex in some ways than most political institutions, and it also helps to make the Court an interesting case study in political behavior.

The Court as a Policy Maker

This book will be concerned with the Supreme Court in general, but it will give particular emphasis to the Court's role in the making of public policy—the authoritative rules by which government institutions seek to influence the operation of government and to shape society as a whole. Legislation to provide subsidies for wheat farmers, a trial judge's sentence of a convicted criminal, and a Supreme Court decision laying down rules of procedure for an administrative agency are all examples of public policy. Thus the Court may be viewed as part of a policy-making system that includes lower courts as well as the legislative and executive branches of government. It will be useful at this point to look at some important aspects of the Court's policy-making role.

Policy Through Legal Interpretation. As I have noted, the Supreme Court makes public policy through the interpretation of provisions of law. Issues of public policy come to the Court in the form of legal questions that the Court is to resolve. In this respect the Court's policy making differs fundamentally in form from that of Congress.

The Court does not face legal questions in the abstract. Rather, the Court addresses these questions in the process of settling specific controversies between parties ("litigants") that bring cases to it. In a sense, then, every decision by the Court has three levels: a judgment about the specific dispute brought to it, an interpretation of the legal issues involved in that dispute, and a position on the policy questions that are connected to the legal issues.

In a specific dispute, the Court determines how the parties to the case should be treated. In a tax case it may decide whether a business must pay taxes claimed by the Internal Revenue Service. In a criminal case it may choose to uphold a conviction, or it may overturn the conviction while allowing a retrial of the defendant. As this second example indicates, the Court often does not determine the final outcome of a case for the parties but instead directs a lower court in its further consideration of the case.

The Court's treatment of the parties is tied to its interpretation of the legal issues in the case. Some legal issues involve the interpretation of federal statutes, and statutory issues dominate many economic fields. The Court may rule in favor of a taxpayer on the basis of its reading of a section of the federal tax code. About half of the Court's decisions, including most of its decisions in civil liberties fields, rest on interpretations of the Constitution. In these cases the Court's task usually is to determine whether some government policy violates a provision of the Constitution. The Court may uphold the conviction of a criminal defendant on the ground that a disputed search for evidence in the case did not violate the Fourth Amendment.

Finally, the Court's legal interpretations also express policy positions, explicit or implicit. An interpretation of the Fourth Amendment may establish a position favorable to the search powers of law enforcement agencies. Often the Court's policy positions emerge most clearly from a series of decisions, such as a string of decisions in environmental law that support rigorous enforcement of environmental regulations. The positions that the Court establishes in a field such as tax law comprise part of the body of policy made by the various government institutions which work in that field.

The Court's Significance in Policy Making. Through its interpretation of law the Supreme Court plays a very important role in the policy-making system of the federal government. The significance of that role is illustrated by some of the Court's major decisions during the 1970s and early 1980s:

—In *Roe v. Wade* (1973), the Court drastically limited the power of states to prohibit abortions.[1] Over the succeeding decade the Court struck down a variety of state laws regulating abortions but upheld legislation that limited government funding of abortions.[2]

—In a series of decisions, the Court first struck down the capital punishment laws of most states and then approved selectively a new set of death penalty statutes.[3]

—In a 1983 decision the Court held unconstitutional a provision that allowed Congress to veto certain decisions of the Immigration and Naturalization Service. In doing so the Court called into question more than one hundred legislative veto provisions through which Congress had sought to exert control over the president and the bureaucracy.[4]

—In *Sony Corporation v. Universal City Studios* (1984), the Court held that the sale of videotape recorders to consumers did not violate the copyright laws. By doing so the Court provided at least a temporary resolution of a major legal battle among industries over a new technology.

—Most important in its immediate effect was the Court's decision in *United States v. Nixon* (1974), perhaps the pivotal event in the process that led to the resignation of President Nixon.

The Court's development of this role has been based on a favorable conjunction of circumstances. As the French observer Alexis de Tocqueville noted more than a century ago, "Scarcely any political question arises in the United States that is not resolved, sooner or later, into a judicial question." [5] Policy disputes tend to reach the courts largely because of the existence of a written Constitution, whose provisions provide a basis for challenges to the legality of government actions. Because so many major policy questions come to the courts, the Supreme Court has the chance to rule on a large number of significant policy questions. Moreover, for much of its history the Court has welcomed that opportunity, first insisting on its supremacy as legal arbiter in the early nineteenth century and later making frequent use of its chances to speak on major issues. By doing so, of course, the Court has encouraged the tendency to bring major policy issues to it.

Reaction to the Court's Role: Activism vs. Restraint. Inevitably, the Court's involvement in deciding major issues of public policy has led to controversy. Some of this controversy concerns the substance of the Court's decisions. Legal scholars debate the merits of the Court's rulings in relatively genteel terms. Supreme Court policies also are subject to less genteel discussion in the political arena, as exemplified by criticism of Court decisions on school prayer and abortion.

More fundamentally, people disagree about the Court's general role as a policy maker. That disagreement has taken many forms, but frequently it centers on the dichotomy between judicial activism and judicial restraint. The term *judicial activism* is used in many ways; one key element of the concept is a court's willingness to make significant changes in public policy, particularly in policies established by other institutions. [6] The most visible element of judicial activism is the issuance of decisions that overturn legislative and executive policies, but activism can take other forms. Judicial restraint is simply the avoidance of activism.

Some members of the Supreme Court, such as the late Felix Frankfurter, and some commentators, such as legal scholar Raoul Berger, argue strongly for restraint. [7] In their view, the Court should work to limit its role in policy making and particularly to minimize its interference with the policies of the other branches. Supporters of judicial restraint attack activism on several grounds, of which three are especially important: activism is illegitimate because the Court is a relatively undemocratic institution; it is risky because the Court is vulnerable to attack when it takes controversial positions; it is unwise because courts lack the capacity to make effective policy choices.

Others, such as scholar Arthur Selwyn Miller and federal judge J. Skelly Wright, defend and support judicial activism. Some proponents of activism see it as a duty under the Constitution. Perhaps most important, proponents of activism see an activist Court as protecting fundamental values, such as liberty, that may be ignored elsewhere in government. Largely for this reason, the supporters of activism applaud the Supreme Court's assertion of a major policy-making role in civil liberties in the last 30 years—a development that many advocates of judicial restraint have criticized.

As we would expect, views about activism and restraint often reflect evaluations of the Court's decisions. Liberals who argued for judicial restraint in the 1920s and 1930s when the Court attacked government regulation of the economy later approved the Court's activism in defense of civil liberties in the 1960s. Today judicial activism continues to be used primarily to support liberal policies, so it is not surprising that conservatives generally advocate judicial restraint. Indeed, President Reagan has been a strong supporter of restraint. But the debate over judicial activism is more than a dispute about the Court's policies. The Supreme Court's involvement in the making of important public policies raises fundamental questions about the appropriate role of a court, questions that transcend the substance of the Court's decisions at a given time.

Limitations on the Court as a Policy Maker. The debate over activism and restraint underlines the importance of the Supreme Court's part in the policy-making process. But the Court's role in policy making is inherently limited by several factors. First, there is only so much that the Court can do with the rather small number of decisions that it makes each year. In the average year, the Court hands down decisions with full opinions in approximately 150 cases. In contrast, federal administrative agencies published about the same number of regulations in the first six working days of 1984. In deciding such a small number of cases, the Court addresses only a select set of policy issues. Inevitably, there are whole fields of policy that it barely touches. Even in the fields in which the Court does act it can deal only with a limited number of the disputes that exist at a given time.

Second, even the most activist-minded justices support judicial restraint in some situations. This support stems in part from judges' training in a legal tradition that emphasizes the value of restraint, and in part from practical considerations. Judicial self-restraint is reflected in the Court's refusal to hear some important and controversial cases, such as the legal challenges brought against American participation in the war in Vietnam.[8] Another reflection of judicial restraint is a set of guidelines that the Court frequently uses to avoid deciding constitutional issues where it is possible to decide or dispose of a case on another basis. These guidelines are listed in a frequently cited opinion by Justice Louis Brandeis in *Ashwander v. Tennessee Valley Authority* (1936).

Finally, even a highly activist Court is limited in its impact by the actions of other policy makers. The Court seldom is the final policy maker to deal with the issues that it addresses. A decision to desegregate school systems must be implemented by lower courts and school boards, which retain some discretion in determining how the decision will go into effect. Congress can overcome the Court's interpretations of the tax laws by amending those laws. The difference between what the Court rules on an issue and the public policy that ultimately results from government action on that issue may be considerable.

For these reasons, those who see the Supreme Court as the dominant force in American government probably are wrong. But if not dominant, the Court does play a very important part in the policy-making process. Certainly the extent of its role in that process is extraordinary for a court.

The Court in the Judicial System

In some respects the Supreme Court is unique among the courts of the United States. But it is also part of a system of courts, and it cannot be understood except in the context of that system. Accordingly, it is important to examine the structure of courts and the Supreme Court's place in that structure.

Structure of the System

Strictly speaking, it is inaccurate to refer to a single court system in the United States. In reality, the courts are divided between the federal system and a separate system in each state.

The federal system may be distinguished from the state systems in terms of jurisdiction, the power to hear and to decide a class of cases. Most of the jurisdiction of the federal courts can be placed in three categories. First are criminal and civil cases that arise under federal laws, including the Constitution. Second are all cases to which the United States government is a party. Finally, in civil cases involving citizens of different states, if the amount in question is at least $10,000, either party may bring the case to federal court; otherwise, it will be heard in state court. Only a small minority of all cases fall into these categories. In 1982 about 240,000 cases were brought to the primary federal trial court, while 2.7 million came to the trial courts of a single state, California.[9] The average federal case, however, is more significant than the average state case.

State Court Structure. The states vary considerably in the structures of their court systems. But a few general patterns can be described, and these are illustrated in Figure 1-1. Most states have two sets of trial courts, one to handle major criminal and civil cases and the other to deal with minor cases. Major cases on the criminal side usually are those defined under the law as felonies, while major civil cases are those

Figure 1-1.　Most common forms of state court structures

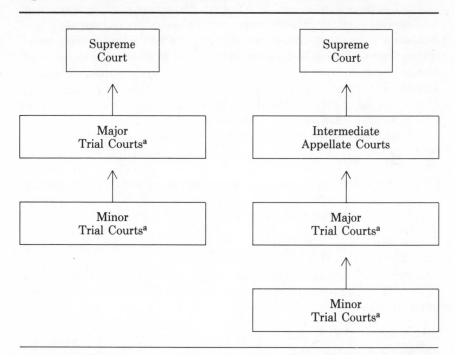

---

[a] In many states, major and/or minor trial courts are composed of two or more different sets of courts. For instance, minor trial courts in California include Municipal Courts and Justice Courts.

NOTE: Arrows indicate most common routes of appeals.

---

involving relatively large sums of money. Most often, appeals from decisions of minor trial courts are heard by the major trial courts. A few states have a single comprehensive trial court.

Courts that hear primarily appeals—appellate courts—are structured in two different ways. These alternative structures are illustrated in Figure 1-1. In about one-third of the states, including most of the less populous states, there is a single appellate court; this is usually called the state supreme court. All appeals from major trial courts go to this supreme court. The other two-thirds of the states have a set of intermediate appellate courts below the supreme court. These intermediate courts initially hear most appeals from major trial courts. The state supreme court may be required to hear certain appeals brought directly from the trial courts or from the intermediate courts, but for the most part it has discretionary jurisdiction over appeals from the decisions of the intermediate courts. The term *discretionary jurisdiction* means simply that a court has the right to hear some appeals and to refuse to hear others.

Federal Court Structure. The structure of federal courts is shown in Figure 1-2. The base of the federal court system is the federal district courts. There are 94 district courts in the United States, one to four in each state along with a court in the District of Columbia and in some of the territories. The district courts hear all federal cases at the trial level, except for a few specialized classes of cases that go to the Tax Court, the Court of International Trade, and the Claims Court.

Above the district courts are the 12 courts of appeals. Each court of appeals has jurisdiction over appeals in one of the federal judicial circuits. The District of Columbia constitutes one circuit, while the other 11 each include three or more states. Appeals from the district courts in a circuit generally go to the court of appeals for that circuit, along with appeals from the Tax Court and from some administrative agencies. Patent cases and some claims against the federal government go from the district courts to the specialized Court of Appeals for the Federal Circuit, as do appeals from the Claims Court and Court of International Trade.

The Supreme Court stands at the top of the federal judicial system. The Court's jurisdiction requires a detailed examination, which follows in the next subsection.

The Court's Jurisdiction

The jurisdiction of the Supreme Court is summarized in Table 1-1. That authority can be divided into two parts. First, the Constitution gives the Supreme Court jurisdiction over certain specified classes of cases as a trial court, what is called original jurisdiction; those cases may be brought directly to the Court. The Court's original jurisdiction includes some cases to which a state is a party and cases involving ambassadors. Disputes between two states can be heard only by the Supreme Court. Other cases under the Court's original jurisdiction can be heard alternatively by a district court. Relatively few cases come to the Court in this way.

Second, under its appellate jurisdiction the Court may hear cases brought by parties dissatisfied with decisions of the federal courts of appeals and the specialized appellate courts in the federal system. The Court may hear cases brought directly from the district courts in certain cases in which an act of Congress was held unconstitutional. Cases also may come directly from special three-judge district courts that are set up to hear a few classes of cases designated by Congress.

Cases can come to the Supreme Court after decisions by the state supreme courts if they involve claims under federal law or the Constitution. More precisely, a case can come to the Court from the highest state court with the power to hear it. The case of *Thompson v. City of Louisville* (1960) was brought to the Court directly from the police court

Figure 1-2. Basic structure of federal court system

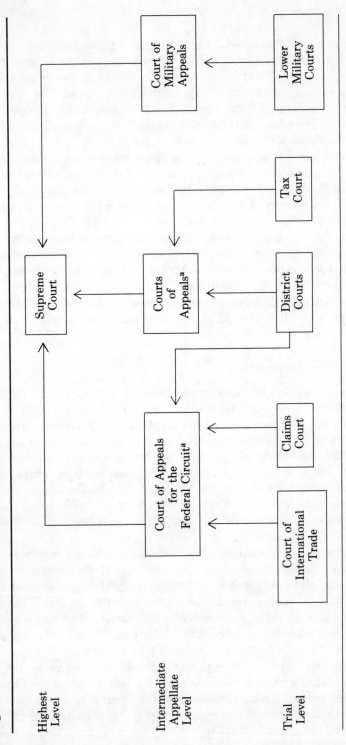

[a] These courts also hear appeals from administrative agencies.

NOTE: Arrows indicate most common routes of appeals. Some specialized courts of minor importance are excluded.

Table 1-1. Summary of Supreme Court jurisdiction

I. Original jurisdiction
    A. Mandatory cases (must be heard by the Court)
        1. Disputes between states
    B. Discretionary cases (Court need not hear)
        1. Cases brought by a state
        2. Disputes between a state and the federal government
        3. Cases involving foreign diplomatic personnel

II. Appellate jurisdiction[a]
    A. Mandatory cases
        1. Cases in which a federal court has held an act of Congress unconstitutional, if the federal government is a party; any cases in which a state supreme court has held an act of Congress unconstitutional
        2. Cases in which a state court has upheld a state law against a claim that it conflicts with the Constitution or federal law
        3. Cases in which a federal court has overturned a state law on grounds that it conflicts with the Constitution or federal law
        4. Decisions of special three-judge federal district courts

    B. Discretionary cases
        1. All decisions of federal courts of appeals except those in mandatory categories
        2. All decisions of the highest state court with jurisdiction over a case, involving issues of federal law, except those in mandatory categories

---

[a] Some minor categories not listed.

of Louisville, Kentucky, because it involved a fine for loitering and disorderly conduct that was too small under state law to be appealed to any higher state court.

The rule by which state cases come to the Supreme Court may be confusing; as I noted earlier, cases arising under federal law ordinarily are brought originally to federal court rather than state court. However, cases that are brought to court on the basis of state law, so that they are heard in state court, frequently contain issues of federal law as well. This distinction can be illustrated with reference to criminal cases. A person who is accused of violating a state criminal law will be tried in a state court. But during the state proceedings the defendant may argue that rights under the Constitution were violated in a police search or interrogation. The case eventually can be brought to the Supreme Court on that issue. If so, the Court will have the power to rule only on the federal issue, not on the issues of state law involved in the case. The Court cannot rule as to whether the defendant actually violated a state criminal law.

For the most part, cases brought to the Court are under its discretionary jurisdiction. They come to the Court in the form of petitions for a writ of certiorari, a legal device by which the Court brings up the case for decision. Some classes of cases from lower courts are under the Court's mandatory jurisdiction; the Court must decide them. These cases are brought to the Court as "appeals." The Court has developed mechanisms by which it gives some appeals only limited consideration so that in practice their handling is similar to the handling of appeals.

The Supreme Court actually hears only a minute proportion of the cases brought to federal and state courts. Even within the federal court system, the Court hears fewer than 1 percent of the cases handled by the district courts. Moreover, the lower courts make important policies in the cases that they decide. In focusing our attention on the Supreme Court, we must be careful to avoid what Jerome Frank called the "upper-court myth," the belief that little of consequence happens at the lower levels of the court system.[10]

A First Look at the Court

The Court's Physical Structure

The Supreme Court did not move into its own building until 1935. Prior to that time the Court sat in quarters borrowed from other institutions. Originally the Court met in the Royal Exchange Building in New York, then the Old City Hall in Philadelphia. The Court moved to Washington with the rest of the federal government at the beginning of the nineteenth century. For the next 130 years the Court sat at various places in the Capitol, as a "tenant" of Congress. In 1860 the Court obtained "permanent" quarters in the old Senate chamber in the Capitol.

The Court's accommodations in the Capitol increasingly were regarded as inadequate. The justices lacked office space and did most of their work at home. Largely at the behest of Chief Justice William Howard Taft, Congress appropriated money for a Supreme Court building in 1929. The building was completed in 1935, but the justices who served at that time found their quarters in the building too opulent for their tastes. "What are we supposed to do, ride in on nine elephants?" one justice asked.[11] Some chose to continue working at home rather than to use their new chambers, which were occupied only as new justices came to the Court.

The Court's building *is* impressive. It occupies a full square block across from the Capitol and is five stories tall. The primary building material is marble, with liberal use of oak inside. The style is Corinthian, intended to give the Court building the same majesty as the neighboring congressional buildings. Not surprisingly, it has been referred to as a "marble palace."

The Court houses all the functions necessary for its operation as an institution. The most important rooms are on the first floor. The Court's formal sessions are held in the courtroom. The justices sit behind their bench at the front of the courtroom, with other participants and spectators in sections in the back and along the sides. Near the courtroom are the chambers that house offices for the associate justices and their staffs. Behind the courtroom is the conference room, where the justices meet to decide cases. The chief justice's chambers are attached to the conference room.

The Court's Personnel

The Justices. The Constitution requires that members of the Supreme Court be nominated by the president and confirmed by a majority of the Senate. It also establishes that they will hold office "during good behavior"—that is, for life unless they relinquish their posts voluntarily or are removed by impeachment proceedings. Beyond these basic rules, such issues as the number of justices, their qualifications, and their duties have been settled by law and tradition, rather than specified in the Constitution. The qualifications and selection of the justices will be covered in greater detail in Chapter 2.

We are accustomed to a Court of nine members, but the number of justices was changed several times during the Court's first century. The Judiciary Act of 1789 provided for six justices. Later statutes changed the number successively to five, six, seven, nine, ten, seven, and nine. The changes were made in part to accommodate the justices' duties in the lower federal courts, in part to serve partisan and policy goals of the president and Congress. The final change to nine members was made in 1869, and the Court has remained at that size; any further changes appear quite unlikely. In 1937 President Franklin Roosevelt's effort to gain ideological control of the Court by increasing the number of justices was defeated in part because the number nine had become well established.

As of 1984 the associate justices received salaries of $100,600, the chief justice $104,700. The primary duties of the justices, of course, involve participation in the collective decisions of the Court: determining which cases to hear, deciding the cases that they hear, writing and contributing to opinions.

Ordinarily, formal Court decisions are made by the full nine members. On occasion, however, fewer than nine justices sit on a case. During some periods the Court has had only eight members because a departing justice has not yet been replaced. A justice may miss some sessions because of poor health. Sometimes a member does not participate in a particular case because of a possible conflict of interest. Justices who have served as solicitor general, for instance, do not help to decide cases that they handled as solicitor. The individual justice alone decides whether it would be appropriate to participate in a case.

When only eight justices participate in a decision on the merits of a case, of course, the Court may divide 4-4. In the case of a tie vote, the lower court decision is left standing. Individual votes are not announced and no opinions are written. Nor are the legal issues in the case resolved, and the Court sometimes comes back to those issues in a later case.

A quorum for decision on a case is six members. The Court seldom fails to achieve a quorum, but in two related cases in 1983 four justices disqualified themselves, and the Court could not act.[12] This failure, like a tie vote, resulted in affirmance of the lower court decisions.

Along with their participation in collective decisions, the justices have decision-making functions as individuals, primarily in their service as circuit justices. The country always has been divided into federal judicial circuits. Since 1891 each circuit has contained a court of appeals whose members decide appeals from district court decisions. Originally, appeals within a circuit generally were heard by ad hoc courts composed of a federal trial judge and two members of the Supreme Court assigned to that area as circuit justices. The circuit duties were arduous, particularly before the development of modern transportation systems. The justices' "circuit-riding" responsibilities were reduced in several stages, the first coming in 1793, until they were eliminated altogether by the creation of the courts of appeals in 1891.

The 12 judicial circuits continue to have circuit justices assigned to them, with three justices doing double duty. The current duties of the circuit justices are largely ceremonial. However, the circuit justices have primary responsibility to deal with applications for special action, such as a request to stay a lower court decision (preventing it from taking effect) until the Court decides whether to hear a case. Typically, such an application goes first to the circuit justice. If the circuit justice rejects an application, under some circumstances it then can be made to another justice, but other justices usually concur with the circuit justice's rejection. A justice who has received an application during the Court's term, while other members are available, sometimes refers it to the Court as a whole.

This part of the Court's work has become more significant in recent years with an increasing number of requests to the Court to stay executions. Often these requests come very close to the scheduled time of execution, putting great pressure on the circuit justice or on the Court as a whole. In 1983 Justice Byron White issued one stay of execution half an hour before an execution scheduled for 1 a.m. Washington time.[13] Stays of execution have become a matter of contention within the Court, in part because of sharp disagreements about the death penalty itself. In 1983 the Court granted a stay of execution by a 5-4 vote; in 1984 it dissolved a lower court stay of execution by a 5-4 vote, and five different opinions were issued with the decision.[14]

The chief justice has special duties associated with the position. Some of these duties concern the Court itself, such as presiding over public sessions and conferences. Others concern the federal judicial system, such as chairing the Judicial Conference of the federal courts. Some chief justices have sought to exert leadership in the legal system as a whole. Warren Burger has been particularly active in this respect, serving as a vocal advocate for causes such as prison reform and new approaches to training for lawyers.

The justices may take on a variety of tasks external to the Court, officially or unofficially. A few have been pressed into official service by the president. In 1963, for instance, Earl Warren was selected to head the commission that investigated the assassination of President Kennedy. Justices also have consulted informally with presidents and members of Congress, worked with nongovernmental groups such as organizations of lawyers, and spoken and written about public issues.

A few justices have remained quite active in politics outside the Court. Recent books by Bruce Allen Murphy and by Nelson Lloyd Dawson describe the concerted but hidden efforts by Justice Louis Brandeis to influence government policy, using future justice Felix Frankfurter as a conduit for these efforts.[15] The secrecy of Brandeis's activity reflects the general feeling that justices should remain free from associations and activities that might compromise their objectivity, and this feeling seems to have become stronger over time.

Law Clerks and Other Support Staff. The justices are supported by a staff that now includes about 320 people. The largest group serves custodial and police functions under the marshal of the Court. About 30 people work for the clerk of the Court, who is responsible for clerical processing of all the cases that come to the Court. The reporter of decisions supervises preparation of the official record of the Court's decisions, the *United States Reports*. The librarian is in charge of the set of libraries in the Supreme Court building.

Each justice is served directly by secretaries and law clerks. (There also are a counsel and a staff counsel for the Court as a whole who examine certain special motions and applications to the Court.) The law clerks are the most important part of the support staff. In 1984 seven of the justices employed four clerks, while Justice William Rehnquist chose to use three and Justice John Paul Stevens only two. The clerks traditionally are recent law school graduates who have compiled exceptional records, primarily in prestigious schools. Most Supreme Court clerks in recent years already have served as clerks for judges in lower federal courts. Usually clerks serve a justice for one year, though some stay for two or more years. After leaving the Court, clerks frequently go on to distinguished careers. Among the 18 law clerks who worked in the 1957 term, by 1983 one was Deputy Secretary of State, a second was president of the American Civil Liberties Union, and a third was president of the Pacific Stock Exchange; three others were judges on state supreme courts and a federal court of appeals.[16] Three of the justices in 1984 (Rehnquist, Stevens, and White) once were law clerks in the Court.

Clerks serve their justices in several ways. Most clerks spend the largest part of their time on the petitions for hearing by the Court, digesting information in the petitions and lower court records and summarizing this information for the justices. Because of the large number of cases brought to the Court, this function is indispensable. The clerks also help with tasks such as the research work used as a basis for deciding cases that the Court has accepted for full consideration and for the drafting of opinions. Many justices give their clerks considerable responsibility for the actual writing of opinion drafts.

It is difficult to assess the influence of the clerks on the Court's decisions. Because so much work is delegated to clerks, it is inevitable that they have some impact on what the justices do. At the same time, most justices seem to work hard to retain control over their decisions. It seems likely, as Justice Rehnquist suggested after his own service as a clerk,[17] that law clerks have greater influence over decisions about which cases to hear than over decisions on the merits of the cases that the Court does hear. The availability of clerks as drafters probably encourages justices to write separate opinions expressing their own views in cases and increases the length and complexity of opinions.

The Court's Schedule

The Schedule by Year. The Court holds one "term" each year, which lasts from the first Monday in October until the business of the term is completed, usually in late June or early July. The term is designated by the year in which it begins. Prior to the beginning of the term, the justices meet to dispose of the large number of petitions for hearing that have accumulated during the summer. Once the term begins, new petitions are disposed of on a regular basis as they come to the Court.

Most of the term is divided into "sittings" of approximately two weeks and "recesses" of almost two weeks, sometimes longer. During the sittings the Court meets in open session and holds internal conferences. Some conferences are held during the recesses as well. The Court departs from this schedule in mid-May, holding one or more sessions each week for the rest of the term.

Early in the term the Court hears oral argument in cases but issues few decisions on argued cases, because the process of decision for most cases takes from several weeks to several months. Later the Court begins to hand down significant numbers of decisions. Oral argument for the term generally is completed by late April. From this point on the Court's sessions will be devoted chiefly to the announcements of its decisions. The term ends when the Court has reached and announced decisions in all the cases that it heard during the term. Cases that the Court accepted for hearings but that were not argued during the term are carried over until the next term.

During the summer the justices spend some time away from Washington but continue their work on the petitions for hearing that arrive at the Court. During that time the Court and individual circuit justices respond to applications for special action, and on rare occasions the Court holds a special summer hearing on an urgent case such as *United States v. Nixon* (1974). When the justices meet at the end of summer to dispose of the accumulated petitions, the cycle begins again.

The Schedule by Week. The schedule of activities during the week, like the annual schedule, is fairly regular. During the sittings, the Court holds sessions on Mondays, Tuesdays, and Wednesdays. In recent terms the most common pattern has been to hold sessions Monday through Wednesday of two weeks and Monday of the third week. As I noted, toward the end of the term one or more sessions is held each week to announce decisions in the form of orders and opinions.

The sessions generally are held from 10:00 a.m. until about 3:00 p.m. with a one hour break at noon. Oral arguments are held in each session except the last Monday of the sitting. They may be preceded by several types of business. On Mondays the Court announces the filing of its order list, which reports the Court's decisions on petitions for hearing and other action in its conference on the preceding Friday. Opinions in cases that the Court has resolved may be announced or read. New members of the Supreme Court bar, attorneys who may handle cases before the Court, are admitted early in the sessions.

The oral arguments consume most of the time of the sessions. Most often one hour is allocated for argument in a case, divided equally between the two sides. Thus the Court generally hears four cases in a session.

During sittings the Court holds two conferences each week. The Wednesday afternoon conference is used to discuss the cases that were argued on Monday. A longer conference on Friday includes discussion of the cases argued on Tuesday and Wednesday, as well as all the other matters that must be taken up by the Court. Most numerous of these matters are the petitions for hearing.

The Court also holds a Friday conference during the last week of each recess to deal with the continuing flow of business to the Court. The remainder of the justices' time during recess periods is devoted to their individual work: preparatory work on petitions for hearing and cases scheduled for argument, the writing of opinions, and reaction to other justices' opinions. These activities continue during the sittings, but less time can be devoted to them then.

The Court's History

This book is concerned primarily with the Supreme Court at present and in the recent past. However, to understand the current Court it is necessary on occasion to look to its history. To provide some context for the excursions into history later in the book, it will be useful at this point to examine some relevant highlights of Supreme Court history.

The Court from 1790 to 1865

The Constitutional Context. The Constitution explicitly created the Supreme Court, giving Congress discretion as to the creation of lower federal courts. But the Constitution said much less about what the Court would be than it did about Congress and the president. Article III laid out the Court's basic jurisdiction and gave Congress power to regulate the appellate part of that jurisdiction. The Constitution also indicated the mode of selection and the tenure of Supreme Court justices. Otherwise it was silent as to the Court's position in government and role in the making of policy.

The Judiciary Act of 1789, which set up the federal court system, used the Court's jurisdiction under the Constitution as a basis for granting it broad powers. The Court explicitly was given power to hear certain cases brought from lower federal courts as well as from state courts. It also was given power to direct action by federal judges and any other federal officials. Still, what the Court would do with its powers was uncertain, in part because the scope of those powers was somewhat ambiguous. Perhaps the most important of the uncertainties was the issue of judicial review: did the Court have the power to declare statutes or other government action void on grounds of inconsistency with the Constitution?

A Slow Start. During its first decade, between 1790 and 1799, the Court decided only about 50 cases. A few of these decisions were significant. The Court's ruling in *Chisholm v. Georgia* (1793) embroiled it in controversy; the decision, which allowed a citizen of one state to sue another state in federal court, was attacked and quickly overturned with passage of the Eleventh Amendment. In some other cases justices seemed to claim the power of judicial review, though they did not exercise that power clearly. But the Court was not yet a major participant in national policy making.

The Court's relative unimportance was reflected in matters of personnel. Several people rejected offers of nominations to the Court. Chief Justice John Jay and Justice John Rutledge left the Court for more attractive opportunities in state government.

John Marshall and Judicial Review. The rise in the Court's fortunes following this early period was directed by John Marshall, chief justice from 1801 to 1835. Marshall, a last-minute appointment by President John Adams, came to dominate the Court to a degree that no other justice has matched. He used his dominance to advance the policies that he favored as well as the position of the Court itself.

The key assertion of power by the Court under Marshall probably was its famous decision in *Marbury v. Madison* (1803), in which Marshall's opinion for the Court held a federal law to be unconstitutional and offered a justification for the Court's supremacy in interpreting the Constitution. A few years later Marshall also claimed the right of judicial review over state acts, and during his tenure the Court overturned more than a dozen state statutes on constitutional grounds.

The Court's aggressiveness brought denunciations and threats, including an effort by President Jefferson to secure the removal of at least one justice through impeachment. But Marshall's finesse helped to protect the Court from a successful attack. Gradually the powers that he claimed for the Court and the Court's central role in the policy-making process came to be accepted by the other branches of government and by the citizenry in general.

This acceptance was tested by the Court's decision in *Scott v. Sandford* (1857). Until that decision the Court had overturned only one federal statute, the minor law involved in *Marbury v. Madison*. In the *Dred Scott* case, however, Chief Justice Roger Taney held for the Court that Congress had exceeded its constitutional powers in adopting the Missouri Compromise prohibiting slavery in some territories. That decision was intended to resolve the legal controversy over slavery. Instead, the level of controversy increased and the Court was vilified in the North. Yet, although the Court's prestige suffered mightily, the Court itself and its basic powers survived without serious challenge. This survival demonstrated the success of the assertions of power that Marshall had undertaken.[18]

The Court and Federalism. During this period the Court was concerned with more than its own position. It addressed major issues of public policy as well. The primary area of its concern was federalism, the legal relationship between the national and state governments.

Under Marshall, the Court gave strong support to national powers. Marshall was especially interested in restricting state policy where that policy interfered with activities of the national government, especially its power to regulate commerce. His position was exemplified by *Gibbons v. Ogden* (1824), which overturned a state monopoly over steamboat transportation that impinged upon national control over interstate commerce, and by *McCulloch v. Maryland* (1819), which limited state power to tax a nationally chartered bank.

Marshall was succeeded by Chief Justice Roger Taney, who served from 1836 to 1864. During this period the Court's position was more complex and less uniformly favorable to the national government. Taney and his colleagues did not reverse the direction of the Court under Marshall, however. As a result the constitutional power of the federal government remained strong; the Court had subtly altered the lines between national and state governments in support of the former.

The Court from 1865 to 1937

Issues of Economic Regulation. In the first two decades after the Civil War, the Court was faced with several issues arising out of that conflict. The Court did not address the constitutionality of the Reconstruction policy of military control over the South, in part because Congress acted to limit the Court's jurisdiction in that area. However, the Court did rule against the use of military courts to try civilians in *Ex parte Milligan* (1866). In 1870 a narrow majority ruled that the Civil War policy of issuing paper money without backing in coin was unconstitutional in part. One year later, after two new appointments, the Court reversed its position. This abrupt shift later was cited by Chief Justice Charles Evans Hughes as one of the Court's "self-inflicted wounds." [19]

Gradually, however, the Court turned its attention primarily to issues of government authority to regulate private economic behavior. By the late nineteenth century, all levels of government had begun to adopt laws regulating business activities. Among those laws were the federal antitrust laws, state regulations regarding railroad practices, and federal and state laws concerning employment conditions. Inevitably, much of this legislation was challenged in the courts on constitutional grounds, and the Court's work in this area increased.

Early in this period, the Supreme Court's position on government authority to regulate business was quite mixed. But the Court increasingly became unfriendly to regulatory policies. That position was reflected in the development of constitutional doctrines that limited government powers to control business activities. Those doctrines were used with increasing frequency to attack regulatory legislation; in the 1920s, the Supreme Court held unconstitutional more than 130 regulatory laws.[20] Federal statutes were overturned because the Court viewed them as unsupported by the Constitution's grants of powers to Congress; state and local laws were overturned primarily as violations of economic rights protected by the Fourteenth Amendment.

The New Deal Conflict. This line of policy was criticized heavily by supporters of regulatory legislation. By the 1920s liberals freely attacked the Court for what they perceived as its friendliness toward business interests. However, the Court did not face a serious threat until the 1930s, when its majority brought it into direct conflict with President Franklin Roosevelt and the New Deal.

Roosevelt's program to combat the Great Depression included sweeping measures to control the economy. The Agricultural Adjustment Act was an effort to limit farm production in order to stabilize commodity prices. The National Industrial Recovery Act was established to bring about agreements on labor and trade practices within whole industries.

In a series of decisions in 1935 and 1936 the Court struck down these two acts and other federal recovery legislation, generally by 6-3 and 5-4 margins.[21] As a result, the New Deal program was weakened seriously. Inevitably, the Court was criticized with a new fervor. Roosevelt led the criticism, and after his overwhelming re-election in 1936 he proposed to deal with the situation through legislation under which an additional justice could be added to the Court for every sitting justice over 70 years old. The result would have been to increase the Court's size temporarily to 15, allowing Roosevelt to "pack" the Court with justices favorable to his programs.

While this plan was being debated in Congress, the Court took away most of the impetus behind it. In a series of decisions in 1937, the Court upheld New Deal legislation and similar state legislation by narrow margins, taking positions contrary to its collective views in recent cases.[22] This shift came because Chief Justice Hughes and Justice Owen Roberts changed their votes to establish majority support for the Roosevelt-sponsored legislation, and thereby turned the Court around. They almost surely did so in response to the conflict between the Court and the president and the resulting threat to the Court's autonomy. As a result of this shift, which became known as "the switch in time that saved nine," the Court-packing plan died.

A second event during the congressional debate was the resignation of one of the conservative justices. That resignation was followed by several others in the next few years, so that Roosevelt was able to obtain the ideological control of the Court that he had sought through the Court-packing legislation. The new Court created by his appointments accepted unequivocally the economic regulation that its predecessor had viewed unfavorably.

The Court from 1937 to the Present

A Shift to Civil Liberties Concerns. Since the Court's retreat in the late 1930s, it has continued to accept major government economic policies. The Court hears many cases involving economic regulation, but this field has become less important as part of its work and as a source of major decisions.

Instead, the Court's emphasis in the current era is on civil liberties. More precisely, the Court has focused primarily upon the interpretation of constitutional guarantees of protection for freedom of expression and freedom of religion, for the procedural rights of criminal defendants and other persons, and for equal treatment of racial minorities and other disadvantaged groups by the government. These issues had concerned the Court since the late nineteenth century, but not until the current era did they become the primary focus of the Court's work.

The Court's general position on civil liberties issues has varied a good deal during this period. That position has been especially sensitive to changes in the composition of the Court. The appointment of one or two new justices may affect the handling of civil liberties issues a great deal. The one constant factor has been the willingness of most justices to give serious consideration to claims of violations of civil liberties.

Activism in the Warren Court. The Court was most uniformly supportive of civil liberties and most activist in its policy making during the period in which Earl Warren was chief justice (1953-1969), particularly during the last half of that period. As a result, the policies of the Court during that period often are identified with Warren. However, other liberal justices played roles of at least equal importance. Especially important were Hugo Black and William Douglas, Roosevelt appointees who served through Warren's entire tenure, and William Brennan, an Eisenhower appointee.

Probably the best known decision of this period was *Brown v. Board of Education* (1954), which ordered a desegregation of Southern school systems and began the long process of desegregation that continues today. The Court also supported the rights of black Americans in several other areas of policy. During the 1960s, the Court expanded the rights of criminal defendants in state trials, most notably in landmark decisions on the right to counsel (*Gideon v. Wainwright,* 1963), police search and seizure practices (*Mapp v. Ohio,* 1961), and questioning of suspects (*Miranda v. Arizona,* 1966). The Court supported freedom of expression by expanding First Amendment rights in several fields, particularly obscenity and libel. In a series of cases beginning with *Baker v. Carr*

(1962), the Court required that legislatures be apportioned according to population.

These policies led to heavy criticism of the Court. In the late 1950s members of Congress attacked the Court for a series of liberal decisions, particularly those concerning the rights of allegedly subversive persons, and proposed legislative action against the Court. These proposals failed, in part because the Court engaged in a more limited version of its retreat in the New Deal period. The liberal policies of the 1960s drew further criticism in Congress and elsewhere. Some legal scholars joined in the criticism, charging the Court's majority with taking untenable positions and engaging in unjustified activism. The Court also had a good many defenders, and the level of controversy over its work reached a level unprecedented since the 1930s.

Partial Retrenchment in the 1970s and 1980s. Earl Warren retired in 1969 and was replaced as chief justice by Warren Burger, President Nixon's first appointment to the Court. Nixon made three more appointments in 1970 and 1971, producing a Court whose aggregate viewpoint was more conservative. The Court's membership was remarkably stable over the next dozen years, with only two appointments during that period. But both President Ford's 1975 appointment of John Paul Stevens and President Reagan's 1981 selection of Sandra Day O'Connor brought to the Court justices who were more conservative than their predecessors.

These changes did not make the Court's policies uniformly conservative, as some observers had expected. One collection of commentaries on the Burger Court was subtitled *The Counter-Revolution That Wasn't*.[23] Rather, the Court became less uniform and less predictable in its tendencies.

In some fields the Court did move in a conservative direction. In criminal procedure the Court became less sympathetic to defendants, interpreting procedural rights narrowly in a series of mostly undramatic decisions. For instance, it expanded the power of police officers to search automobiles without warrants in *United States v. Ross* (1982). In freedom of expression the Court's decision in *Miller v. California* (1973) gave government more power to regulate obscene materials, and the Court reduced protection of the mass media against libel suits in decisions such as *Wolston v. Reader's Digest Association* (1979).

Even in these fields there were important exceptions to the dominant pattern, and in other fields the Court was more favorable to civil liberties. It was in the 1970s that the Court gave its first significant support to legal equality for women, striking down a variety of laws that treated women and men differently. The Court showed a willingness to support other disadvantaged groups as well; that willingness was symbolized by its decision in *Plyler v. Doe* (1982), holding that the children of people who entered the country illegally have a right to a public education. In *Roe v. Wade* (1973), the Court virtually eliminated the power of states to prohibit abortions, and over the next decade it reinforced that decision by restricting the power of states to regulate abortions.

The Court's ruling in *United States v. Nixon* in 1974, along with the response to that ruling, underlined the Court's continued importance as an independent and powerful participant in the political process. The Court held unanimously that President Nixon must yield recordings of his conversations to a federal court and thereby overcame one of his last lines of defense against impeachment. The expectation of compliance with that decision was so great that Nixon had little choice but to comply, even though the result was to expose evidence fatal to his position. Beyond its immediate effects on the nation, the decision in this case demonstrated that the efforts begun by John Marshall to make the Court a major participant in national policy making had succeeded.

The Court's decision in *United States v. Nixon* was unusual in its unanimity; generally, the Court of the 1970s and early 1980s was deeply divided in major cases. That division reflected a close balance between liberals and conservatives, with a middle group of moderates who usually determined the Court's position. Meanwhile, the Court collectively had become relatively old in years. Thus it was not surprising that Court appointments became an issue in the presidential election of 1984, because the successful candidate might well have a chance to tilt the Court's balance in one direction or the other.

Notes

1. Full legal citations to cases mentioned in this book are provided in the Index of Cases.
2. *City of Akron v. Akron Center for Reproductive Health* (1983); *Harris v. McRae* (1980).
3. See *Furman v. Georgia* (1972) and *Gregg v. Georgia* (1976).
4. *Immigration and Naturalization Service v. Chadha* (1983).
5. Alexis de Tocqueville, *Democracy in America*, trans. Henry Reeve, rev. Francis Bowen (New York: Alfred A. Knopf, 1945), 1:280.
6. Bradley C. Canon, "A Framework for the Analysis of Judicial Activism," in *Supreme Court Activism and Restraint*, ed. Stephen C. Halpern and Charles M. Lamb (Lexington, Mass.: Lexington Books, 1982), 385-419.
7. The views on activism and restraint mentioned in this subsection are presented in *The Supreme Court in American Politics: Judicial Activism vs. Judicial Restraint*, ed. David F. Forte (Lexington, Mass.: D. C. Heath & Co., 1972); and in *Supreme Court Activism and Restraint*, ed. Halpern and Lamb. See also Raoul Berger, *Government by Judiciary: The Transformation of the*

Fourteenth Amendment (Cambridge: Harvard University Press, 1977); and Arthur Selwyn Miller, *Toward Increased Judicial Activism: The Political Role of the Supreme Court* (Westport, Conn.: Greenwood Press, 1982).

8. *Mora v. McNamara* (1967); *Massachusetts v. Laird* (1970); *Sarnoff v. Shultz* (1972).

9. These figures exclude federal bankruptcy cases and traffic and parking cases in the California courts. Administrative Office of the United States Courts, *1982 Annual Report of the Director* (Washington, D.C.: Government Printing Office, 1983), 92, 132; Judicial Council of California, *1983 Annual Report of the Administrative Office of the California Courts* (San Francisco, 1983), 97, 124.

10. Jerome Frank, *Courts on Trial* (Princeton: Princeton University Press, 1950), 222.

11. Richard L. Williams, "Supreme Court of the United States: The Staff That Keeps It Operating," *Smithsonian,* January 1977, 42.

12. *Arizona v. Ash Grove Cement Company* (1983); *Arizona v. United States District Court* (1983).

13. *Autry v. Estelle* (1983). The case is discussed in Linda Greenhouse, "New Issue 'Compelled' a Justice to Bar Execution, Despite Policy," *New York Times,* October 6, 1983, A1, A28.

14. *Stephens v. Kemp* (1983); *Woodard v. Hutchins* (1984).

15. Bruce Allen Murphy, *The Brandeis/Frankfurter Connection: The Secret Political Activities of Two Supreme Court Justices* (New York: Oxford University Press, 1982); Nelson Lloyd Dawson, *Louis D. Brandeis, Felix Frankfurter, and the New Deal* (Hamden, Conn.: Archon Books, 1980).

16. James F. Clarity and Warren Weaver, Jr., "High Court Graduates," *New York Times,* October 7, 1983, B9.

17. William H. Rehnquist, "Who Writes Decisions of the Supreme Court?" *U.S. News and World Report,* December 13, 1957, 74-75.

18. Robert G. McCloskey, *The American Supreme Court* (Chicago: University of Chicago Press, 1960), 98-100.

19. Charles Evans Hughes, *The Supreme Court of the United States* (Garden City, N.Y.: Garden City Publishing Co., 1936), 50. The cases were *Hepburn v. Griswold* (1870) and the *Legal Tender Cases* (1871).

20. That figure was calculated from data in Congressional Research Service, *The Constitution of the United States of America: Analysis and Interpretation* (Washington, D.C.: Government Printing Office, 1973).

21. The cases included *Carter v. Carter Coal Co.* (1936), *United States v. Butler* (1936), and *Schechter Poultry Corp. v. United States* (1935).

22. The cases included *National Labor Relations Board v. Jones & Laughlin Steel Corp.* (1937), *Steward Machine Co. v. Davis* (1937), and *West Coast Hotel Co. v. Parrish* (1937).

23. Vincent Blasi, ed., *The Burger Court: The Counter-Revolution That Wasn't* (New Haven: Yale University Press, 1982).

The Justices 2

The attention given to Supreme Court appointments in the 1984 presidential campaign underlines the importance of the Court's membership. What any policy-making body does is determined in part by the attitudes and perspectives of the people who serve in it. This is particularly true of the Supreme Court, whose members are relatively free from the electoral controls that legislators face and from the organizational constraints that limit the choices of administrators. Indeed, the single most important factor shaping the Court's policies at any given time may be the identity of its members.

This chapter is concerned with the members of the Supreme Court: their selection, backgrounds, and tenure on the Court. First, I will examine the process by which justices are selected. Second, I will discuss the characteristics of those who become justices and the implications of those characteristics for the court's policies. Finally, and more briefly, I will discuss how and why justices leave the Court.

Through 1983 there have been 139 nominations to the Supreme Court, and 102 people have sat on the Court. Three people were nominated and confirmed twice, eight declined appointments or died before beginning service on the Court, and 26 failed to secure Senate confirmation.[1] In discussing the recruitment process I will focus on the 53 nominations that were made and the 45 justices who were selected during this century (see Table 2-1).

The Process of Selection

The selection of a Supreme Court justice begins with the creation of a vacancy, when a member of the Court dies or steps down from the Court. Inevitably, vacancies occur at an irregular rate. There were no vacancies to fill in Franklin Roosevelt's first term, but five in his second term. Four justices left the Court in Richard Nixon's first three years in office. The absence of any vacancies in the four years from 1977 through 1980 made Jimmy Carter the first president in more than a

Table 2-1. Twentieth-Century nominations to the Supreme Court

Name	Nominated by	Replaced	Years served
Oliver Wendell Holmes	T. Roosevelt	Gray	1902-32
William Day	T. Roosevelt	Shiras	1903-22
William Moody	T. Roosevelt	Brown	1906-10
Horace Lurton	Taft	Peckham	1910-14
Edward White (CJ)[a]	Taft	Fuller	1910-21
Charles Evans Hughes	Taft	Brewer	1910-16
Willis Van Devanter	Taft	White	1911-37
Joseph Lamar	Taft	Moody	1911-16
Mahlon Pitney	Taft	Harlan	1912-22
James McReynolds	Wilson	Lurton	1914-41
Louis Brandeis	Wilson	Lamar	1916-39
John Clarke	Wilson	Hughes	1916-22
William Howard Taft (CJ)	Harding	White	1921-30
George Sutherland	Harding	Clarke	1922-38
Pierce Butler	Harding	Day	1923-39
Edward Sanford	Harding	Pitney	1923-30
Harlan Fiske Stone	Coolidge	McKenna	1925-45
Charles Evans Hughes (CJ)	Hoover	Taft	1930-41
John Parker	Hoover	(Sanford)	Defeated for confirmation, 1930
Owen Roberts	Hoover	Sanford	1930-45
Benjamin Cardozo	Hoover	Holmes	1932-38
Hugo Black	F. Roosevelt	Van Devanter	1937-71
Stanley Reed	F. Roosevelt	Sutherland	1938-57
Felix Frankfurter	F. Roosevelt	Cardozo	1939-62
William Douglas	F. Roosevelt	Brandeis	1939-75
Frank Murphy	F. Roosevelt	Butler	1940-49

Name	President	Seat	Years
James Byrnes	F. Roosevelt	McReynolds	1941-42
Harlan Fiske Stone (CJ)[a]	F. Roosevelt	Hughes	1941-46
Robert Jackson	F. Roosevelt	Stone	1941-54
Wiley Rutledge	F. Roosevelt	Byrnes	1943-49
Harold Burton	Truman	Roberts	1945-58
Fred Vinson (CJ)	Truman	Stone	1946-53
Tom Clark	Truman	Murphy	1949-67
Sherman Minton	Truman	Rutledge	1949-56
Earl Warren (CJ)	Eisenhower	Vinson	1953-69
John Harlan	Eisenhower	Jackson	1955-71
William Brennan	Eisenhower	Minton	1956-
Charles Whittaker	Eisenhower	Reed	1957-62
Potter Stewart	Eisenhower	Burton	1958-81
Byron White	Kennedy	Whittaker	1962-
Arthur Goldberg	Kennedy	Frankfurter	1962-65
Abe Fortas	Johnson	Goldberg	1965-69
Thurgood Marshall	Johnson	Clark	1967-
Abe Fortas (CJ)[a]	Johnson	(Warren)	Nomination withdrawn, 1968
Homer Thornberry	Johnson	(Fortas)	Nomination became moot, 1968[b]
Warren Burger (CJ)	Nixon	Warren	1969-
Clement Haynsworth	Nixon	(Fortas)	Defeated for confirmation, 1969
G. Harrold Carswell	Nixon	(Fortas)	Defeated for confirmation, 1970
Harry Blackmun	Nixon	Fortas	1970-
Lewis Powell	Nixon	Black	1971-
William Rehnquist	Nixon	Harlan	1971-
John Paul Stevens	Ford	Douglas	1975-
Sandra Day O'Connor	Reagan	Stewart	1981-

[a] Nominated as chief justice while serving as associate justice.
[b] When Fortas's nomination for chief justice was withdrawn, no vacancy for his seat as associate justice existed.

century—and the only president who served a full term—not to select any justices.

The formal selection process for justices is rather simple. When a vacancy occurs, the president makes a nomination, and the nomination must be confirmed by a majority of those voting in the Senate. When the chief justice's position is vacant, the president may nominate a sitting justice to that position and also nominate a new associate justice, or simply nominate a person as chief justice from outside the Court. Most of the time presidents have taken the latter course, chiefly to have a wider field from which to select this important leader.

Ordinarily the president's nominee is not actually "appointed" and cannot join the Court until confirmed by the Senate. In a few circumstances the president may make a "recess appointment" to the Court that becomes effective immediately, without Senate approval. The most important of these circumstances is when a vacancy occurs in the last month of a Senate session or when the Senate is not in session. The Senate retains the power to vote on the appointee's confirmation when it returns, but the confirmation process inevitably is affected by the fact that the person in question is already acting as a justice. Four of President Eisenhower's five nominations were recess appointments, and in 1960 the Senate expressed its disapproval of the practice. There have been no recess appointments since that time, in part because congressional recesses have become much shorter.

The actual process of selection, of course, is far more complicated than the simple formal procedure would suggest. The president and Senate make their decisions in an environment of individuals and groups highly interested in these decisions, and the process by which they reach their decisions is quite complex. In examining this process it will be useful first to discuss the roles of unofficial participants in the selection of justices, and then to discuss how the president and Senate reach their decisions.

Unofficial Participants

Because of the importance of appointments to the Supreme Court, a variety of individuals and groups seek to influence the president and Senate. Apart from members of the president's administration, whose activities will be discussed later in this section, the most important of these participants fall into three categories: the American Bar Association and the legal community in general; nonlegal interest groups; and members of the Supreme Court. The roles of each of these participants, along with the activities of those who seek nominations for themselves, will be discussed in turn.

The ABA and Legal Community. The American Bar Association (ABA) is a national voluntary organization of attorneys organized in 1878. Because of its large membership and national scope, the ABA has come to be accepted as the major voice of the legal profession in the United States.

Much of the ABA's activity concerns politics and government policy, and among the most important of its policy interests is the selection of judges. At the state level the ABA and other bar associations have worked for the adoption of so-called merit selection of judges, by which the explicit role of partisan politics in judicial recruitment would be reduced. These efforts have been a major factor in the growing adoption of merit selection by the states.

At the federal level the ABA generally has accepted the existing formal method for the selection of judges, but it has sought to influence the selections that are made. Its attempts to influence judicial selection were unsystematic and occasional until the creation of its Committee on the Federal Judiciary in 1946. This committee is composed of 14 members selected by the ABA president on a regional basis. It has sought to obtain a regular role in the selection process, particularly the opportunity to approve or disapprove of potential nominees before the president's final choice is made.

Presidents and senators have been relatively cooperative with the ABA in appointments below the Supreme Court level. The committee regularly is allowed to make recommendations to the president's administration concerning the qualifications of serious candidates for lower court judgeships. This participation is accepted in part because it serves presidential purposes in avoiding unqualified nominees, particularly where senators are supporting candidates who appear to be unqualified. However, presidents have been less willing to give the committee a significant role in Supreme Court nominations. In 1969, for instance, the Nixon administration gave the committee a veto power over nominations to all federal courts except for the Supreme Court. This difference stems from the fact that presidents care far more about Supreme Court nominations than they do about lower court judgeships, and wish to minimize constraints over their nominations to the Court.

The ABA committee's participation in Supreme Court nominations has varied according to the attitudes of the existing presidential administration. Generally, its role has been limited to rating nominees as "qualified" or "not qualified" after their nominations are made public. Acting after a nomination is made, the committee is understandably reluctant to call nominees unqualified. Indeed, it has never done so—even in the case of G. Harrold Carswell, a nominee of seemingly dubious qualifications who was defeated for confirmation by the Senate in 1970.

The committee would prefer to help screen prospective nomi-nees before the president makes a choice. The Eisenhower adminis-tration consulted with the committee on its later nominations to the Court, but presidents Kennedy and Johnson did not follow this practice. After two Nixon nominees for the same vacancy on the Court were defeated in the Senate, the Nixon administration allowed the ABA committee to screen potential nominees. The committee investigated and supported the qualifications of Harry Blackmun for the still-vacant seat; Blackmun's nomination was confimed by the Senate.

When two additional vacancies appeared in 1971, the Nixon admin-istration gave the committee six prospective nominees to investigate, asking it to concentrate on two: Mildred Lillie, a California appellate judge, and Herschel Friday, an Arkansas lawyer. After its investigation the committee unanimously voted Lillie "unqualified" and split on Friday, six finding him unqualified and six "unopposed." The votes quickly became public, embarrassing the administration, and Attorney General John Mitchell angrily retracted the administration's acceptance of the committee's pre-screening.

President Ford allowed the ABA to screen 15 potential nominees for the one vacancy that he filled; the committee gave John Paul Stevens, the eventual nominee, a very high rating. In contrast, President Reagan did not ask the ABA to consider Sandra Day O'Connor until the day that he announced her nomination. Two months later the ABA committee gave O'Connor a qualified endorsement, expressing some concern about her limited experience as a lawyer and judge. By that time O'Connor's confirmation was virtually assured.

The ABA committee is by far the most important participant from the legal community in the selection process. Its power is a matter of some controversy. Some lawyers see the committee as reflecting "estab-lishment" values to the exclusion of other perspectives within the bar, and some people think it is inappropriate for any group to gain the special position that the ABA is accorded. Whatever the merits of these criticisms, they underline the significance of the role that the ABA committee has attained.

At particular times other legal groups and individual lawyers have played a significant part in the selection process. In 1932, for instance, President Hoover nominated Benjamin Cardozo in response to the lobbying activities of a number of legal scholars. In recent years the most notable example of non-ABA legal influence was the criticism of Nixon's nominees Clement Haynsworth and Carswell by prominent attorneys. This criticism helped to counterbalance the ABA's official judgment that the nominees were qualified. For instance, legal scholar Louis Pollak apparently had some impact when he stated that Carswell "presents more slender credentials than any nominee for the Supreme Court put forth in this century." [2]

Other Interest Groups. The decisions of the Supreme Court affect the interests of most organized interest groups in the United States. While the Court's work in the general area of civil liberties is best publicized, the Court is also active in economic fields such as antitrust and labor law, and certainly most major economic interests have a real stake in the Court's policies.

Yet open lobbying over appointments by interest groups is relatively limited. To some degree it may be limited by the continuing hold of the mythology that the Court is "nonpolitical," making overt lobbying over its membership seem inappropriate. More important is the relative secrecy in which presidential nominations, the key decisions in the process, are made. To the extent that groups seek to influence nominations, private efforts are likely to be the most effective.

For this reason it is difficult to determine the extent and character of group activity at the nomination stage. Certainly we can assume that groups associated with the president's party and political fortunes will have some impact on the nomination decision even without active lobbying. A Democratic president, for instance, probably would not select a candidate whose views are opposed to those of organized labor. In addition, groups that enjoy close relations with the administration may communicate their general concerns or their feelings about particular candidates to the president. Some groups, such as those concerned with the interests of blacks and women, do lobby openly for the selection of particular kinds of candidates.

Once a nomination is announced, groups may work for or against confirmation in the Senate. Group opposition to a nominee is especially interesting, because it constitutes an effort to overcome the presumption in favor of confirmation. In this century, liberal groups frequently have sought to defeat nominees whom they perceived as too conservative on relevant issues. In 1930, labor groups and the National Association for the Advancement of Colored People (NAACP) opposed the confirmation of federal judge John Parker, a Hoover nominee, because of his conservative decisions on labor relations and racial issues. Parker's eventual defeat by a two-vote margin in the Senate was made possible by their activity. Forty years later, the same groups opposed President Nixon's nominations of Haynsworth and Carswell on similar grounds, and again they were successful by small margins in the Senate.

Liberal groups have opposed other conservative nominees with less success. Labor unions unsuccessfully fought the nominations of Horace Lurton in 1909 and Mahlon Pitney in 1912. More recently, the American Civil Liberties Union worked to defeat the nomination of William

Rehnquist in 1971 because of his lack of support for civil liberties, but Rehnquist was confirmed by a fairly wide margin. The National Organization for Women (NOW) opposed Ford's selection of John Paul Stevens in 1975 because of his decisions on women's rights as a lower court judge, but Stevens was confirmed easily.

Conservative groups also have opposed some nominees. A variety of individuals and groups attacked the nomination of Louis Brandeis in 1916, because they regarded Brandeis as a dangerous radical. They succeeded in delaying, but not preventing, Brandeis's confirmation. Since the 1950s anti-civil rights groups have attacked some nominees with whose views they disagreed, most notably Thurgood Marshall in 1967, without great success.

Group reactions to Sandra Day O'Connor in 1981 were intriguing. As a conservative Republican nominated by another conservative Republican, O'Connor might have been expected to draw support from conservative groups and opposition from liberal groups. The actual pattern was quite different. Liberal groups offered no opposition, in part because they approved the selection of a woman, and liberal women's groups such as NOW endorsed O'Connor. Meanwhile some conservative groups attacked O'Connor as insufficiently conservative, especially on the abortion issue, and representatives of antiabortion groups testified against her in the Senate committee hearings.

Group campaigns against nominees are similar in form to other kinds of lobbying campaigns. Group representatives seek to mobilize sympathetic senators to oppose the nominee, and together they try to build a convincing case that will sway other senators. The opposition to Carswell in 1970 was led by the Leadership Conference on Civil Rights, which secured the support of other liberal interest groups and of liberal senators such as Birch Bayh of Indiana and Joseph Tydings of Maryland. The core group of supportive senators and senatorial aides helped the interest groups to build a case against Carswell, a case that ultimately persuaded a majority of the Senate. In this instance, as in others, the outcome reflected not only group efforts but also factors beyond the groups' control, such as the party composition of the Senate and the nominee's qualifications.

Sitting Justices. Sitting members of the Supreme Court frequently have played active roles in the selection process. The extent of their activity may be surprising, because we might expect justices to remain aloof from politics outside the Court. But members of the Court frequently have participated in external politics when the stakes seemed sufficiently high, and there are few matters as important to justices as the selection of new colleagues. Whether they wish to obtain ideologically compatible colleagues, to maintain the Court's collective competence, or to bring friends onto the Court, they frequently will have an interest in intervening in the selection process.

Indeed, research by two political scientists identified 65 separate efforts by justices to influence Supreme Court nominations in this century.[3] Most of these efforts were in support of potential nominees. Often the lobbying was relatively mild, involving no more than a letter of recommendation for an individual, and in several instances it came at the request of the administration. In a few cases, however, justices have engaged in rather intensive lobbying. When Justice Oliver Wendell Holmes retired in 1932, Justice Harlan Stone undertook a strong campaign in favor of New York Judge Benjamin Cardozo, while six of his colleagues worked against Cardozo by supporting another candidate. Cardozo eventually was nominated, although Justice Stone's efforts probably were less significant than other sources of support for Cardozo.

By far the most active Supreme Court lobbyist in the twentieth century was Chief Justice William Howard Taft, who intervened continually during his tenure in the 1920s. Taft, a former president, felt no hesitancy about tendering his advice to his successors. Indeed, Taft personally directed a successful campaign for the nomination and confirmation of Pierce Butler in 1922. In recent years Chief Justice Warren Burger suggested the name of his long-time friend Harry Blackmun to the attorney general in 1970, and William Rehnquist gave a strong endorsement of his law school classmate Sandra Day O'Connor to the White House in 1981.[4] In general, chief justices have been particularly active in the selection process, perhaps because their position gives them a special interest in appointments and greater credibility with the president than their colleagues have.

It is difficult to gauge the effects of judicial intervention. Active justices such as Taft have obtained the desired outcomes more often than not, but their activity may not have been the crucial factor in producing these outcomes. Taft did appear to have considerable influence over President Harding. In a few instances, such as Burger's suggestion of Blackmun, the intervening justice played a key role by putting the eventual nominee's name into consideration. Where several members of the Court stand together on a recommendation, as occasionally has happened, their views may carry particular weight. But most justices lack the leverage to secure decisive influence over selections, and concerted campaigns may even backfire if the president resents interference. Felix Frankfurter's pressure on Franklin Roosevelt to select federal Judge Learned Hand in 1943 was one reason that Roosevelt chose Wiley Rutledge instead of Hand; "This time," Roosevelt reportedly said, "Felix overplayed his hand."[5]

Prospective Nominees. People who wish to become members of the lower federal courts often engage in very active campaigns for these positions, seeking to secure support from the officials who select judges and from those with influence over these officials. Indeed, such campaigns are almost a necessity. In most circumstances, Joel Grossman has written, "the candidate who does not make at least a minimum effort in his own behalf is likely to remain a private citizen."[6]

The Supreme Court appears to be somewhat different. People often are chosen as justices without campaigning actively for the job. Because presidents see Court appointments as so important, they look for candidates who best serve presidential purposes rather than restricting their choices to people who seek the job openly. Further, the Court's standing makes some potential justices hesitant to conduct campaigns on their own behalf.

Some people do work to obtain appointments, however, and some of them are successful. Of the successful campaigns, the best documented and almost surely the most elaborate was conducted by William Howard Taft. Taft was a somewhat reluctant president who really wanted to be chief justice of the Supreme Court. Even as president he worked toward his eventual selection by appointing a relatively aged chief justice, Edward White, to help guarantee a vacancy in that position in the foreseeable future. White returned the compliment by refusing to retire or die, despite his extreme disability, until a Republican replaced President Wilson. When White died early in President Harding's term, Taft was appointed to replace him; the appointment came after an intensive campaign by Taft that had begun even before Harding's election. It is appropriate to speak of Taft as "virtually appointing himself Chief Justice," as one commentator has said.[7]

According to Justice William Douglas, Sherman (Shay) Minton obtained his nomination in 1949 through a far simpler campaign. President Truman had agreed to nominate another candidate for a vacancy on the Court when Minton, a federal judge and close personal friend, walked into the White House to see Truman. Douglas reported that the following conversation ensued:

"What can I do for you, Shay?"

"Harry, I want you to put me on the Supreme Court to fill that new vacancy."

"Shay, I'll do just that." [8]

Other justices who reportedly worked to obtain their nominations were Douglas himself, Truman appointee Tom Clark, and Warren Burger. In the account of President Nixon's aide John Ehrlichman, Burger "wanted a seat on the Supreme Court so passionately that he would have agreed to almost anything to get it." Ehrlichman claimed that Burger even promised to retire before the end of Nixon's tenure as president so that Nixon could appoint a younger chief justice to serve for a long period.[9]

While some people actively seek appointments to the Court, some others are reluctant to accept them. Several people have declined nominations or taken themselves out of the running when they appeared likely to be nominated. John W. Davis, a highly successful lawyer and later a presidential nominee, declined a possible nomination in 1922. One reason was financial; Davis explained to a friend that "I have taken the vows of chastity and obedience but not of poverty." [10] Abe Fortas also had financial reasons to remain in private practice, but President Johnson got Fortas to accept a nomination in 1965 through the kind of persuasive effort that so often succeeded for Johnson.

Such cases, however, are exceptions. Whether or not they worked for a position on the Supreme Court, most of those who are offered a nomination have little difficulty in accepting it.

The President's Decision

Every president must make thousands of appointments to positions in the executive and judicial branches. For most of these posts, the real process of selection is handled by subordinate officials. The president's time is considered too important to be spent in filling posts that are not viewed as critical.

In particular, the president is not a major participant in the selection of judges for the lower federal courts. The task of identifying candidates and negotiating with other participants in the selection process falls chiefly to officials in the Department of Justice, although the Carter administration instituted a system of commissions of private citizens to identify possible nominees. The president ordinarily does little more than ratify these choices. This willingness to delegate responsibility reflects the belief of most presidents that lower court judges are relatively insignificant figures.

The president plays a much more active role personally in the selection of Supreme Court justices. Presidents recognize the importance of the Court and of its membership. As a result, they give nominations to the Supreme Court a degree of personal attention that is paralleled only by that given to Cabinet appointments. There is, however, some variation among presidents in this respect: Taft scrutinized potential nominees with great care, while Eisenhower played only a peripheral role in the selection process.

In identifying candidates for nomination to the Supreme Court and making a final selection, the president receives help from the attorney general and other officials in the Justice Department. The attorney general often suggests candidates to the president and usually plays an important part in the president's final selection. Attorney General Edward Levi was decisive in President Ford's selection of John Paul Stevens, whom Levi had known in Chicago. Attorney General William French Smith was in charge of the search process that led to President Reagan's nomination of Sandra Day O'Connor.

In making their selections the president and attorney general hear from a variety of individuals and groups. To some extent administrations encourage this kind of participation to obtain desired information and to build congressional support for the president's ultimate nominee.

Presidents make selections based on a broad range of considerations. These considerations can be placed in four general categories: the "objective" criteria of competence and ethics; policy preferences; reward to political and personal associates; and the pursuit of future political support. Each of these categories merits consideration in some detail.

Competence and Ethics. In the selection of judges to the lower federal courts, "objective" qualifications traditionally have played a relatively limited role. Because of the perceived unimportance of the lower courts, the Justice Department and relevant senators often elevate other considerations over a candidate's merits. As a result, the perceived quality of lower court nominees varies from very high to fairly low.

Quality plays a more important role in the selection of nominees for the Supreme Court, because presidents have strong incentives to select persons of high competence and ethical behavior. A candidate who falls short on either of these standards is likely to embarrass the president and may even attract enough opposition to be defeated in the Senate. A highly skilled justice has relatively great influence on the Court; if such a justice shares the president's policy goals, the president's own effect on the Court is thereby increased. Finally, most presidents have sufficient respect for the Supreme Court that they wish to uphold high standards in selection.

In general, the choices made by presidents have reflected a concern for competence. In this century, as Robert Scigliano points out, the great majority of nominees had achieved eminence in political or legal careers.[11] Oliver Wendell Holmes and Benjamin Cardozo, for instance, were distinguished state appellate judges. This does not mean that all nominees are highly skilled in the law, but only in a few cases has the competence of a nominee to serve on the Court been questionable.

Even where a justice eventually is rated as a "failure" by students of the Supreme Court, this does not mean that the appointing president disregarded competence in selecting that person. For instance, Charles Whittaker, one of Eisenhower's appointees, is widely regarded as a failure on the Court. According to one legal scholar, "He had two fatal defects: lack of intellectual capacity and inability to reach decisions."[12] Whittaker resigned after five years of service, in part because of a feeling that he could not handle his work as a justice. Yet he had had a successful career in private practice and experience as a federal judge, and there may have been no reason to expect that he could not serve well on the Court.

The ethical behavior of the great majority of nominees has been unexceptionable, at least so far as that behavior was known. There have been a few exceptions in this century. Louis Brandeis was accused of improper practices as a private attorney when he was nominated by President Wilson. More recently, Abe Fortas (when nominated for chief justice) and Clement Haynsworth were attacked for alleged financial improprieties, and Fortas also was criticized for his continuing consultation with President Johnson after he had joined the Court. The charges against Fortas and Haynsworth aided in producing their defeats in the Senate. These outcomes help to explain why presidents give attention to ethical standards in their nominations.

Competence and ethics can be considered screening criteria for potential nominees. These criteria may eliminate some people from consideration, but enough candidates survive the screening process to give presidents a wide range of choices for a nomination. In one instance, President Hoover's nomination of Benjamin Cardozo, these criteria played a more central role; Cardozo was so well respected for his work as a state judge that Hoover received very strong pressure to elevate him to the Supreme Court. Ordinarily, however, a concern for objective qualifications leaves the president with a great deal of freedom.

Policy Preferences. By policy preferences, I mean a person's attitudes toward policy issues. Until recently, these preferences generally were of limited importance in the selection of lower federal judges. Now, with the policy-making role of the federal courts increasingly apparent, presidents are giving more attention to the attitudes of prospective nominees for lower court judgeships. The Carter administration sought to appoint liberals, while conservatism on issues such as abortion is an important criterion for the Reagan administration.

For the Supreme Court, policy preferences are the president's single most important consideration. No president can fail to understand the significance of the Court's decisions or the role that its members' attitudes play in shaping these decisions. Accordingly, all presidents have sought to put on the Court people whose views on important policy questions are similar to their own.

The seriousness of this effort has varied among presidents. For some presidents a person's ideological position was the overwhelming criterion for selection, because they had special reason to be concerned with the direction of Supreme Court policy. Thwarted by the Court's attacks on his economic policies, Franklin Roosevelt was careful to select justices who supported his views on the economic powers of the federal government. It was only after he had gained a clear majority for his position on the Court that Roosevelt's interest in nominees' attitudes declined somewhat. President Nixon felt that the Court's liberalism on criminal procedure questions in the 1960s had helped to weaken law enforcement, so he was meticulous in finding conservatives to put on the Court. Presidents less concerned with the Court's direction, such as Harry Truman, have put less emphasis on policy preferences as a basis for their choices.

A president who is interested in the attitudes of a potential nominee first must find out what those attitudes are. This may not be easy to do. It generally is easiest for sitting judges, who have made a record on many of the kinds of issues that they would face as justices. When Richard Nixon nominated Warren Burger as chief justice, he could be reasonably certain of his nominee's conservatism: Burger had served for 13 years as the most vocal conservative on the U.S. Court of Appeals for the District of Columbia. After his disappointment with Earl Warren, a California governor who was selected partly as a reward for his political support, President Eisenhower decided to select only from lower court judges in order to increase his chances of predicting a potential nominee's behavior on the Court. But William Brennan, one of the judges promoted by Eisenhower, also surprised the president with his liberal decisions as a justice. This was at least partly because the Eisenhower administration gave limited scrutiny to Brennan's judicial record prior to his nomination. Because administrations usually do examine a judge's record with some care, sitting judges as a group have been less likely to disappoint their nominators with their Supreme Court decisions than have other justices.[13]

When a candidate has not served as a judge, it may be difficult to determine that person's preferences. A president may have a good sense of a nominee's views from personal association, such as the friendship between Lyndon Johnson and Abe Fortas. Partisan affiliation provides one indicator of preferences; in the present era, Democrats are likely to be liberal, Republicans conservative. This tendency helps to explain presidents' preference for nominees from their own party. A nominee's public expressions on relevant issues also may offer some clues to the president.

Sometimes presidents or their representatives question prospective nominees directly about their views, even when the candidate is a sitting judge. Harry Blackmun reports that before his nomination by President Nixon, "I was rather cross-examined by two members of the Department of Justice," and it is likely that one prominent subject was his policy preferences.[14] (One of the cross-examiners was William Rehnquist, who joined Blackmun on the Court a year later.) Sandra Day O'Connor was questioned by two sets of administration officials and then by President Reagan himself, with whom she discussed abortion and other issues.

Observers of the Court give considerable attention to the instances in which justices have dismayed the presidents who selected them with their policies on the Court. The liberal Wilson was shocked by the extreme conservatism of James McReynolds, just as conservative Coolidge later was upset with Harlan Stone's liberalism. Eisenhower was unhappy with the liberalism of both Warren and Brennan; asked if he had made any mistakes as president, Eisenhower replied, "Yes, two, and they are both sitting on the Supreme Court." [15]

Such instances are not rare; Robert Scigliano has estimated that at least one-quarter of the justices have deviated from the expectations of their appointers.[16] But most justices do turn out to be ideologically compatible with the presidents who appoint them. Moreover, presidents who were especially careful to select compatible justices have suffered relatively few disappointments. Both Franklin Roosevelt and Richard Nixon, for instance, did rather well in getting what they wanted from the justices that they selected, although Harry Blackmun's increased liberalism over time has marred the Nixon record of success somewhat. Presidents who have emphasized other criteria or who chose with less care often have done less well.

No justice, of course, will please the appointing president with every decision. This is inevitable for an appointee to any position. It is particularly common for judges because the facts of particular cases and the state of the law may move them to reach decisions contrary to their general predispositions. Whatever his pleasure with most of his appointees' votes on the Court, President Nixon could not have been happy with their votes against his position in *United States v. Nixon* (1974), in which a unanimous Court required him to yield recordings of his conversations as president. As this decision illustrates, even the most careful selections do not provide a president with "control" over the Supreme Court.

Certainly the power of appointment does provide presidents with an opportunity to shape the Court's general direction. The impact of this power on the Court's policies will be examined in Chapter 5.

Political and Personal Reward. Nominations to the Supreme Court are among the most important prizes that presidents can bestow. It should not be surprising that they frequently offer these prizes to people who have been political associates or personal friends. Not only do such people seem deserving of positions on the Court, but a president can have the most confidence in the ability and ideological "correctness" of associates and friends.

Indeed, about 60 percent of the nominees to the Court personally knew the nominating president.[17] Of the most recent presidents, Franklin Roosevelt, Harry Truman, John Kennedy, and Lyndon Johnson all selected primarily acquaintances. Johnson, for instance, chose Abe Fortas, one of his longest and closest political associates, and Homer Thornberry, a colleague from Texas politics (Thornberry's nomination was never considered by the Senate because it was contingent on Fortas's elevation to chief justice). For Truman, reward for political associates seemed to be the predominant criterion for selection. Presidents Nixon, Ford, and—thus far—Reagan have shown less of a tendency to select associates.

Occasionally appointments to the Court are rewards of a more direct sort. Presidents may feel the need to compensate someone for past service with an appointment of this magnitude. Dwight Eisenhower selected Earl Warren to serve as chief justice of the Supreme Court in part because of a debt owed for Warren's crucial support of Eisenhower's cause in the 1952 Republican convention. As governor of California and leader of that state's delegation, Warren had provided needed votes on a preliminary issue concerning contested state delegates, and Eisenhower's success in that contest helped to secure his nomination. Franklin Roosevelt nominated James Byrnes in 1941 partly to compensate for Byrnes's being denied the Democratic vice-presidential nomination in 1940 after his loyal service to Roosevelt.

A rather different kind of "reward" is the use of a Supreme Court appointment to remove a troublesome individual to a presumably safer place. It has been suggested that Wilson's appointment of James McReynolds and Coolidge's appointment of Harlan Stone came about in part because these individuals had created difficulties as attorney general. If these allegations are true, then Wilson and Coolidge "deserved" the disappointments that they received from these men as justices. Earl Warren's appointment to the Court served the purposes of rival California Republicans, including Vice-President Nixon, in removing him from the political scene, and this fact apparently played a role in his selection.

About 90 percent of all nominees to the Court have been members of the president's party. This statistic, similar to those for the lower federal courts, reflects several factors: the relationship between party and ideology, the tendency for presidents' associates to come from the same party, and the desire to reserve the patronage of seats on the Supreme Court for the party faithful. Nominees who were not of the president's party have been appointed because they appealed to the president on other grounds. Harold Burton, for instance, had served with Truman in the Senate, and they were close friends. Eisenhower chose William Brennan in part to appeal to Democratic and Catholic voters in the 1956 election. Lewis Powell, nominated by Nixon, was an eminent lawyer who fulfilled the president's goal of putting a Southerner on the Court.

Pursuit of Political Support. Like other appointments, such as those to the Cabinet, seats on the Supreme Court provide means for a president to build political support. By selecting justices with particular characteristics, presidents often have sought to gain the gratitude of voters who share those characteristics. Similarly, presidents seek to avoid choices which will alienate people. It is for this reason that presidents often welcome advice from groups such as the American Bar Association or organized labor. This advice helps them to make nominations which will appeal to significant sectors of the public.

For most of our history, efforts to obtain political support with appointments to the Court focused heavily on geography. Presidents sought to provide each region of the country with representation on the Court in order to please a maximum number of voters. This interest was strengthened by the practical value of geographical diversity. Until 1891 the justices "rode circuit," helping to staff the lower federal courts in designated regions of the country, and it made most sense to select justices from the circuits that they would represent.

Geography has continued to be a consideration in some nominations. For instance, Franklin Roosevelt nominated Wiley Rutledge in 1943 partly because of Rutledge's Iowa residence. Occasionally geography becomes very important, as it was when Nixon struggled mightily to put a Southerner on the Court to strengthen his electoral support in that region. But in general, geography has become a less important criterion. As circuit-riding responsibilities declined and then were abolished, one important rationale for concern with geography disappeared. Presidents also seem to have perceived a decline in sectional consciousness, so that geography has become less important to them as a means of building support. As a result of both factors, the Court has become less balanced geographically.

During the twentieth century an interest in providing representation to religious minority groups has affected some presidents' choices, such as Eisenhower's selection of Brennan and Kennedy's selection of Goldberg. There has been at least one Catholic member of the Court throughout nearly the whole period since 1894, and at least one Jewish member from 1916 to 1969. Once these groups had obtained representation on the Court, there was some tendency to view this representation as an "entitlement" that should not be taken away. Understandably, presidents have been somewhat reluctant to court disfavor by disappointing people who hold this view.

Representation by race and sex has become more important than religion. Thurgood Marshall's selection in 1967 brought the first black member to the Court, and in the future presidents will feel some pressure to maintain black representation on the Court. The pressure for the appointment of a woman to the Court in 1981 would have been difficult for President Reagan to resist, and even while Sandra Day O'Connor remains on the Court presidents may see some advantage to appointing additional women.

The two parties stand in somewhat different positions in relation to group representation on the Court. The Democrats today receive disproportionate support from Jewish and female voters and even more from black voters, and prospective Supreme Court justices in these groups tend to be liberal Democrats rather than conservative Republicans. These factors are counterbalanced by the incentive for Republican presidents to try to increase their support from these groups through Court nominations. During the 1980 campaign Ronald Reagan sought to shore up his support from female voters by promising to name a woman to "one of the first Supreme Court vacancies in my administration," [18] and his continuing problems with women voters made it imperative to keep that promise with his first nomination the next year.

The use of nominations to build political support may be rather futile. Important through they are, Supreme Court appointments seldom are conspicuous to most voters—the O'Connor appointment was a striking exception—and in themselves it is unlikely that they have great impact on election results. But the practice of using judicial and other appointments to build political support is so well established that it almost surely will continue even in the absence of any clear effect.

Summary. As the discussion of these four kinds of considerations should suggest, nominations to the Supreme Court rest on a variety of criteria, and most appointments serve multiple goals. Perhaps the only safe generalizations are that all four categories of considerations are important and that their relative importance varies considerably.

The perceived importance of the Court has at least two effects on the criteria for selection of justices. First, it makes presidents weigh all the criteria more carefully than their representatives generally do for lower court nominations. Second, it gives emphasis to the factors of competence and policy preferences as opposed to the "political" considerations of reward and support building. If Supreme Court justices are better jurists and better reflections of their nominators' views than are lower court judges, it is largely because presidents have an interest in producing both of those results.

The Role of the Senate

Once the president has nominated someone for a vacancy on the Supreme Court, the nomination goes to the Senate for confirmation. Ordinarily the nomination is referred to the Judiciary Committee, which holds hearings and then votes its recommendation for Senate action. After committee action the nomination is referred to the floor, where it will be debated and a confirmation vote taken. The length of this process depends on the degree of controversy concerning the nomination. If there is no opposition to a nominee, hearings may be pro forma and take only a single day, the nomination will be reported to the full Senate rather quickly, and the nominee will be confirmed quickly with little debate. However, hearings on Thurgood Marshall, Clement Haynsworth, and Abe Fortas all lasted five days or more, and the Judiciary Committee reported Louis Brandeis's nomination 122 days after it was made.[19] Most important, some nominations have been debated vigorously on the floor, and three have been defeated since 1968.

A Reactive Role. The role of the Senate in the selection of Supreme Court justices can best be understood in contrast with its role at the district court level. For district judges the practice of "senatorial courtesy" has given a quasi-veto power to senators of the president's party from the state for which an appointment is made; if they disapprove of a nomination, their colleagues will defeat it. Since the late 1970s senatorial courtesy has become a bit less automatic, but home-state senators retain considerable veto power. This power gives the Department of Justice a strong incentive to consult with the relevant senators before making a recommendation for the president's nomination. In practice, many senators play a very active role at the nomination stage, not only indicating their disapproval of potential nominees but suggesting and sometimes insisting upon particular candidates. Although the administration officials also hold considerable power in the process, the ultimate veto power held by particular senators ensures that they will take a meaningful part in the nomination decision if they wish to do so.

A degree of senatorial courtesy existed for the Supreme Court in the nineteenth century, in that the senators from the nominee's state possessed some veto power. That power seems to have disappeared. This does not mean that senators play no role in the nomination process. Individual senators occasionally will participate in the president's decision-making process or voice support or opposition to a possible nominee. For example, Sen. Barry Goldwater worked to secure the nomination of Sandra Day O'Connor, a fellow Arizona Republican. When a vacancy appeared in 1937, the Senate as a body actually endorsed its majority leader, Joseph Robinson, for the nomination. If Robinson had not died shortly afterwards, President Roosevelt might have had little choice but to nominate him. But the role of senators in selecting the president's nominee is far more limited than it is for the district courts.

In some respects this difference increases the president's freedom in making Supreme Court nominations. In choosing a nominee the president generally need not give heavy weight to a particular senator's views and never needs to determine whether a potential nominee would be vetoed by a single senator. In addition, the fact that the Senate is responding to nominations already made rather than helping to make a choice puts it at something of a disadvantage in the confirmation process. However, Supreme Court nominations are given a collective scrutiny that district court nominations seldom receive. For that reason the president must take the Senate's likely reaction into account in making a nomination.

The Senate's Record. Through 1983 the Senate had failed to confirm 26 of the president's nominations to the Supreme Court, either through an adverse vote or through a refusal to act. These 26 cases constituted about 20 percent of the nominations that the Senate considered. This proportion of defeats is higher than for any other position to which the president makes appointments. For instance, only eight cabinet nominees have been defeated.

Presidents have been more successful with Supreme Court nominations in the twentieth century than in the nineteenth. Since 1900, only four of the 52 nominations considered by the Senate have failed: Hoover's nomination of John Parker in 1930, Johnson's elevation of Abe Fortas to chief justice in 1968 (withdrawn after Fortas's supporters failed to end an anticonfirmation filibuster), and Nixon's nominations of Clement Haynsworth in 1969 and G. Harrold Carswell in 1970 for the same vacancy. Moreover, only one successful nominee was confirmed by less than a two-thirds margin in the Senate (Mahlon Pitney, a Taft nominee, was confirmed by a 50-26 vote), and only eight others suffered as many as 10 negative votes.

This record of success is impressive, but it may be a bit misleading. During two periods in this century a high proportion of nominees have faced serious opposition. The first was between 1910 and 1930, when several nominees were attacked by senators on ideological grounds. The second began in the late 1940s and continues today. Of the 20 nominees considered by the Senate from 1949 through 1981, three were defeated, five others received more than 10 negative votes, and still others were opposed seriously. The Senate votes in this period are shown in Table 2-2. Meanwhile, Senate care in scrutinizing nominations, as indicated by such measures as the length of time spent in hearings, has increased markedly. Although nominations usually have been successful even during these periods, clearly the Senate has not adopted a policy of automatic confirmation for nominees.

The relative success of nominations to the Court in this century and the serious opposition that frequently arises both can be understood in terms of the sources of opposition to nominees. I will examine those sources in general terms and then illustrate their impact by looking at the most recent instances of serious opposition to presidential nominees.

Table 2-2. Senate votes on Supreme Court nominations, 1949-1981

Nominee	Year	Vote
Tom Clark	1949	73-8
Sherman Minton	1949	48-16
Earl Warren	1954	NRV[a]
John Harlan	1955	71-11
William Brennan	1957	NRV
Charles Whittaker	1957	NRV
Potter Stewart	1959	70-17
Byron White	1962	NRV
Arthur Goldberg	1962	NRV
Abe Fortas	1965	NRV
Thurgood Marshall	1967	69-11
Abe Fortas[b]	1968	withdrawn[c]
Homer Thornberry	No action	
Warren Burger	1969	74-3
Clement Haynsworth	1969	45-55
G. Harrold Carswell	1970	45-51
Harry Blackmun	1970	94-0
Lewis Powell	1971	89-1
William Rehnquist	1971	68-26
John Paul Stevens	1975	98-0
Sandra Day O'Connor	1981	99-0

[a] No recorded vote.
[b] Elevation to chief justice.
[c] Nomination withdrawn after Senate vote failed to end filibuster against nomination; vote was 45-43 to end filibuster, and 2/3 majority was required.

SOURCE: Congressional Quarterly, *The Supreme Court: Justice and the Law* (Washington, D.C.: Congressional Quarterly Inc., 1983), 179.

The Sources of Opposition. Nominees to the Supreme Court have attracted opposition on a variety of grounds, and confirmation defeats have resulted from very different mixes of negative factors. Still, it is possible to identify four sources of opposition to nominees that have been particularly important. Of these, two are related to the president who makes the appointment, two to the nominee.

For the president, the likelihood of defeat increases a good deal with the strength of the opposition party in the Senate. Indeed, whether or not the president's party has a Senate majority seems to make a tremendous difference in the confirmation decision. When the president's party has a majority, 91 percent of the nominees have been confirmed; when the president faces an opposition majority, only 48 percent have been confirmed.[20]

The timing of a nomination in the president's term also has an effect on the chances for confirmation. Historically, only about two-thirds of the nominations made in the last year of the term have been confirmed. Timing is important in part because a president's power sometimes declines toward the end of the term. More important, partisanship may increase in presidential election years, and the opposition may seek to delay an appointment until its own candidate can come into office. When the Senate was controlled by the opposition party, nominations made in the presidential election year or during the "lame duck" period between the election and the inauguration of a new president were defeated 11 out of 15 times.

One important characteristic of nominees is their objective qualifications, as assessed by senators. Nominees who appear to lack the competence to do their job effectively or the ethical standards demanded of justices tend to attract great opposition. Scrutiny of qualifications seems to have increased in this century.

Another important characteristic of nominees in the Senate has been their policy preferences. Where a nominee's views are anathema to a significant number of senators, the nomination is likely to face difficulty. Interest groups play an important role in calling ideology to the attention of senators. When organized labor opposes a nominee on grounds of unfriendliness to the labor movement, for instance, liberal senators will be moved to examine the candidate from an ideological perspective.

In the twentieth century, nominees' policy preferences have been the primary source of Senate opposition to nominations. Where nominees in this century have received 10 or more negative votes, the most important reason for opposition nearly always has been disagreement about policy. During the 1950s and 1960s, for instance, the 11 votes cast against John Harlan and Thurgood Marshall and the 17 opposed to Potter Stewart were based primarily on conservative Southern disagreement with the nominees on racial issues. Similarly, several conservative nominees have received negative votes from liberal senators.

The relative success of twentieth-century presidents in obtaining confirmation for their nominees stems in part from the infrequency of unfavorable circumstances. Only 13 of the 53 nominations in this century were made when the Senate was controlled by the opposition party, and few have been made in election years except under conditions favorable to the president's nominee. Presidential success also seems to stem from an increased willingness of the Senate to defer to the president's choice if that person's competence and adherence to ethical standards are clear. Although party and policy disagreement frequently produce opposition to a nomination, that opposition is unlikely to be successful unless it can be buttressed with weaknesses in the nominee's competence or ethics. The existence of such weaknesses provides a rationale for opposition and helps to attract ideological moderates to the opposition cause. Their absence makes opponents appear to be unfair and partisan, and it increases the difficulty of building a coalition against the candidate.

These generalizations may be illustrated by a discussion of the four most recent instances in which a nominee faced serious opposition in the Senate. In the first three instances, defects in the candidate's qualifications served to reinforce opposition based on partisan and policy oriented motives. In the fourth, the absence of such defects limited the effectiveness of an ideologically based opposition.

Abe Fortas. President Lyndon Johnson nominated Abe Fortas to the Supreme Court in 1965, and Fortas was confirmed with little opposition. In June 1968 Chief Justice Warren indicated his intention to retire, and Johnson nominated Fortas to replace Warren as chief justice. The nomination immediately attracted opposition, for two reasons. First, Fortas's demonstrated liberalism on the Court, symbolic of the Warren Court's direction, caused conservative senators to oppose him. Second, Republicans sought to prevent President Johnson from filling Warren's seat because they expected that a Republican would be elected in November and they preferred to reserve the appointment for the new president.

These grounds alone would have produced sufficient opposition to threaten the nomination. But partisan and ideological objections to Fortas were strengthened by two activities of the nominee that raised doubts about his fitness. The first was Fortas's continued consultation with Johnson while a member of the Court. Some senators saw this consultation as threatening his neutrality on some matters that might come before the Court, such as the war in Vietnam. The second was an arrangement by which Fortas gave nine lectures at American University for a fee of $15,000 raised from businesses; the fee struck some as excessive and improper.

The Judiciary Committee approved the nomination by an 11-6 vote, but it ran into a filibuster on the Senate floor. A vote to end the filibuster was favored by 45-43, 14 votes short of the two-thirds majority then required. Fortas was supported by a 33-4 margin by Northern Democrats, but Republican and Southern opposition was sufficiently strong to leave him short of the needed majority. After the unsuccessful vote Fortas asked that his nomination be withdrawn, and President Johnson did not make another. Thus, for the first time since 1930 and the second time since 1894, a nomination was defeated.

Clement Haynsworth. Chief Justice Warren finally was replaced in 1969 when President Nixon's nomination of Warren Burger was confirmed. In the same year, Justice Fortas resigned from the Court under pressure after revelations of financial dealings that raised further questions about his ethical standards. To replace Fortas, Nixon selected Clement Haynsworth of South Carolina, chief judge of the federal Court of Appeals for the Fourth Circuit.

Haynsworth attracted opposition from labor groups and from the NAACP, both of which interpreted his record on the court of appeals as unsympathetic to their interests. This opposition was supported by liberals in the Senate, some of whom were motivated in part by their anger over the Republicans' treatment of Fortas. Indeed, it is likely that Fortas's defeat helped to overcome the "habit" of supporting nominations that had developed since 1930.

Still, Haynsworth almost surely would have been confirmed had charges of unethical conduct not arisen. It was learned that he sat in two cases involving subsidiaries of companies in which he owned stock, and that in another case he bought the stock of a corporation between the time of his court's decision in its favor and the announcement of the decision. These disclosures were seized upon by Haynsworth's opponents, and they helped to attract additional opposition from Senate moderates—including a good many Republicans. The nomination was defeated by a 45-55 vote. The margin of defeat came from nearly unanimous opposition by Northern Democrats, but 17 of the 41 Republicans also voted against Haynsworth.

G. Harrold Carswell. A few months after Haynsworth's defeat, President Nixon nominated G. Harrold Carswell, a member of the Fifth Circuit Court of Appeals from Florida, to fill the same vacancy. After the fight over Haynsworth, most senators were inclined to support the next choice. But Carswell drew quick opposition from civil rights groups for what they perceived as his hostility to their interests. Their cause gradually drew strength from a series of revelations about Carswell that suggested an active opposition to black civil rights. The behavior in question ranged from apparent efforts to slow the pace of desegregation in cases before him to nonjudicial statements and actions favorable to segregation.

While Carswell was being attacked for his racial views, he also was criticized for an alleged lack of judicial competence. Legal scholars attested to his limited abilities, and their testimony was strengthened by data showing that an unusually high proportion of his decisions were reversed on appeal. Carswell's supporters were not able to counter this attack successfully. Republican senator Roman Hruska, floor manager for the nomination, offered the following support: "Even if he were mediocre, there are a lot of mediocre judges and people and lawyers. They are entitled to a little representation, aren't they, and a little chance?" [21] His statement seemed to support the charges of incompetence; in any case, the nomination was defeated by a 45-51 vote, with the lineup similar to that on Haynsworth.

William Rehnquist. In 1971 President Nixon sought to fill one of the two vacancies that had developed on the Court with William Rehnquist, an assistant attorney general originally from Arizona. Liberals opposed his confirmation because his record indicated a strong conservatism on civil rights and civil liberties issues. The Leadership Conference on Civil Rights led the opposition and was joined by the American Civil Liberties Union, opposing a nomination for the first time.

The opposition to Rehnquist was weakened, however, by the general agreement that he was a highly competent person who would serve effectively as a justice. The opposition thus had to rest entirely on ideological grounds, and even for some liberals those grounds were insufficient to justify a negative vote. As a result, Rehnquist was confirmed by a 68-26 vote, with conservative and moderate supporters joined by several Democratic liberals.

The Present Picture. The three defeats of nominees between 1968 and 1970 constituted a striking exception to the pattern of general Senate acquiescence in nominations since 1930. However, it should be recalled that the defeats were possible only because of circumstances particularly adverse to the nominees: the selection of Fortas late in Johnson's term, the liberal Democratic strength in the Senate of 1969-1970, and the existence of credible challenges to the nominees' objective qualifications.

Senate reactions to the five nominations that followed Carswell's defeat were strongly positive. Rehnquist was opposed by a significant number of senators but was confirmed fairly easily. Harry Blackmun, Lewis Powell, John Paul Stevens, and Sandra Day O'Connor received close scrutiny, but ultimately all were confirmed with little or no dissent. Only in O'Connor's case was the Senate controlled by the president's party. The other cases show that even when a Democratic Senate is faced with Republican nominees who seem conservative, ordinarily those nominees will be able to secure confirmation. Undoubtedly, future candidates frequently will be challenged and occasionally will be defeated. Notwithstanding the events of 1968 to 1970, however, the Senate probably will continue to accept the great majority of nominations to the Court.

Who Is Selected

From the process of selecting Supreme Court justices, we turn to the characteristics of those who have been selected. These characteristics should be examined to determine what kinds of people reach such exalted positions in the American political system and how they reach the point of being considered for selection. This examination is useful for a second reason as well. The characteristics of the justices potentially have a major impact on their policy choices, so observers of the Court who wish to understand those choices need to take into account the backgrounds of justices.

First, I will examine the major paths by which people reach the Court. These paths are significant in themselves. In addition, they help in understanding why justices tend to share certain characteristics. Those characteristics themselves will be the subject of the second part of the section.

As in the preceding section, I will focus on the justices selected in the twentieth century. Because paths to the Court have changed somewhat even in this century, I will give particular attention to the period beginning with the presidency of Franklin Roosevelt, which includes the 27 justices selected from Hugo Black in 1937 through Sandra Day O'Connor in 1981. Some important characteristics of those justices are listed in Table 2-3.

Career Paths

The Legal Profession. It may be surprising to learn that the Constitution does not restrict membership on the Supreme Court to attorneys. In practice, however, this restriction has been absolute. Most people involved in the selection process have assumed that a person must have legal training to serve effectively on the Court, although Justice Black thought otherwise.[22] Certainly the large number of attorneys in the Senate and the strength of the organized bar help to ensure that this rule never will be violated.

What this means is that a person who does not undertake legal training early in life is disqualified from consideration for the Supreme Court; the willingness and capacity to obtain a legal education, then, is the first and least flexible requirement for recruitment to the Court. For the first century of the Court's history, most justices had undergone apprenticeship under a practicing attorney, as was the predominant pattern at that time. In several cases the practicing attorney was a leading member of the bar.[23] More recently, law school education has predominated, with James Byrnes (chosen in 1941) the last justice to study law through apprenticeship. A high proportion of justices have gone to the more prestigious schools. Of the nine justices sitting in 1984, for instance, five had been educated in the Harvard, Yale, or Stanford law schools.

High Positions. If legal education is a necessary first step in the path to the Court, almost as necessary as a last step is the holding of a high position in government or the legal profession. The importance of such a position stems largely from the credibility that it gives a person for consideration by the selectors. Obscure private practitioners or state trial-court judges might be superbly qualified for the Court, but their qualifications would be questioned because of their lowly positions. A high government or legal position also helps to make a person visible to the president and others involved in the nomination process and helps to bring about the acquaintanceship with presidents that has been a factor in a great many nominations.

The 27 appointees since 1937 have held four kinds of positions at the time that they were selected. Ten held federal administrative positions. Seven of the 10 served in the Justice Department, either as attorney general or in a lower administrative position. The attorney general's central role in the selection process certainly has much to do with this large number. The other three served as chairman of the Securities and Exchange Commission (Douglas), Secretary of the Treasury (Vinson), and Secretary of Labor (Goldberg).

Ten of the justices in the most recent period have been appellate judges, eight on the federal courts of appeals and two (Brennan and O'Connor) on state courts. The predominance of federal judges is a recent phenomenon, in large part because the intermediate appellate courts in the federal system were not created until 1891. We might expect many justices to come from the District of Columbia circuit, because of its visibility in Washington, but only two (Rutledge and Burger) were serving on that court when they were selected.

Four justices came from high elective office, three as senators (Black, Byrnes, and Burton) and the fourth as the governor of California (Warren). It may be more than coincidence that the three members of Congress were from the Senate and that the governor was from a major state. These positions provide more visibility and prestige than do the House of Representatives and governorships of small states.

The other three recent justices held positions outside government, in private practice or university teaching. Each had acquired unusual success and prestige in his field. Felix Frankfurter was a renowned legal scholar who had worked a good deal in the federal government, both formally and informally. Abe Fortas was a highly successful Washington lawyer who had held positions in the executive branch, argued an important Supreme Court case, and advised a president. Lewis Powell was a leader of the bar whose important positions included the presidency of the American Bar Association. Even among successful attorneys, their records were extraordinary.

The Path Between. The discussion thus far has described the first and last rungs of the ladder by which people ascend to the Supreme Court. Also important is the path between these stages. By what process

Table 2-3. Selected characteristics of justices appointed since 1937

Justice	Age[a]	State of residence[b]	Law school	Position at appointment[c]	Years judge	Elective office[d]	Admin. position[e]
Black	51	Ala.	Alabama	Senator	1	Senate	—
Reed	53	Ky.	Columbia	Solicitor General	0	State leg.	Solicitor General
Frankfurter	56	Mass.	Harvard	Law professor	0	—	Subcabinet
Douglas	40	Wash.	Columbia	Chairman, Sec. & Exchange Comm.	0	—	Sec. & Exchange Comm.
Murphy	49	Mich.	Michigan	Attorney General	7	Governor	Attorney General
Byrnes	62	S.C.	None	Senator	0	Senate	—
Jackson	49	N.Y.	Albany	Attorney General	0	—	Attorney General
Rutledge	48	Iowa	Colorado	U.S. Ct. App.	4	—	—
Burton	57	Ohio	Harvard	Senator	0	Senate	—
Vinson	56	Ky.	Centre (Ky.)	Sec. of Treasury	5	House of Rep.	Sec. of Treasury
Clark	49	Texas	Texas	Attorney General	0	—	Attorney General
Minton	58	Ind.	Indiana	U.S. Ct. App.	8	Senate	Asst. to president
Warren	62	Calif.	Calif.	Governor	0	Governor	—
Harlan	55	N.Y.	New York	U.S. Ct. App.	1	—	Asst. U.S. Attorney

Brennan	50	N.J.	Harvard	State Sup. Ct.	7	—	—
Whittaker	56	Mo.	Kansas City	U.S. Ct. App.	3	—	—
Stewart	43	Ohio	Yale	U.S. Ct. App.	4	City council	—
White	44	Colo.	Yale	Dep. Atty. General	0	—	Dep. Atty. General
Goldberg	54	Ill.	Northwestern	Sec. of Labor	0	—	Sec. of Labor
Fortas	55	D.C.	Yale	Private practice	0	—	Subcabinet
Marshall	59	N.Y.	Howard	Solicitor General	4	—	Solicitor General
Burger	61	Minn.	St. Paul	U.S. Ct. App.	13	—	Asst. Attorney General
Blackmun	61	Minn.	Harvard	U.S. Ct. App.	11	—	—
Powell	64	Va.	Wash. & Lee	Private practice	0	—	State Bd. of Education
Rehnquist	47	Ariz.	Stanford	Asst. Atty. General	0	—	Asst. Atty. General
Stevens	55	Ill.	Northwestern	U.S. Ct. App.	5	—	—
O'Connor	51	Ariz.	Stanford	State Ct. App.	6	State leg.	State Asst. Atty. General

a Age at time of appointment.
b Primary state of residence prior to selection.
c In this and following columns, positions are federal except where noted otherwise.
d Highest office.
e Highest appointive administrative position. Minor positions omitted.

SOURCES: Leon Friedman and Fred L. Israel, *The Justices of the United States Supreme Court 1789-1969: Their Lives and Major Opinions* (New York: R. R. Bowker Co., 1969; 1978 supplement); Harold W. Chase and Craig R. Ducat, *Constitutional Interpretation*, 2d ed. (St. Paul: West Publishing Co., 1979), 1361-1376; Congressional Quarterly, *The Supreme Court and Its Work* (Washington, D.C.: Congressional Quarterly Inc., 1983), 169-187.

do people move from membership in the bar to the high positions from which justices are selected? There are several recognizable career paths that the justices have taken.

One common path is through partisan elective office. Throughout the Supreme Court's history, many of its members have had careers in politics, advancing in office until they reach positions in which they can be considered for the Court. Eight of the last 27 justices fit into this category. Some, such as Earl Warren, spent virtually all of their careers in political office. Warren practiced law for only three years, then held a series of appointive and elective offices. He was elected state attorney general at the age of 47, then was elected governor three times, becoming a party leader and serious candidate for the Republican nomination for president (he was the vice-presidential nominee in 1948). For others, the final move from private practice into politics as a career came somewhat later. Hugo Black held some minor offices in Alabama early in his career, but he did not leave private practice permanently until he was 40 years old, when he was elected to the Senate; his next step was to the Court.

A majority of the recent justices have followed a second path. This path begins with a private practice, followed at some point by elevation to a high administrative or judicial position from which the selection to the Court was made, or to a series of positions in administration and the judiciary and then to the Court.

The careers of the justices who fit into this category have differed in the length of time that the person spends in the "intermediate" positions. For some justices, this is a relatively long period that constitutes an important part of their pre-Court work. For instance, after a private practice of about 20 years, Warren Burger served for three years in the Department of Justice, then 13 years on the Court of Appeals for the District of Columbia before his elevation to the Court. For other justices, the intermediate position is only a very short way station. President Kennedy's appointees, Byron White and Arthur Goldberg, served in his administration for less than two years before they were selected as justices. In instances such as these, the intermediate position provides a stamp of legitimacy for the person in question and gives the president more information about that person's views, but it does not constitute a significant part of the pre-Court experience.

A smaller third group of justices has come to the Court directly from the private sector, skipping intermediate positions. The three recent justices in this category—Frankfurter, Fortas, and Powell—all have been discussed. In each case the justice had achieved eminence through the practice or teaching of law, and each had gained attention through governmental service during his professional career.

As this discussion makes clear, there are multiple paths from membership in the bar to the positions from which Supreme Court appointments are made. Certainly the careers of the persons selected as justices differ a great deal. At any given time, the nine members of the Court are likely to have brought with them a broad range of career experiences. What they will share is their membership in the legal profession and their success at reaching the higher levels within that profession or within government.

Implications of the Career Paths

On the basis of this analysis of paths to the Supreme Court, it is possible to explore some significant issues concerning the kinds of people who become justices. These issues include age at time of appointment; the role of "social background" characteristics such as class, race, and sex; the significance of prior judicial service; partisan political activity as a requisite for selection; and the role of chance in recruitment to the Court.

Age. Young people are not appointed to the Supreme Court. Most of the justices selected in this century were in their 50s when they joined the Court, and of the remainder most were over 60 years old. William Douglas was the youngest appointee at 40, and only two other appointees—Potter Stewart and Byron White—were under 45.

This pattern is surprising in at least one sense. We might expect presidents to select relatively young people in order to increase the length of time during which "their" justices would serve. In this way, presidents could increase their indirect influence over the Court's future policies. Given this advantage of young appointees, why do presidents generally choose persons over 50 and frequently choose persons over 60?

One major reason for the predominance of older justices is the time required to achieve the high positions from which most justices are selected and to attain the eminence that makes one a "candidate" for selection. The groups from which justices are chosen, such as appellate judges and high administrators, are populated chiefly by people of at least middle age. Another reason is that at least some participants in the selection process would regard truly young persons as lacking the experience to serve effectively on the Court. The American Bar Association prefers more than a decade of experience as an attorney even for prospective lower court judges. Thus it is easiest for presidents to select older persons as justices, even though in doing so they are limiting their own influence over the Court.

Class, Race, and Sex. The Supreme Court's membership has been quite unrepresentative of the general population in social class backgrounds, with most justices coming from upper-status families. John Schmidhauser has concluded that "only a handful of the members of the Supreme Court were of essentially humble origin." [24] Schmidhauser's definition of humble origin may be overly restrictive, but he is certainly correct in pointing out that rather few children of the working class and poor have reached the Court.

The period since 1937 has differed somewhat from the general pattern, in that the number of justices from relatively low-status backgrounds has been fairly high. Two commentators noted in 1976 that "the Supreme Court of 1968-1969 contained the largest number of justices from humble beginnings ever to sit on the Court at one time," [25] and since 1969 the Court has continued to be relatively heterogeneous in the class backgrounds of its members. Although the group of recent justices is still of higher average status than the population as a whole, the gap is narrower than in any previous period.

The tendency for justices to come from higher-status backgrounds can be understood in terms of the career paths that justices take. First and most important, a justice must obtain a legal education. To do so is easiest for people with high status, because of the costs of law training and the education that precedes it. When apprenticeships provided the major source of legal education, high social status was important in obtaining an apprenticeship with a leading practitioner. Second, people of high-status backgrounds have a variety of advantages in their post-educational careers. Those who can afford to attend elite law schools, for instance, have the easiest time finding positions in successful law firms.

The partial deviation from this pattern since 1937 may be explained in part by the increasing availability of legal education. Warren Burger, with few financial resources, could attend law school at night while selling insurance during the day. It may also be that the growth of the legal profession, the judiciary, and the federal government has opened access to high positions in these sectors for people of lower-status backgrounds who might have been shut out of the limited opportunities that existed earlier. If these explanations have some validity, then we should expect that the proportion of justices from lower-status backgrounds will remain relatively high and perhaps increase in the future.

With the exceptions of Thurgood Marshall and Sandra Day O'Connor, the Supreme Court has been composed entirely of white males. This pattern is not difficult to understand. Until very recently, women and blacks had extreme difficulty pursuing legal educations due to legal and other restrictions. As a result, the pool of potential justices from these groups who passed the first barrier to selection was quite small. Moreover, prejudice against women and members of racial minority groups has limited their ability to advance in the legal profession and in politics, so that very few people from these groups could reach the high positions from which justices are selected. It is notable that Thurgood Marshall became a renowned attorney not through the usual process of advancement in a major law firm—which would have been nearly inconceivable—

but through his work for the NAACP. Similarly, Sandra Day O'Connor graduated near the top of her class at Stanford Law School but found the law firms of Los Angeles and San Francisco unwilling to hire her as an attorney.

The representation of women and racial minority groups on the Court probably will increase significantly in the future. One reason, already noted, is the growing willingness of presidents to consider women and blacks in selecting justices from those holding high positions. More important, increased educational and career opportunities for both groups will augment their representation in those positions. Still, the various advantages of white males are likely to keep them numerically dominant on the Court for some time.

If the Court has been composed primarily of white men from upper-status backgrounds, what impact has this composition had on its policies? The impact of these characteristics is difficult to ascertain, but some tentative judgments are possible. In the case of race and sex, the claims of racial minority groups and of women might have been taken seriously at an earlier time had these groups enjoyed even limited representation on the Court. During the 1960s Congress took its first steps to support equality for women, largely through the efforts of its female members; during the same decade, the all-male Supreme Court gave no support to those litigants who brought sex discrimination complaints to the Court despite its general support for civil liberties.

For social class the picture is more complicated. Certainly a person of high socioeconomic status tends to develop certain attitudes that differ from the predominant attitudes in lower-status groups. But this is only a tendency. Moreover, some of those born relatively poor became fairly wealthy in adulthood; Warren Burger is one example. The sympathies of those who have "climbed" from low-status backgrounds may differ little from those who started out with social and economic advantages. Notably, the justices from humble backgrounds have included solid conservatives such as Warren Burger as well as liberals such as Earl Warren. If the Supreme Court's decisions have reflected "essentially the conscience of the American upper middle class," it is only in part because most justices originated in that class.[26]

Prior Judicial Service. A majority of all the justices have served as judges on state courts or in lower federal courts. The importance of such service has been debated. For some observers of the Court, experience as a lower court judge is a prerequisite to superior work on the Supreme Court. Indeed, in recent years members of Congress have made several efforts to create a formal requirement of such experience. These efforts have stemmed largely from conservatives' belief that judicial activism is encouraged by an absence of lower court service. On the other side, a number of commentators—including Justice Felix Frankfurter—have argued that lower court experience is not a necessity for a justice. A few have even suggested that nonexperienced justices have a better record on the Court. Certainly it is not difficult to find justices without prior experience who have distinguished themselves on the Court, from John Marshall to Earl Warren.

Of the 14 justices since 1937 who had lower court experience, the longest experience was 13 years (Burger), and eight justices had been lower court judges for five years or less. Undoubtedly even a short period on a lower court provides experiences that shape a justice's perspective, but a stint of three or five years—or even of 13 years—is not likely to have as much impact on a person's thinking and approach to judicial policy issues as the much longer period of education and professional development that preceded it.

For this reason, it is not surprising that justices with lower court experience have not behaved very differently as a group from justices without that experience. Service on lower courts may offer one benefit, that of easing the difficulties of new justices. But even this benefit is limited by the differences between the Supreme Court and other courts, which make the Court's work a challenge for experienced judges as well as other persons.

Partisan Political Activity. Most justices have had significant involvements in partisan politics prior to their selection, as holders of partisan offices and participants in political campaigns. This pattern differs from that in many other countries, and it is a source of dissatisfaction for many observers of the courts.

The use of nominations as political rewards causes presidents deliberately to select politicians for some vacancies. But the importance of partisan activity also can be understood as a result of the established paths to the Court. First, high partisan office has come to constitute one recognized source of potential nominees, both because of the achievement that it signifies and because of the visibility of those who hold such offices. Second, appointment to the high judicial and administrative posts that constitute the major source of Supreme Court justices in the current period is itself heavily based on partisan politics.

Whether the preponderance of politicians on the Court is desirable constitutes a more difficult question. Certainly people uninvolved in partisan activities have a substantial disadvantage in reaching the Court; some highly qualified but less visible people have little chance of appointment. Yet there always will be far more qualified people available than vacancies on the Court, and this would be the case even if justices were recruited only from professional politicians. Moreover, it can be argued that involvement in partisan politics is useful preparation for the Court, particularly insofar as it provides a broad understanding of the policy issues that the Court's decisions touch. In any case the current pattern is unlikely to change radically.

The Role of Chance. Perhaps the clearest conclusion to be reached from an examination of the path to the Supreme Court is that people do not become justices through an inevitable process. At any given time the number of people considered eligible for appointment to the Court because of their high positions in government or the bar will be very large. Even those people who attain high positions are a small proportion of those who might have reached them. Nor are these two kinds of advancement based on a rational selection of the most able or a "survival of the fittest." Rather, much of the advancement from membership in the bar to the Court is a result of luck as much as anything else. Chance factors such as geography and a president's need to appeal to a major interest group may be decisive in determining whether a person becomes a justice. For this reason an ambitious person hardly could guarantee eventual selection to the Court by choosing a particular career path.

The impact of luck is clear when we consider that presidents ordinarily select members of their own party, and that when they do cross party lines they seldom cross ideological lines at the same time. All the appointments to the Court between 1969 and 1984 were made by Republican presidents. As a result, potential justices who were liberal Democrats and who were of prime age for appointment in this period have had to watch their chances slip away.

Indeed, most justices probably would not have reached the Court under any other president. The case of Byron White is typical of many. White was a highly successful attorney in Denver who became involved in John Kennedy's campaign for the presidency because of their personal friendship. When Kennedy was elected, White received first a position in the Department of Justice and then a Supreme Court appointment. Had Kennedy not become president, it is almost certain that White never would have reached the Court.

The role of luck in the selection of justices does not mean that the Court's direction, as determined by its membership, is entirely random. Although Warren Burger's selection as chief justice was hardly inevitable, President Nixon was certain to select a political conservative for the position. However, this discussion does suggest that membership on the Supreme Court, like other high positions in government, is attained through good fortune as well as a person's own qualities. "You have to be lucky," said Sandra Day O'Connor;[27] that statement reflects realism as well as modesty.

Leaving the Court

Thus far, this chapter has examined the process by which people get to the Supreme Court. Also of importance is the process by which justices' careers end, and in this final section I will examine that process briefly.

Voluntary Resignation and Retirement

When the Supreme Court's importance as a policy maker was established, one effect was to increase the willingness of justices to remain on the Court. In the Court's first decade, its members frequently resigned to seek more attractive opportunities. For instance, John Jay, the first chief justice, left the Court to become governor of New York. Since the early years, however, the great majority of Supreme Court justices have stayed on the Court either until their death or until they were overtaken by age or ill health.

Some notable exceptions to this rule have occurred, including several in this century. Charles Evans Hughes resigned in 1916 on receiving the Republican nomination for president; he lost a close race, and 14 years later he returned to the Court as chief justice. James Byrnes left the Court in 1942 to become director of the Office of Economic Stabilization, a crucial post during World War II. Arthur Goldberg resigned in 1965 to become U.S. ambassador to the United Nations. John Clarke in 1922 and Charles Whittaker in 1962 both resigned largely because of dissatisfaction with the Court and their life on it. But these cases *are* exceptions. Most justices have found the Court sufficiently attractive to remain on it until the end of their professional lives.

In the nineteenth century the desire of some justices to remain on the Court created problems, because these justices refused to resign despite serious infirmities that limited their contributions. In at least a few cases, their colleagues attempted to apply gentle pressure on them to induce retirement. The results were mixed. The classic story concerning these attempts involved Justice Stephen Field, who served in 1870 on a committee of justices that helped to convince Justice Robert Grier to retire. Years later, when age severely limited Field's own capacities, one of his colleagues was delegated to remind him of his encounter with Grier and thus to suggest the desirability of resignation. But when the colleague asked Field if he remembered his visit to Grier, Field replied, "Yes, and a dirtier day's work I never did in my life." [28]

Since 1869 Congress has encouraged aging justices to leave the bench by providing that their salaries will continue if they do so. Today justices who are at least 70 years old and who have served for at least 10 years may resign and continue to receive the salaries that they earned prior to resignation. Justices who meet those criteria, or who are 65 years old with 15 years of service, may retire and still obtain any salary increases granted those still on the Court. (A person who resigns relinquishes the position of justice, whereas one who retires retains that position formally. In either case, the person gives up a seat on the Court and ceases to participate in the Court's decisions.) These financial benefits seem to have had the desired effect, in combination with an apparent growth in the responsibility that justices feel for the Court's work. In the twentieth century, unlike the nineteenth, a majority of justices have left the Court prior to their deaths. Indeed, as Table 2-4 shows, none of the 10 justices who left the Court between 1962 and 1981 died in office, although Black and Harlan died soon afterward. The table also shows that old age and health problems have been the primary reasons for voluntary resignation and retirement in recent years.

Potter Stewart exemplifies the justices who wish to leave the Court before their performance begins to decline. Stewart retired in 1981. He was 66 years old but remained healthy and vigorous, and after retirement he began a busy round of activities that included service on presidential commissions and as a visiting university scholar. In explaining his retirement, he said that "I've always been a firm believer in the principle that it's better to go too soon than to stay too long." [29]

By no means have all recent justices taken Stewart's path. Some have clung to their positions more tenaciously, in some cases because of ideological concerns about the Court. In 1975 William Douglas delayed his retirement until it was absolutely clear that he could not recover from his physical problems, and his delay disrupted the Court's work during that year. Douglas did not want to yield his liberal voice on the Court when his replacement would be chosen by the conservative Gerald Ford—who had, not so incidentally, sought to impeach Douglas a few years earlier. With his mental faculties weakened, Douglas apparently tried to participate in the Court's decisions even after his retirement.[30]

The Court of the early 1980s stood out for the refusal of several members to retire despite advanced age. After Stewart retired, five older colleagues remained on the bench. By the beginning of 1984, those five justices, still on the Court, all were at least 75 years old. In the case of the more liberal justices, especially Brennan and Marshall, the prospect of their replacement by President Reagan undoubtedly helped to keep them from retiring. For conservatives such as Burger, enjoyment of their position and power may have been the primary consideration. Although some of the older justices suffered from health problems, in no case were they as serious or as disruptive as the incapacities of some past justices; in that sense the tenacity of the older justices did not constitute a difficulty for the Court.

Table 2-4. Reasons for leaving the court, since 1960

Year	Justice	Age	Primary reasons for leaving	Length of time from leaving until death
1962	Whittaker	61	Unhappiness on Court, ill health	12 years
1962	Frankfurter	79	Age and ill health	2 years
1965	Goldberg	56	Appointment as ambassador to U.N.	—
1967	Clark	67	Son's appointment as attorney general	10 years
1969	Fortas	58	Pressures based on possible ethical violations	13 years
1969[a]	Warren	78	Age	5 years
1971	Black	85	Age and ill health	1 month
1971	Harlan	72	Age and ill health	3 months
1975	Douglas	77	Age and ill health	4 years
1981	Stewart	66	Age	—

[a] Warren originally announced intent to leave Court in 1968.

SOURCES: Congressional Quarterly, *The Supreme Court: Justice and the Law* (Washington, D.C.: Congressional Quarterly Inc., 1983), 165-183, 244-245; other biographical sources.

External Pressure

Beyond the provision of retirement benefits, Congress and the president can influence specific justices to leave the Court in several ways. First, presidents can offer inducements for justices to take other positions. Franklin Roosevelt was able to appeal to Justice Byrnes to resign from the Court to accept a central position in the war effort in World War II, and it would have been difficult for Byrnes to refuse under the circumstances. A quarter century later Justice Goldberg resigned to take the ambassadorship to the United Nations only under heavy pressure from President Johnson, and apparently only because of an implied understanding that he would be reappointed later. The understanding, of course, was never fulfilled.

Second, the president can try to encourage a justice to leave the Court through indirect pressure. Theodore Roosevelt sought to induce the resignations of Chief Justice Melville Fuller and Justice John Marshall Harlan, in part through leaks to newspapers. Roosevelt's efforts only stiffened the two justices' resolve to stay on the Court; they reportedly made a pact not to resign "until they have to take us out feet foremost." [31] Lyndon Johnson effectively brought about Justice Tom Clark's retirement by appointing Clark's son Ramsey as attorney general. Because the federal government is a party to a high proportion of Supreme Court cases, Justice Clark had little choice but to leave his post.

Third and very different is impeachment or its threatened use. Under the Constitution justices, like other federal officials, can be removed through impeachment proceedings for "treason, bribery, or other high crimes and misdemeanors." [32] President Jefferson actually sought to gain control of the largely Federalist (and thus anti-Jefferson) judiciary through the liberal use of impeachment, and Congress did impeach and convict a federal district judge in 1803. Meanwhile, Justice Samuel Chase made himself vulnerable to impeachment through his participation in President John Adams's campaign for reelection in 1800 and some injudicious and partisan remarks to a Maryland grand jury in 1803. He eventually was impeached, with the action justified chiefly by his handling of political trials, but the Senate acquitted him in 1805. His acquittal effectively ended Jefferson's plans to bring impeachment against other members of the Court.

This episode discredited impeachment as a means to remove justices. Later, the near-success of the effort to remove President Andrew Johnson from office through impeachment helped to establish a belief that impeachment was a potentially dangerous procedure that should be reserved for extraordinary situations. In this century impeachment proceedings have been brought against a few federal judges, but each instance involved clear corruption. In more ambiguous situations, such as judicial senility, impeachment has proved to be a useless procedure.

It is true that justices, like presidents, occasionally are subject to demands for impeachment from their opponents. The ultraconservative John Birch Society engaged in a prolonged campaign to impeach Chief Justice Warren, but there was never any real possibility that Congress would respond to its urgings. Somewhat more serious were several efforts to remove Justice Douglas, with his strong liberalism as the underlying motivation. The most significant of these efforts came in 1969 and 1970, based publicly on his financial connections with a foundation and on his outside writings. The public leader of this effort was House minority leader Gerald Ford, who apparently was set in motion by President Nixon.[33] The impeachment resolution against Douglas was disapproved by a special committee and died.

Justice Fortas is the one exception in this century to the general rule that justices need not fear impeachment; had he not resigned from the Court in 1969, he might well have been removed through impeachment proceedings. Fortas had been criticized for his financial dealings when he was nominated unsuccessfully for chief justice in 1968. A year later it was disclosed that he had a lifetime contract as a consultant to the Wolfson Foundation and had received money from that foundation at a time when its head was being prosecuted by the federal government. The Nixon administration orchestrated a campaign of pressure on Fortas through the mass media and through the Court itself, and after Fortas's explanation of his conduct proved unsatisfying, he resigned fairly quickly. The resignation came too early to determine how successful an impeachment effort would have been, but almost certainly it would have been serious.

A repetition of the Fortas episode may be unlikely, if only because the justices have become more aware of the dangers of questionable financial conduct. Notably, Justice Douglas severed his own foundation connection shortly after Fortas's resignation, and Justice Brennan cut back on his investments and other extra-Court activities. Although the effort to impeach President Nixon in 1974 seemed to revive impeachment as a serious option for Congress, it is still likely to remain a last resort and one used only in extreme circumstances.

Thus the timing of a justice's leaving the Court is chiefly a matter of that person's own inclinations, health, and longevity. Other people seeking to influence the Court's composition may have their say when a vacancy occurs, but they have relatively little control over the vacancies.

Conclusion

One theme that emerges from this chapter is that the recruitment process for Supreme Court justices is affected considerably by the Court's accepted importance. The importance of the Supreme Court in the political system gives presidents an interest in controlling these appointments and causes them to stress competence and policy preferences as well as "political" considerations in selecting justices. For the same reason, the Senate gives nominations to the Court a degree of scrutiny that is unusual for presidential appointments. The prestige attached to the Court helps to limit the selection of its members to those who have achieved high positions in the law or in politics. Finally, the attractiveness of the Court has reduced the willingness of justices to leave it before they are overtaken by old age or death.

Beyond this generalization, it should also be clear that the recruitment of justices is a complex process, whether seen from the perspective of the president or from the perspective of those who aspire to the Court. The Supreme Court is not a body to which people "rise" in an orderly and rational fashion. Rather, people reach the point of being considered for the Court and actually obtain appointments through a process that involves a great many participants, in which a great many considerations are weighed, and in which chance plays a considerable role.

The significance of the recruitment process lies largely in the impact of the Court's membership on its decisions. That impact will be discussed in succeeding chapters, in the examination of the factors that shape the Court's policy choices and determine its general direction.

Notes

1. The three who were nominated and confirmed twice include two individuals elevated from associate justice to chief justice (Edward White and Harlan Stone) as well as one (Charles Evans Hughes) who resigned from the Court and was later appointed chief justice.
2. U.S. Congress, Senate, *Congressional Record,* 91st Cong., 2d sess., 1970, 116, pt. 3:2860.
3. Henry J. Abraham and Bruce Allen Murphy, "The Influence of Sitting and Retired Justices on Presidential Supreme Court Nominations," *Hastings Constitutional Law Quarterly* 3 (Winter 1976): 37-63.
4. Abraham and Murphy, "Influence of Sitting and Retired Justices," 49; Aric Press, "A Woman for the Court," *Newsweek,* July 20, 1981, 17.
5. William O. Douglas, *Go East, Young Man: The Early Years* (New York: Random House, 1974), 332.
6. Joel B. Grossman, *Lawyers and Judges: The ABA and the Politics of Judicial Selection* (New York: John Wiley & Sons, 1965), 42.
7. Henry J. Abraham, *Justices and Presidents: A Political History of Appointments to the Supreme Court* (New York: Oxford University Press, 1974), 174.
8. William O. Douglas, *The Court Years 1939-1975: The Autobiography of William O. Douglas* (New York: Random House, 1980), 247.

9. John Ehrlichman, *Witness to Power: The Nixon Years* (New York: Simon and Schuster, 1982), 114-115. The quotation is on p. 114.

10. William H. Harbaugh, *Lawyer's Lawyer: The Life of John W. Davis* (New York: Oxford University Press, 1973), 192.

11. Robert Scigliano, *The Supreme Court and the Presidency* (New York: Free Press, 1971), 107-108.

12. Bernard Schwartz, *Super Chief: Earl Warren and His Supreme Court—A Judicial Biography* (New York: New York University Press, 1983), 216.

13. Data supporting this conclusion are presented in David W. Rohde and Harold J. Spaeth, *Supreme Court Decision Making* (San Francisco: W. H. Freeman & Company, 1976), 107-109.

14. John A. Jenkins, "A Candid Talk with Justice Blackmun," *New York Times Magazine,* February 20, 1983, 24.

15. Abraham, *Justices and Presidents,* 246.

16. Scigliano, *Supreme Court and the Presidency,* 147-148.

17. Ibid., 95.

18. Lou Cannon, "Reagan Pledges He Would Name a Woman to the Supreme Court," *Washington Post,* October 15, 1980, A6.

19. Data on the length of the process are collected in Joel B. Grossman and Stephen L. Wasby, "The Senate and Supreme Court Nominations: Some Reflections," *Duke Law Journal* (1972): 563-566.

20. These figures and those in the following paragraph are based primarily on data in Scigliano, *Supreme Court and the Presidency,* 97-99.

21. "CQ on the Floor," *Congressional Quarterly Weekly Report,* March 20, 1970, 776.

22. "Justice Black and the Bill of Rights," *Southwestern University Law Review* 9 (1977): 939-940.

23. For this observation and much of the information on which the analysis in this section is based, I am indebted to John R. Schmidhauser, *Judges and Justices: The Federal Appellate Judiciary* (Boston: Little, Brown & Co., 1979), 41-100.

24. Ibid., 49.

25. Sheldon Goldman and Thomas P. Jahnige, *The Federal Courts as a Political System,* 2d ed. (New York: Harper & Row, 1976), 67.

26. Schmidhauser, *Judges and Justices,* 99.

27. Laurence Bodine, "Sandra Day O'Connor," *American Bar Association Journal* 69 (October 1983): 1394.

28. Quoted in Robert Shogan, *A Question of Judgment: The Fortas Case and the Struggle for the Supreme Court* (Indianapolis: Bobbs-Merrill Co., 1972), 250.

29. Fred Barbash, "Student Query Moved Stewart to Quit," *Washington Post,* June 20, 1981, A9.

30. James F. Simon, *Independent Journey: The Life of William O. Douglas* (New York: Harper & Row, 1980), 452-454.

31. John E. Semonche, *Charting the Future: The Supreme Court Responds to a Changing Society, 1890-1920* (Westport, Conn.: Greenwood Press, 1978), 202.

32. U.S. *Constitution,* Art. 2, sec. 4.

33. Ehrlichman, *Witness to Power,* 122.

The Cases 3

In recent years the Supreme Court has decided an average of about 150 cases with full opinions each term. In these cases the Court not only rules on the legal rights of specific parties but also lays down general principles that apply to the nation as a whole. It is primarily these cases that the Court uses to make law and policy.

These 150 cases, of course, involve only a minute proportion of the disputes that might have resulted in full Supreme Court decisions. This fact gives great importance to the process that determines which cases the Court does decide, the Court's agenda-setting process. This chapter will examine that complex process, with the goal of understanding the roles of the various participants who help to set the Supreme Court's agenda. The first section will take a brief, general view of the agenda-setting process. The following two sections will look at how cases are brought to the Court and how the Court chooses which of these cases it will hear. A final section will discuss the growth in the Court's caseload and its significance for the Court's capacity to function.

A General View

Steps in the Process

The Supreme Court's agenda-setting process ordinarily involves several successive steps. First, a case is initiated in a state or federal trial court. This first step is significant, since only a small minority of the legal disputes which might be taken to court actually result in civil suits or criminal prosecutions.

In the second step, that case must proceed through the court system to a court from which a dissatisfied party can bring a case to the Supreme Court. This means, of course, that the parties have not settled the case somewhere along the way; approximately 90 percent of all civil and criminal cases are settled prior to a trial-court decision. It also means that at least one of the parties must appeal from the court's decision at each step.

Third, the party who is dissatisfied with the decision of a court below the Supreme Court—usually a federal court of appeals or a state supreme court—petitions the U.S. Supreme Court to hear the case. Petitions are brought in only a minority of cases. One study found that 30 percent of the losing parties in the federal courts of appeals took their cases to the Supreme Court.[1] The petition rate from state supreme courts is lower; a high proportion of cases in state supreme courts are ineligible for hearing by the Supreme Court because they involve no issues of federal law.

Finally, the Supreme Court agrees to accept the case for decision on the merits and then renders a decision with full opinion. By its own rule the Court does not accept a case for decision on its merits unless four justices agree that the case should receive that treatment; this is the "rule of four." Even when the Court does accept a case, it may render only a summary decision rather than a full ruling on the legal issues. The Court is highly selective in its choices; for every case which it accepts and decides fully, more than 20 are rejected or decided summarily.

Two classes of cases take routes to the Court that differ somewhat from the one that I have described. Some cases originate in federal administrative agencies and go next to the courts of appeals, only one step below the Supreme Court. A few cases arise under the Court's original jurisdiction and come directly to the Court. Like other cases, however, these cases reach the Court's ultimate agenda through action by one or more parties and by the Court itself.

The Participants

In the agenda-setting process for the Supreme Court, three sets of participants play crucial roles. The first is Congress, which influences the agenda in several ways. Most broadly, Congress has general power over the Court's appellate jurisdiction. Through this power Congress can determine what classes of cases may come to the Court and from what courts they may be brought.

Congressional legislation can affect the agenda in a variety of other ways. For instance, Congress occasionally adopts statutes that allow certain kinds of parties, such as persons subject to racial or sexual discrimination, new or expanded rights to bring cases to federal court. By doing so it increases the potential business of the Supreme Court. Major changes in environmental or tax statutes are likely to create new questions of interpretation that the Court ultimately may resolve. When Congress creates a large number of new federal judgeships, as it did in 1978, it may reduce the delay in lower federal courts and thus encourage litigants to use those courts, and in turn a larger number of cases may reach the Supreme Court. Although the impact of a specific congressional action on the Court's agenda frequently is too subtle to measure, the overall impact of Congress on that agenda is tremendous.

The impact of litigants and potential litigants is much more direct. Like most courts, the Supreme Court cannot hear a case on its own initiative. Thus the Court is totally dependent upon people and institutions that bring cases to court originally and that bring cases up to the Supreme Court. Moreover, the Court must address the facts of the particular cases which come to it. It cannot reach out for a case with a "better" set of facts if no such case has been brought to it. Litigants also help to determine the Court's range of options with the issues that they raise.

Finally, the Court itself plays a most important role in the process. The Court has total control over its agenda in a negative sense by retaining an absolute power to forgo full decision in any given case. No matter how many cases are brought to the Court concerning a particular issue, no matter how urgent that issue seems, nobody can require the Court to give a case full consideration. When the Court does agree to hear a case, it can determine which issues in the case it will address, and in this respect too the Court is master of its own agenda. One striking example is *Mapp v. Ohio* (1961), in which the Court turned what had been brought to it and argued before it as an obscenity case into a landmark decision on searches and seizures.

The Court also can encourage and discourage cases in particular areas through the cues that its decisions provide for potential litigants. If the Court evinces sympathy for aliens who are subject to government discrimination, for instance, cases which challenge discrimination against aliens are likely to reach the Court in increased numbers.

Assessing the Court's Position

In a general way, the Supreme Court's position in the setting of its agenda may be considered a hybrid of the positions of most courts and that of Congress. In its dependence on the legislative branch for most of its jurisdiction and on litigants to bring cases the Court is similar to other courts but very different from Congress. Unlike the Supreme Court, Congress can address whatever policy questions it chooses. It is subject to few constraints from other institutions in this respect, and it can act on an issue whether or not it has received any requests for such action. In this sense Congress has a significant degree of freedom which the Court lacks.

In its capacity to choose from the cases brought to it, however, the Supreme Court is more typical of a legislature than of a court. All courts have some ability to screen the litigation brought to them, but few have as complete a freedom to reject cases as does the Supreme Court.

Moreover, the very large number of requests for hearings allows the Court to be highly selective.

The Court's control over its agenda is greater than this hybrid position might suggest. First, the practical impact of the Court's enforced passivity is more limited than it appears to be. As I have noted, the Court can encourage and discourage litigation of a particular type through its pattern of decisions. Moreover, because so many cases are brought to the Court, justices probably will find in these cases nearly all the questions that they would like to decide.

The Court also draws freedom from its relative isolation in the political system. While Congress technically is totally free to decide which issues it will address seriously, in practice its choices are dictated in part by pressures upon it to act. Since the mid-1970s, for instance, Congress often has had little choice but to grapple with energy problems. Further, Congress is burdened by recurring issues such as the budget which must be addressed regularly. The Court is nearly free of those constraints. An occasional case will be regarded as so important that the Court feels some pressure to decide it, but for the most part the Court has practical as well as technical freedom to turn aside whatever litigation it chooses.

Thus the Supreme Court has almost as much control over its agenda as does Congress, despite the seemingly fundamental differences between their positions. Certainly the Court possesses great freedom to determine the issues it will address.

Reaching the Court:
Litigants, Attorneys, and Groups

In the 1983 term about 4,200 cases were filed in the Supreme Court.[2] These cases came from a great many different courts, primarily federal courts of appeals and state supreme courts. Their subject matter was diverse; the largest number arose from criminal prosecutions, but the others included a wide variety of policy issues in civil cases. What all of these cases had in common, of course, was a request for action by the Supreme Court.

In this section I will consider how and why these cases came to the Supreme Court by examining the roles of three sets of participants: the litigants who are parties to the cases; the attorneys who represent them; and the interest groups that frequently play either central or peripheral roles in the litigation process. After discussing these sets of participants, I will give separate attention to the litigation activities of the federal government, the single most frequent participant in Supreme Court cases and one whose role is rather distinctive.

Litigants

Every case which comes to the Supreme Court has at least two formal parties, one on each side, and frequently more than two. For a case to reach the Court, of course, one or more of the parties must have taken action to initiate the litigation and to move it upward through the court system. Parties who have played this role in Supreme Court cases may be referred to generally as litigants.

As we would expect, litigants in the Supreme Court are a rather diverse lot. Many are individuals. Most individual litigants are criminal defendants, but individuals also appear in disputes concerning such civil matters as civil rights issues or personal injuries. Others are private institutions, including businesses, labor unions, colleges, foundations, and an array of other categories. Still others are state and local government agencies, most commonly the local agencies responsible for prosecution of criminal cases. Finally, a variety of agencies of the federal government become litigants in the Court. As this range of litigants suggests, it is difficult to generalize about the participants in Supreme Court cases.

The Motivations of Litigants. Perhaps the most important question concerning litigants is why they have become involved in court cases and carried them to the Supreme Court. The significance of this question is underlined by the fact that most people seek to avoid litigation or to terminate it as early as possible, chiefly because of its expense and the conflict and risk that it engenders. The motives of litigants can be thought of as taking two general forms, resulting in two "ideal types" of Supreme Court litigation. In reality some litigation falls between the two types, because it is based on mixed motives, but the distinction is still a useful one.

The first type may be called "ordinary" litigation because of its relative frequency. Ordinarily, people bring cases to court or appeal adverse judgments because of a direct personal or organizational interest that they seek to advance. Plaintiffs take personal injury suits to court because they perceive that they will obtain a monetary advantage from litigation. Prosecutors file criminal cases in order to fulfill the goals of the prosecuting agencies for which they work. Similarly, litigants usually appeal court decisions because they believe that their potential gain from a successful appeal and the likelihood of success are sufficient to justify additional trouble and expense.

The second type may be called "political" litigation. Here the goal of litigants is not self-interest but the advancement of policies that they favor. Most often, political litigation involves an effort to obtain a judicial decision that supports the litigant's policy goals. For instance, a person concerned with environmental protection might bring a suit to obtain a stringent interpretation of a statute that regulates air pollution. Someone who seeks to promote equality for disabled people may challenge the constitutionality of a state law that allegedly discriminates against the disabled.

The proportion of litigation that can be classified as political increases with each step upward in the judicial system, and political litigation is most common in the Supreme Court. This pattern is not accidental. Ordinary litigation tends to be terminated at a relatively early stage because participants find it more profitable to settle their dispute or even to accept a defeat than to fight on. In contrast, political litigants often can obtain significant victories only by getting a case to the highest levels of the system; a favorable verdict at the local level may do little to advance their policy goals. Moreover, political litigation often attracts support from interest groups that help to shoulder financial and other burdens of carrying a case through the judicial system.

Still, most of the cases brought to the Supreme Court would be classified as ordinary litigation. A large share are criminal cases in which the primary goal of the convicted defendant who seeks a hearing is to get out or stay out of prison. Other cases involve business corporations that have a sufficient economic stake in the outcome to justify a petition to the Court. Still other cases involve a variety of individual grievances, big or small, in which the aggrieved party cannot resist going to the Supreme Court for one final effort at redress.

Political litigation is more common in the set of cases that the Court agrees to hear, because these cases are more likely to involve the broad issues in which the justices are interested. Yet by no means is ordinary litigation absent from this set of cases. Even in the biggest cases, the ones that attract attention from large numbers of interest groups, the litigants themselves sometimes are motivated primarily by personal self-interest.

Some Examples. A few examples of Supreme Court litigants will suggest the range of goals that motivate them. Cecelia Young is a good representative of the litigant with a personal grievance. Young lived on the edge of Atlantic Beach, North Carolina. She kept two goats and a pony on her property. In 1979 Atlantic Beach passed an ordinance barring residents from keeping on their property a number of animals, including horses and goats. When town officials tried to evict Young's animals, she argued in court that her animals fell under a "house pets" exception in the ordinance. After the state supreme court ruled against her, Young took her case to the Supreme Court on constitutional grounds. While she may have been trying to make a point, her primary interest was in keeping her animals. Her case attracted the attention of neither interest groups nor the Supreme Court itself; her petition for a hearing was turned down in June 1983.[3]

Allan Bakke's case was of far more interest to other people. His challenge to an affirmative action program at a University of California medical school attracted national publicity and the submission of legal briefs to the Court in the names of more than one hundred interest groups. But Bakke simply wanted to get into medical school, and he brought suit for that purpose. After the Supreme Court accepted his case—the university appealed from a state court decision favorable to him—Bakke avoided journalists and refrained from speaking about the litigation. When the Court ruled in his favor in 1978, he spoke not of the policy issues in the case but of his pleasure at the prospect of attending medical school. Whatever his case was to the rest of the nation, for Bakke it was ordinary litigation.[4]

Edward Lawson was a black man with long hair in the Rastafarian style who frequently took evening walks in San Diego districts that were primarily white and upper-middle class. This combination of circumstances resulted in his being stopped several times by police officers, after which he would refuse to identify himself. Because of this refusal he was arrested or detained approximately 15 times between 1975 and 1977 under a California loitering statute that required people on the streets to provide identification and account for their presence when requested with justification by a police officer. Eventually Lawson brought a lawsuit asking, among other things, that the applicable statute be declared unconstitutional. After Lawson won that declaration in the lower federal courts, the defendants brought the case to the Supreme Court. Lawson's motives for the case appear to be complex, combining a personal interest in protection from police interference with a more general interest in protection of civil liberties. Lawson did take full advantage of his case as a means to garner personal publicity. He freely gave interviews to the press and even sought as a nonlawyer to argue the case himself before the Supreme Court. He was turned down in that effort, but the Court ultimately ruled in his favor in 1983.[5]

One example of "pure" political litigation is the case arising from a city-sponsored nativity scene in Pawtucket, Rhode Island. The case was brought in 1980 by four individuals, some of whom were members of the Rhode Island affiliate of the American Civil Liberties Union (ACLU), and by the affiliate itself. The individual plaintiffs had nothing to gain personally from the litigation; indeed, people who challenge government involvement with religion sometimes suffer abuse for their efforts. Rather, the lawsuit was an expression of the goals of the ACLU in supporting the separation of church and state. After winning in the lower federal courts, the opponents of the nativity scene lost in the Supreme Court in 1984.[6] The loss, like the case itself, was on the level of the plaintiffs' policy goals rather than their personal interests.

Lawyers

In about half of the cases that come to the Supreme Court, the parties seeking a hearing from the Court are represented by attorneys; most of the others are cases brought by indigent prisoners. In nearly all cases that reach the Court, attorneys have been involved at the lower court level. Thus an examination of Supreme Court litigation must take into account the role of lawyers.

The participation of attorneys in cases that reach the Court varies considerably in form. In some cases a litigant is represented by the same attorney from the initiation of the case through the Supreme Court decision. Allan Bakke and his attorney Reynold Colvin worked together throughout Bakke's legal efforts to obtain admission to medical school. Criminal defendants are more likely to be represented by a series of attorneys as their case progresses and, if they are indigent, to draft their petition for a hearing in the Supreme Court without legal representation. If the Court accepts such a case, it will appoint an attorney to represent the successful petitioner.

When attorneys are involved in cases, they tend to become the primary decision makers for their side. By hiring a lawyer, a person makes a kind of tradeoff, gaining the benefit of the attorney's expertise but losing some control over the handling of the case. This loss of control is significant, since it makes the litigant dependent upon the attorney's competence and willingness to serve the litigant's interests faithfully.

Attorneys may not fully serve their clients' interests where attorney and client view the case from different perspectives. This is seldom a problem in economic cases before the Court. If a corporation's officers pursue an antitrust case without concern for its general policy implications, the corporation's attorneys can be expected to view the case in much the same way.

The potential for divergent perspectives is greater in civil liberties cases. In this field a litigant may pursue a case for reasons of self-interest while the attorney is motivated by broader policy concerns. This is particularly true when an attorney donates services to the client because of an individual or group interest in the policy issues in a case. In his research Jonathan Casper found that attorneys with the ACLU who volunteered their services to criminal defendants tended to view their work in terms of principles rather than clients. Speaking of the defendants in most of these cases, one attorney said: "They're pretty scurvy little creatures, and what *they* are doesn't matter a whole hell of a lot. It's the principle that we're going to be able to use these people for that's important." [7] An attorney with such an attitude may subordinate the client's interest in getting out of prison to the pursuit of more general principles of civil liberties. For instance, the attorney may ignore narrow legal issues that might win the case but that would cost the case any general significance.

Members of the Court and other observers have complained about the competence of many attorneys who appear before the Court. Justice William Douglas, a harsh critic, concluded: "Few truly good advocates have appeared before the Court. In my time 40 percent were incompetent." [8] In 1972 a study group on the Court's caseload reported that "the average level of oral advocacy in the Court is judged to be disappointingly low." [9]

To the extent that problems of competence exist, they stem to some degree from the inexperience of most advocates. In the nineteenth century a high proportion of Supreme Court cases were handled by a few attorneys who argued regularly before the Court, representing many different parties. One lawyer argued 317 cases between 1801 and 1850. [10] Today few attorneys other than those who represent the federal government appear before the Court with any regularity. In the 1982 term, only two nonfederal attorneys participated in oral argument as many as three times. One of the two was Harvard law professor Laurence Tribe, whose eight arguments over four years for a variety of clients make him perhaps the closest current equivalent to the Supreme Court specialists of an earlier period.

In the legal system as a whole, a relationship exists between the wealth of an individual or institution and the quality of the legal services available to that party. In the Supreme Court the relationship between wealth and quality of available services is less clear. Many of the attorneys who do appear before the Court with some frequency and who are most skilled in arguing before the Court represent some of the poorest and most powerless groups in society. Attorneys such as Thurgood Marshall and Jack Greenberg of the NAACP Legal Defense Fund and Hayden Covington of the Jehovah's Witnesses have been frequent and effective advocates for their groups in the Court. Lawyers for state and local governments who must contend with more experienced advocates for civil rights and civil liberties groups often are outmatched, and in response to that situation a State and Local Legal Center was established in the early 1980s to help these government lawyers prepare for Supreme Court cases.

Even a poor person without support from an interest group is likely to get very good legal services in a case that the Court accepts, because the Court appoints some of the best attorneys in the country to represent indigent litigants; a lawyer who is offered such an appointment seldom declines. For instance, Abe Fortas, then a renowned Washington lawyer, was appointed to represent Clarence Earl Gideon in the famous case of *Gideon v. Wainwright* (1963), which concerned the right to counsel for indigent criminal defendants.

Once in a great while a Supreme Court litigant who is not an attorney wishes to argue the case personally. Twice during the 1970s the Court allowed litigants to do so. But in 1982, as I noted, the Court refused that right to Edward Lawson in his fight against the California loitering statute; the relative importance of the issue in the *Lawson* case may explain the difference.

Interest Groups

The Forms of Group Activity. The activity of political interest groups in Supreme Court policy making is greatly circumscribed in comparison with group activity in Congress. It is considered highly illegitimate to lobby judges directly, as a group would lobby legislators; in general, Supreme Court justices seek to avoid contact with litigants and others interested in the outcomes of particular cases. When Thomas Corcoran, a prominent Washington lobbyist, reportedly sought to lobby Justices Black and Brennan in a case in 1969, the justices were said to have been shocked and angered.[11] The justices also are insulated from group influence in the sense that groups have rather little to offer them in comparison with the services which they can perform for legislators or administrators.

Still, interest groups can seek to influence what the Court does in several ways. First, a group can help to get cases to the Court. It may initiate a "test case" designed to obtain a ruling from the Court on a policy issue that is important to the group, locating people who can serve as plaintiffs in the case and directing the litigation from the start. Alternatively, a group can become involved in cases that others already have initiated, helping to bear financial costs and supplying legal services and advice.

Second, a group can attempt to influence the Court's decisions whether to accept cases and how to decide those that are accepted through participation in oral argument or the submission of legal briefs. If a group is effectively in control of a case, its attorneys will submit the brief in support of (or in opposition to) the Supreme Court's acceptance of the case. If the case is accepted for full decision, the group's attorneys will submit further briefs and participate in oral argument.

When a group does not control the case, it still may submit arguments to the Court through what are called *amicus curiae* ("friend of the court") briefs. With the consent of the parties to a case or by permission of the Court, any person or organization may submit an *amicus* brief to supplement the arguments of the parties. (Legal representatives of the various levels of government do not need to obtain permission.) *Amicus* briefs can be submitted on the issue of whether a case should be heard or, after a case is accepted for hearing, directly on

Table 3-1. Examples of interest groups and other parties submitting or joining in *amicus curiae* briefs to the Supreme Court in cases decided in the 1983 term

Private interest groups

Air Transport Association of America
American Civil Liberties Union of Northern California
American Immigration Lawyers Association
Atomic Industrial Forum
Authors League of America
Florida Farm Bureau Federation
League of Women Voters of the United States
Mexican American Legal Defense and Education Fund
Minnesota Public Interest Research Group
Motor Vehicle Manufacturers Association
Mountain States Legal Foundation
National Council of Churches of Christ in the U.S.A.
National Council on Crime and Delinquency
National Education Association
Reporters Committee for Freedom of the Press

Governments and government organizations

American Samoa
City of Norfolk, Va.
Multistate Tax Commission
National Institute of Municipal Law Officers
New Jersey Department of the Public Advocate
State of New York
United States

Businesses

Brooklyn Union Gas Co.
Dow Jones & Company
Minnesota Mining and Manufacturing Co.
Mountain States Telephone and Telegraph Co.
New York Times Company
Sears Roebuck and Co.
TDK Electronics Company, Ltd.

Individuals

Alan Cranston
Bob Dole
Geraldine A. Ferraro
Claude Pepper

the merits of the case. Submission of *amicus* briefs is the easiest and most common form of group involvement in cases. If "commercial" cases are excluded, 53 percent of the cases decided by the Court with full opinions between 1970 and 1980 attracted at least one *amicus* brief.[12] In turn, a high proportion of *amicus* briefs come from interest groups. The large number and diversity of the groups that submit *amicus* briefs are suggested by Table 3-1, which offers a partial listing of the groups and other parties providing such briefs in cases decided during the Court's 1983 term.

Finally, a group can attempt to lobby the Court indirectly. Occasionally a group will hold demonstrations, as civil rights groups did in the *Bakke* case, or initiate a letter-writing campaign directed at the justices. These tactics are regarded as being of questionable legitimacy. Justice Frankfurter once recommended that the Court consider citing the Communist Party for contempt for threatening demonstrations if a decision displeased it.[13] On a more significant level, groups sometimes attempt to get articles favorable to their positions published in law journals and other prestigious outlets. In its efforts to overturn restrictive covenants that limited blacks' access to housing, the NAACP stimulated several publications to publish articles designed to obtain support from the public and the Court.

Taken together, these avenues of potential influence may provide groups with significant roles in Supreme Court policy making. At this point I will focus on the part which groups play in getting cases to the Court. In the next chapter I will discuss their influence over the Court's decisions.

Group Involvement in the Supreme Court. Because Supreme Court decisions are such an important part of public policy making, it is inevitable that groups seek to bring cases to the Court. Over time a great many groups of various types undertake this effort. While most of these groups do so only occasionally, some are fairly regular participants in Supreme Court litigation. These "regulars" are those groups for which litigation seems likely to pay significant dividends, because the policy issues that concern these groups fall within the Court's own concerns and because the Court appears to be sympathetic to these groups' claims.

In the late nineteenth and early twentieth centuries, the groups most prominent in the Court were conservative groups that opposed government regulation of business. Unable to prevent the growth of regulatory legislation, they turned to the more sympathetic courts with claims that much of this legislation was unconstitutional. These claims were fairly successful, as the Supreme Court struck down a good deal of regulatory legislation in the first four decades of this century. But by the late 1930s the Court adopted a more liberal position on economic issues that discouraged further efforts by antiregulation groups.

The Court's growing liberalism encouraged increased efforts by groups that already had begun to litigate on behalf of civil liberties. Most prominent were the ACLU, with general interests in civil liberties, and the NAACP, with its interest in the status of black people. Both groups had found the other branches of government inhospitable to their concerns, while the Supreme Court provided enough support to make litigation efforts worthwhile. Also active were other groups with civil liberties interests such as the Jehovah's Witnesses, who sought to protect the proselytizing activities of their members.

In the last two decades new kinds of groups have played a significant part in the litigation process. The NAACP has been joined by groups that represent more recent civil rights interests, such as the National Organization for Women and the Mexican-American Legal Defense and Education Fund. Groups supporting consumers and environmental protection have also become involved in litigation. The Sierra Club, for instance, has sponsored environmental cases that reached the Supreme Court.

One important structure that has emerged in recent years is the public interest law firm, a concept pioneered by Ralph Nader in the 1960s. These firms devote themselves to cases that they see as serving the public interest in general. They are not tied directly to a particular interest group, and the activities of any particular firm may range broadly. The first public interest firms were ideologically liberal, and these groups have brought litigation with liberal goals such as protection of civil liberties and the environment.

In the 1970s and 1980s conservative groups have become increasingly frequent participants in Supreme Court litigation.[14] During this period several conservative public interest law firms have been created, primarily on a regional basis, and these firms have been responsible for some of the conservative resurgence. Conservative groups give more emphasis to economic issues than do their liberal counterparts; one of their goals is to limit government business regulations that they see as undesirable. As yet, the participation of conservative groups in the Supreme Court generally is limited to the submission of *amicus* briefs; in this respect they play less central roles than do liberal groups that fully sponsor cases. Undoubtedly, conservative groups have been encouraged by the favorable ideological trend in the Court; should the Court become even more conservative with new appointments, conservative groups could be expected to devote even greater efforts to litigation.

The involvement of groups in the Supreme Court clearly has increased over time. Research by Karen O'Connor and Lee Epstein shows that the proportion of cases with *amicus* briefs has grown substantially over the last half century, and group sponsorship of cases also seems to have increased.[15] One reason may be increased awareness of the Court's importance as a public policy maker. Another, probably, is the examples that some groups set for others. Several groups have patterned legal defense funds after the one established by the NAACP, and liberal public interest firms have served as a model for conservative counterparts. Whatever the causes, the Court gradually has become more of a focus for interest group activity.

Group Approaches and Strategies. Of the various groups involved in Supreme Court litigation, some are far more active than others. The groups that involve themselves in the largest number of cases also tend to play the most central roles when they do become involved. It is these groups that merit the closest scrutiny.

These groups differ a good deal in such characteristics as the scope of their activities and the ways that they make litigation decisions. One key similarity among them is the desire to develop effective long-term strategies for litigation. Ideally, a group interested in the favorable development of legal policy in a particular field would bring a series of cases to the Supreme Court through which the Court gradually would move doctrine in the direction the group favors. To achieve this result, groups look for cases which will serve their interests at a particular time. "Good" cases have such characteristics as favorable factual situations and attractive plaintiffs. For instance, in a case attacking government involvement in religion, a devout churchgoer serves as a better plaintiff than an outspoken atheist. Because of the rule of precedent and the caution which frequently characterizes courts, a group ordinarily seeks a case in which the Supreme Court must move only a short distance from its existing position to rule in the group's favor rather than a case in which a favorable decision requires that existing doctrine be uprooted.

This kind of strategy is easier to describe than to achieve. First of all, groups are constrained by limited resources. Litigation is expensive, and many groups have difficulty in financing their court activities. This is especially true of groups with very broad interests, such as the ACLU and the NAACP Legal Defense Fund, which could not possibly finance major campaigns in each area of concern to them. Certainly, what such groups are able to do depends heavily on their success in raising money through memberships, foundation grants, and other sources.

Even if finances are no problem, the task of carrying out an ideal litigation program is complicated by other practical considerations. The case which would meet a group's needs perfectly often does not exist, and a group then must accept a less attractive vehicle for its legal arguments. Further, no group has total control over the initiation of litigation in its area of interest. A group cannot prevent individuals from bringing cases, and in criminal justice the initiative in effect lies with prosecutors rather than with defendants and the groups that support their rights. The groups that work against capital punishment have no choice but to enter cases in which prosecutors have sought and obtained death sentences. Often multiple groups are active on the same side of an issue; this is the case, for instance, with women's rights litigation, in which the ACLU and several women's groups are active. This situation may create problems of coordination, especially when groups have different goals. A large and decentralized group such as the ACLU often has trouble even in coordinating its own activities.

Of course, the courts themselves are not always cooperative. An environmental group may select a case as the appropriate vehicle to establish a principle from which it can work in future cases. But if the Supreme Court refuses to hear that case or explicitly rejects the principle in question, the strategy must be reconsidered.

This discussion suggests that groups must be satisfied with something less than well-coordinated long-term litigation campaigns. "Despite talk of 'strategy,'" Stephen Wasby has concluded, "it is problematic whether interest groups do more than respond idiosyncratically to cases one at a time." [16] From this perspective it is all the more impressive that at least a few groups have enjoyed considerable success over a long period in getting cases to the Supreme Court. It will be useful to take a further look at the two litigating groups that have been the most important over the past two decades.

The NAACP Legal Defense Fund. The NAACP was organized in 1909.[17] Early in its history it began to devote extensive efforts to litigation, largely because the executive and legislative branches were unfriendly to the interests of black citizens. In 1939 the NAACP established the Legal Defense and Educational Fund, usually called the Legal Defense Fund or simply the Fund, as a separate organization for legal activity. The Fund gradually became more independent of the NAACP, and the two organizations now are entirely separate.

The Fund does not have a mass membership, and much of its activity is centralized in a national office in New York City. Its litigation activities operate primarily through the national staff and a network of cooperating attorneys throughout the country. Possible cases come from a variety of sources, and the Fund's staff attempts to choose among them on the basis of priorities and strategic considerations.

The Fund is best known for its work in school desegregation, especially for its management of the attacks on Southern school segregation that led to the Supreme Court's decision in *Brown v. Board of Education* (1954). But the Fund has been involved in a variety of other areas as well. Voting rights is a long-standing and continuing priority.

After Congress adopted the Civil Rights Act of 1964, the Fund initiated a concerted litigation campaign to obtain effective enforcement of its provision on employment.

In part because it is not a membership group, the Fund has some advantages in carrying out general strategies. But its orchestration of the *Brown* case probably has been exaggerated, and in some other instances the organization has been unable to develop and implement effective strategies. One problem is that the Fund cannot always choose the cases that it handles; another is that in most areas of its work other organizations also are engaged in litigation.

Nonetheless, the achievements of the NAACP Legal Defense Fund are impressive. It has brought a substantial number of cases to the Supreme Court concerning legal equality and other issues that affect the status of black citizens. One ironic tribute to the Fund's effectiveness is the efforts that Southern opponents of civil rights expended in the 1950s and 1960s to cripple its litigation activities. A more straightforward tribute is the establishment of similar litigation operations by a variety of other organizations that seek to influence judicial policy.

The American Civil Liberties Union. The ACLU was established after World War I as an organization to protect civil liberties, and it has always emphasized litigation as a means to that end.[18] Its range of interests is even broader than that of the NAACP; it has given particular emphasis to freedom of expression, but by no means does it specialize in that field. During the Supreme Court's 1982 term, the ACLU participated in cases on such issues as the rights of public employees, sex discrimination in pension plans, tax deductions for parochial school tuitions, and access to the ballot for minor political parties.

The ACLU participates in a great many Supreme Court cases as *amicus,* but its central activity is sponsoring of cases. To a great extent, this sponsorship role is triggered by the action of people outside the organization. People bring complaints of civil liberties violations to local ACLU affiliates, which then determine whether to take legal action. Litigation is undertaken primarily by volunteer attorneys attached to affiliates. The national office has a fairly small staff and budget. Its litigation activity comes largely at the Supreme Court level, where it reserves the right to take charge of ACLU cases.

The obvious disadvantage of this system is its fragmentation, which aggravates the difficulty of coordinating litigation and selecting appropriate cases to take to the Supreme Court. The ACLU is not well structured to carry out an ideal litigation strategy. But the ACLU's decentralization makes it accessible to people with civil liberties complaints and thus maximizes the number of potential cases from which the organization can choose. (Not incidentally, ACLU affiliates also can help to solve individual problems without engaging in litigation.)

Certainly the ACLU has been quite active as a Supreme Court litigator. It has aided litigants in such important cases as *Engel v. Vitale* (1962), in which the Court ruled against recitation of prayers in public schools, and *Buckley v. Valeo* (1976), in which the Court struck down part of the Federal Election Campaign Act. Its resources and the skills of its attorneys often make it possible for a significant case to get to the Court and strengthen cases as candidates for hearings by the Court.

In the 1970s and 1980s the ACLU has operated several special projects that undertake concerted campaigns in specific areas. Among the projects set up are those dealing with sex discrimination, children's rights, prisons, and national security. These projects have made a mark; through the Women's Rights Project, for instance, the ACLU has been the primary sponsor of sex discrimination cases decided by the Supreme Court since 1969. Because of the coordination that these projects provide, they offer a useful complement to the traditional mode of ACLU litigation activity.

Conclusions: The Significance of Groups. It is clear that interest groups are heavily involved in Supreme Court litigation, but how important are they in getting cases to the Court? In this respect, cases may be placed in three general categories.

The largest category includes the cases that come to the Court without any participation by interest groups. For the most part, these cases constitute what I have called "ordinary" litigation. The issues in these cases are too narrow to interest any group. These cases get to the Court because the parties and attorneys have sufficient motivation on their own to seek a Supreme Court hearing and sufficient resources to finance the litigation costs. As suggested earlier, these conditions often exist in litigation involving businesses and in criminal cases.

A second category consists of cases in which group help is unnecessary to get to the Court but one or more groups are involved in some way. An interest group may aid one of the parties with legal services or financing to ensure that the case does reach the Supreme Court and to gain some control over its form. More often, a group supplements the legal arguments of a party with an *amicus* brief. The group's participation may enhance the chances of getting a hearing from the Supreme Court, particularly by providing effective legal arguments in favor of hearing the case.

Finally there are the cases that would not reach the Court without the initiative or aid of interest groups. In areas such as civil liberties there often are important legal questions that no individual litigant has sufficient incentive or capability to take to the Supreme Court. Ordinarily it would be impossible for one parent or even several parents to arrange and finance a school desegregation suit on their own. To take another example, a man named Stephen Wiesenfeld believed that he had been subjected to sex discrimination when he was denied Social Security benefits under statutory rules after his wife's death, but a successful suit against the federal government would have cost more than any benefits that he could have gained. When the ACLU offered to handle his case, he asked only one question: "How much will it cost me?" Because the group would pay all the costs, he agreed to pursue the case, which resulted in a significant Supreme Court decision in 1975.[19]

The general importance of interest groups in the agenda-setting process is greater than the proportions of cases in the second and third categories would indicate. Groups are especially likely to participate in and to sponsor the most significant cases, those whose importance gives them the best chance of securing full hearings from the Court. Further, groups have their greatest effect in the civil liberties area that is most central to the Court's work in the current era. Thus interest groups are of considerable significance in setting the agenda.

The Federal Government as Litigant

As a litigant in the Supreme Court, the United States government is distinctive, both because of its importance and because of its handling of litigation decisions. Its importance stems from the fact that the United States is a party in a high proportion of all federal cases. Not only is it the prosecutor in criminal cases, but it is a party in a wide range of civil litigation as well. As a result, the government is involved in a great many cases that might come from lower federal courts to the Supreme Court.

At the trial level, litigation decisions for the government are divided among the United States Attorneys who serve the Department of Justice in each of the federal judicial districts and lawyers for other federal departments. Decisions to appeal, however, are controlled primarily by the Office of the Solicitor General in the Justice Department. Particularly at the Supreme Court level, the solicitor general maintains an effective control over the flow of appeals. By statute, only a few federal agencies are allowed to take cases to the Court without the solicitor general's approval. Moreover, it is the solicitor general's office which drafts petitions for hearing in the Supreme Court and undertakes all other legal action in these cases.

The most striking characteristic of the solicitor general's handling of cases is a restraint in seeking hearings from the Supreme Court. In the Court's 1981 term, for instance, the federal government filed 57 petitions for writs of certiorari, while in 568 other cases the solicitor general decided not to petition. In contrast, in that term the government's opponents petitioned in 1,577 cases.[20] This willingness to forgo petitions for hearing demands explanation.

One reason for the federal government's restraint is its relatively limited stake in many of the cases which it loses. To take an obvious example, a criminal defendant will be unhappier about a conviction than the government will be about an acquittal.

But more important is the quasi-partnership that the solicitor general has developed with the Supreme Court. The federal government as a litigant has a special status in the Court. This status is reflected in the Court's provision of an office for the solicitor general's staff to use at the Court. It is also reflected in the Court's frequent requests to the solicitor general to participate as *amicus curiae* by submitting a brief or offering oral argument in cases to which the federal government is not a party.

As part of this close relationship, the solicitor general's office seeks to avoid bringing all but the most important and "meritorious" cases, in a deliberate effort to lighten the Court's burdens. Erwin Griswold, solicitor general from 1967 to 1973, has expressed his office's perspective as follows:

> In effect, the Solicitor General does most of the screening which is done in other cases by the Supreme Court, for he tries to take to the Court only cases which ... he thinks that the Court will accept.[21]

The solicitor general's restraint in bringing cases before the Supreme Court helps to preserve the federal government's special relationship with the Court. It also helps to bring about an extraordinary level of success for the federal government in obtaining hearings from the Court, which will be discussed in the next section.

All this does not mean that the solicitor general plays a neutral role. What the solicitor general's office does, including which cases it takes to the Supreme Court, is influenced by policies of the administration and the personal views of the solicitor general. The Reagan administration came into office in 1981 with the goal of moving the Court in a conservative direction on a variety of issues. Rex Lee, appointed as solicitor general that year, has played an active and sometimes controversial part in that effort. Lee's active role on behalf of the Reagan administration illustrates the importance of Supreme Court litigation as one vehicle for efforts to shape public policy.

Deciding What to Hear: The Court's Role

The Process of Decision

When a litigant brings a case to the Supreme Court, the Court may dispose of the case in several different ways. Basically, it has three options. First, it may refuse to hear the case at all. The great majority of cases are handled in this way—about 93 percent in the 1982 term.[22] Second, the Court may accept the case for decision with "full treatment," including oral argument before the Court and a decision on the merits with a full opinion explaining the decision. Third, the Court may accept the case but give it less than full treatment. For instance, it may decide the case without oral argument and issue only a brief, uninformative opinion that is labeled *per curiam* (by the Court) rather than being signed by a justice.

The distinction between the second and third categories is important. Of the cases that the Court actually accepts, between half and two-thirds are given full treatment. The others are cases on which the justices would like to rule, but which are not thought to require full argumentation and a full explanation of the decision. For instance, members of the Court may feel the need to settle a minor issue of tax law that has divided the lower courts, but oral argument and a full opinion on that issue may seem unnecessary. Some cases involve legal issues on which the Court already has ruled in other cases, so they can be handled easily.

The judgment that a case merits a decision but less than full treatment is not always unanimous, and in the past few years a controversy has developed within the Court about summary decisions. Justice Stevens has led Brennan and Marshall in complaints that the Court is overusing this mode of decision as a means to overturn liberal rulings by lower courts. Their complaint has several aspects. One is that some of these cases are important enough to merit full treatment or sufficiently complicated to require that the Court receive full information from the parties. Another is that some cases decided summarily are too trivial to justify any kind of decision by the Court. Dissenting in one 1982 case, Stevens noted sarcastically, "Today we exercise our majestic power to enforce a school board's suspension of a tenth grade student who consumed too much alcohol on October 21, 1980." [23] But their most fundamental concern is with the use of summary decisions to reach conservative results. In a 1984 case, Stevens noted that in the last 19 criminal cases involving constitutional rights that the Court had decided summarily, it had overturned decisions favorable to defendants, and he questioned whether this "striking" pattern of results was consistent with the Court's "primary role as the protector of the citizen and not the warden or the prosecutor." [24]

The Handling of Mandatory Cases. As noted earlier, there is an important distinction between cases that fall under the Supreme Court's discretionary jurisdiction and those under its mandatory jurisdiction. The discretionary cases may come to the Court as petitions for certiorari, where a litigant who has lost in a lower court petitions the Supreme Court to review the case, setting out the reasons why review should be granted. If the petition is granted the Court requests from the lower court a certified record of the case. Discretionary cases may also come as requests for extraordinary writs such as habeas corpus, by which prisoners challenge their convictions. The mandatory cases come as appeals. By statute, the Court is required to hear appeals. The major classes of appeals were listed in Table 1-1. Together, the various types of appeals constitute fewer than 10 percent of the cases brought to the Court.

The cases classified as appeals would take a great deal of the Court's time if all of them actually were decided, whether or not they were given full treatment. The justices consider many of them to be undeserving of that time, because of the unimportance of the issues involved in them. Accordingly, the Court uses the device of the summary decision to evade the statutory requirement that appeals must be heard. Parties who bring appeals must file a statement of the grounds on which they contend that their cases merit hearing. Their opponents then may request that the Court dismiss the appeal on any of several grounds, including procedural defects and the absence of a substantial question of federal law in the case. They may also request that the Court summarily affirm the lower court decision. The Court is not reluctant to grant such requests; a survey of the 1971-1973 terms found that more than 70 percent of all appeals were disposed of through dismissal or summary affirmance.[25]

The summary dismissal or affirmance of a lower court decision in an appeal is not strictly equivalent to a denial of certiorari. Dismissal and affirmance are treated legally as decisions on the merits of cases, and they have some weight as precedents for future cases. This is not true of certiorari denials, which have no precedential value. But in terms of the Court's screening process there is virtually no difference between denials of certiorari and the great majority of summary decisions in appeal cases, and for our purposes a summary decision in an appeal case should be considered a refusal to hear a case rather than a decision with less than full treatment.

Under its original jurisdiction, the Court is required to hear disputes between states, such as disagreements between western states over water rights. Even the small number of mandatory original jurisdiction cases might be burdensome to the Court. For that reason it has established a procedure by which it may deny a party leave to file an original case, and it often does deny leave. When the Court accepts an original case and questions of fact are in dispute, a "Special Master" will be appointed to conduct a hearing on the facts and to make a report with a recommended decision, thus reducing the time that the justices must spend on the case.

Paupers' Cases. About half of the requests for hearing which arrive at the Supreme Court are "paid" cases, in which the Court's filing fee of

$200 is paid and all required copies of materials are provided. The other half are filed *in forma pauperis,* by indigent persons for whom the fee and requirement of multiple copies are waived. About 80 percent of the "paupers' cases" are criminal, brought primarily by prisoners in federal and state institutions.

Criminal defendants who have had appointed counsel in the lower federal courts automatically are entitled to file paupers' cases. Other litigants must support with an affidavit their motion for leave to file as paupers. The Court has never developed precise rules as to when a litigant can claim pauper status, and ordinarily it focuses on the petition for hearing rather than passing on the question of pauper status. Recently the Court has taken a harder line, denying motions by litigants such as one who had approximately $1 million in net assets. The four most liberal justices have dissented in some of these cases, arguing that it would be more efficient simply to deny a writ of certiorari when a petition is clearly unmeritorious.[26]

The paupers' cases have been handled by the Court in a somewhat different way from the paid cases. Until 1970 they were placed on a separate docket, and even now they are listed separately on the Court's docket. Prior to the 1970s these cases were reviewed by the chief justice's law clerks, and other justices received materials only on cases deemed to merit serious consideration. Under Chief Justice Burger the procedure for handling paupers' cases has become similar to that for paid cases.

Most of the petitions from indigent persons have little merit. In the 1982 term fewer than 1 percent were accepted for decision on the merits, in contrast with 13 percent for the paid cases.[27] Even so, the paupers' cases are an important source for the Court's decisions on issues of criminal procedure, because few convicted defendants can afford to meet the Court's requirements for paid cases.

Pre-Screening: The Discuss List. The ultimate decision to hear a case is made at the Court's conference. But not all requests for hearing are discussed at conference. The Court now receives more than 4,000 cases each term, and to discuss each case collectively would require an almost intolerable expenditure of time. In addition, a high proportion of cases have essentially no chance of gaining four votes. For instance, a great many petitions for hearing raise rather narrow issues that are most unlikely to interest any justices.

For these reasons, Chief Justice Hughes introduced a procedure by which the chief justice's clerks would screen incoming cases and place on a "special list" those which they and the chief justice deemed clearly unworthy of hearing. Unless another justice objected, these requests for hearing would be denied without discussion. During the 1970s the procedure was reversed, so that the chief justice now places cases on what is called the "discuss list" if they are thought to merit serious consideration. All other cases are denied hearings automatically unless another justice asks that they be added to the discuss list to be considered in conference.

About two-thirds of all cases are denied hearings without conference discussion, so the pre-screening procedure is an important one. But this does not mean that the chief justice obtains an absolute power to eliminate cases through this procedure. Other justices and their clerks seem to take some care to scrutinize the cases not scheduled for discussion, looking for possible disagreements with the chief justice. This is particularly likely to be true of justices whose policy preferences differ from those of the chief. During the period from 1947 to 1958, about a dozen cases a term were rescued from the special list by a justice's objection,[28] and the number of disagreements seems to have risen since that time. Occasionally such a case is accepted for decision on the merits, and one of the Warren Court's landmark criminal justice decisions came in a case originally placed on the special list.[29]

Action in Conference. The cases on the discuss list are considered and voted upon in conference. The chief justice as presiding officer presents the cases and offers a personal summary of the merits of each as it comes up. The other justices then speak in order of seniority. If the justices' positions are not clear from the discussion, a formal vote is taken to determine whether four justices support the grant of a hearing. If there are fewer than four favorable votes, a justice may ask that the case be reconsidered at the next conference.

The brief discussion in conference generally is unlikely to change justices' views about hearing a case. But Justice Brennan reports that a single justice may convince three colleagues to accept a case,[30] and it appears to be common for a justice to "lend" a fourth vote to three colleagues as a courtesy if they are strongly inclined to hear a case.

The justices do disagree frequently about whether to accept cases. In the 1947-1958 period a little more than half the conference decisions were unanimous. In the 1981 term 29 percent of the accepted cases received the bare minimum of four votes, and in one set of accepted cases from the 1972 term only 9 percent received unanimous support.[31]

Of the cases discussed at conference, a majority are denied review. In the 1947-1958 period one-quarter of the discussed cases were accepted by the Court.[32] Because of the Court's increased caseload, the proportion probably is somewhat lower today. Thus the decision to place a case on the discuss list guarantees its consideration but hardly assures that it will be accepted.

When it accepts a case, the Court also decides whether to allow oral argument or to decide the case on the basis of the written materials.

When the Court hears oral argument it generally decides the case with a full opinion, so the case receives what I have called full treatment; when oral argument is bypassed, the decision usually is announced with a very brief *per curiam* opinion. A case that is given less than full treatment may be granted a hearing and decided on the merits at the same conference, so that the two stages of decision in effect become one.

Except for the cases decided on the merits at the same time, the Court's decisions on whether or not to accept cases are announced with very brief notices. Ordinarily the votes of individual justices are not announced. But it has become increasingly common for justices to record dissents from denials of petitions for hearing, sometimes with opinions. In the 1982 term, 418 dissenting votes were recorded in 238 cases. Justices Brennan and Marshall cast by far the largest number of these dissents. These included a great many joint dissents in capital punishment cases, in which they continued their practice of restating their belief that the Court should overturn the death penalty in all cases. Except for recorded dissents, justices' votes on requests for hearing almost never are made public. Occasionally a justice will write an opinion concurring with a denial of certiorari, usually to answer a dissenting opinion. Even rarer is an opinion concurring with the *grant* of a hearing.

The Clerks' Role. Probably the most important function of justices' law clerks is to help in scrutinizing requests for hearings. Until recently, each justice's clerks wrote memoranda which summarized for the justice the relevant facts and the parties' contentions in every paid case. Since 1972 several justices have pooled their resources by designating a single clerk to prepare a memo for their mutual use in each case. As of 1984, all of the justices except Brennan, Marshall, and Stevens participated in this arrangement; it is not surprising that the most liberal members have chosen to remain independent of it.

The press of work makes the usual clerk's memo rather dull and routine, but there are occasional exceptions. One such exception, produced by one of Justice Harold Burton's clerks in the 1954 term, merits quotation to illustrate the weakness of some requests for hearing:

> Petitioner is a big Cadillac dealer who got caught buying the local Alderman; he has been fighting conviction for four years; his case has no merit and his brief is replete with overstatements, innuendo, speculation, and almost untruth. It would be a crime to touch this case.[33]

As noted in Chapter 1, the influence of the clerks has been debated. Indisputably, the justices have delegated significant decision-making power in the screening of petitions to their clerks. In 1982 Justice Stevens reported that his clerks examine all the petitions "and select a small minority that they believe I should read myself. As a result, I do not even look at the papers in over 80 percent of the cases that are filed." [34] For the most part, however, clerks can be expected to exercise this power in a way consistent with the needs and goals of their justices. Moreover, the justices are sensitive to the potential loss of control that their delegation of this responsibility entails, and this sensitivity increases their desire to maintain independence from their clerks' recommendations. Justice Black once returned from a conference in which the Court unanimously had denied a hearing for a case favored by the clerks and proclaimed gleefully, "Today the Justices beat the law clerks." [35]

The Criteria for Decision

The Supreme Court's decisions on requests for hearings clearly are significant ones. These decisions determine which litigants are given a chance to challenge unfavorable decisions. They also determine which policy issues the Court addresses. In this section I will examine the criteria on which these decisions are based, focusing on the Court's selection of cases that are given full treatment in its decisions on their merits.

The Court offers only limited guidance concerning its decisions whether to hear specific cases. Frequently the Court's opinion on a case offers an explanation of its acceptance of that case, but the rationale tends to be brief and unilluminating. Seldom does the Court explain denials of petitions for hearing.

The Court does provide some general guidance on its treatment of petitions. Its Rule 17, shown in Table 3-2, proclaims some of the conditions under which the Court will hear a case. The rule emphasizes the Court's role in enhancing the certainty and consistency of the law: the criteria it lists for accepting a case include the existence of important legal issues that the Court has not yet decided, conflict among courts of appeals on a legal question, conflict between a lower court and the Supreme Court's prior decisions, and departure "from the accepted and usual course of judicial proceedings" in the courts below.

These criteria make sense, but they suggest a conception of the Court's function and of its members' interests that is unrealistically narrow. Accordingly, it is necessary to take a broader view of the criteria for decision. Evidence from the Court's pattern of screening decisions and from other sources suggests the significance of several criteria, which I will discuss in succession.

The Technical Criteria. To merit acceptance by the Supreme Court a case must meet certain technical requirements. First of all, the petition for hearing must comply with the Court's rules. A petition may be denied, for instance, because the petitioner has not supplied the required number of copies of the papers in the case. These requirements are relaxed for the

Table 3-2.   The Supreme Court's Rule 17, Section 1: Considerations
Governing Review on Certiorari

"1. A review on writ of certiorari is not a matter of right, but of judicial
discretion, and will be granted only when there are special and important reasons
therefor. The following, while neither controlling nor fully measuring the Court's
discretion, indicate the character of reasons that will be considered.

"(a) When a federal court of appeals has rendered a decision in conflict with
the decision of another federal court of appeals on the same matter; or has
decided a federal question in a way in conflict with a state court of last resort; or
has so far departed from the accepted and usual course of judicial proceedings, or
has so far sanctioned such a departure by a lower court, as to call for an exercise
of this Court's power of supervision.

"(b) When a state court of last resort has decided a federal question in a way
in conflict with the decision of another state court of last resort or of a federal
court of appeals.

"(c) When a state court or a federal court of appeals has decided an
important question of federal law which has not been, but should be, settled by
this Court, or has decided a federal question in a way in conflict with applicable
decisions of this Court."

paupers' petitions, but even these petitions may be denied if their
deviation from the rules is extreme.

More important, the Court imposes the same kinds of general
technical requirements for the hearing of cases that other courts apply:
the requirements of jurisdiction and standing. The Court's jurisdiction
was discussed in Chapter 1. If the Court receives a case that clearly falls
outside its jurisdiction, it cannot accept the case for hearing. For instance,
the Court could not hear a state case in which the petitioner raised no issues of federal law.

The rule of standing holds that a court may not hear a case unless
the party that brings the case is properly before it. Standing is a complex
concept with several aspects. Most of what is involved in standing
concerns the requirement that a party in a case have a real and direct
stake in its outcome. This requirement precludes hypothetical cases,
cases brought on behalf of another person, "friendly suits" between
persons who are not really adversaries, and cases which have become
"moot" (purely academic) because the parties no longer can be affected
by the outcome.

In the Supreme Court, a primary effect of the standing requirement
is to complicate the task of challenging governmental practices on
constitutional grounds. Individuals or groups unhappy with a particular
practice cannot bring suit in their own names unless they have a direct
personal stake; if they do not, a party with that stake must be found to

serve as the official challenger. The NAACP Legal Defense Fund cannot challenge school segregation in its own name. Rather, in each district it must support cases brought in the names of students in the district.

Because of their complexity and ambiguity, the rules of jurisdiction and standing require occasional interpretation, and as the highest federal court the Supreme Court is the most important interpreter. In recent years the Court has dealt with such issues as the standing of environmental groups to challenge projects which may damage the environment. In deciding these issues, the Court helps to determine access to all federal courts including itself.

The technical requirements are not always easy to interpret, and justices sometimes differ in their interpretations. In two 1983 decisions, for instance, the justices disagreed as to whether cases were moot.[36] Often, such disagreements reflect the views of justices about the underlying merits of cases. The justices most likely to grant standing to environmental groups generally are those who are most favorable to the policy positions of those groups. As this example indicates, the rules of jurisdiction and standing are not only requirements imposed upon the Court but also means by which the Court itself can regulate access to its judgments in accord with its members' goals.

The technical criteria serve as preliminary screening devices by which some cases are eliminated from consideration. But most cases meet these criteria, and the Court must use other criteria to choose among them.

Conflict Between Courts. One of the criteria suggested by Rule 17 is the existence of conflicting legal interpretations between courts, such as a conflict between federal courts of appeals or between a state or federal appellate court and the Supreme Court. The existence of a conflict should provide the justices with an incentive to hear a case, both to enhance the consistency of the law and—where the conflict is with the Court's own decision—to vindicate its authority as the highest court. Indeed, we might expect the Court to accept any case involving intercourt conflict.

In reality, conflict inclines the Court to accept a case, but it is far from an automatic basis for acceptance. With an increased volume of litigation, conflicts have become so numerous that the Court could not hear all conflict cases if it wanted to hear much else. One study of the 1971 and 1972 terms estimated that among the cases rejected during those terms were 93 with direct conflicts between courts of appeals and another 65 with "strong partial" conflicts.[37] Given these numbers, it is understandable that conflict alone is not a sufficient condition for the Court to accept a case.

Whether a case involving conflict between courts is accepted, then, depends upon the other characteristics of the case. Certainly one key characteristic is the effect of the conflict. Some conflicts are so serious that the Court may have little choice but to resolve them. One justice has said, "It's easy to take a case where two or more circuit courts have interpreted an IRS [Internal Revenue Service] rule in different ways. Things like that have to be straightened out quickly." [38] Indeed, in federal tax law the Court has taken cases in recent years primarily where there was a conflict between lower courts.[39] Where a dispute involves less pressing issues the Court may prefer to avoid resolving it. In the mid-1970s the Court refused all requests to rule on the legality of school regulations concerning student hair length, despite the fact that 10 federal courts of appeals had split evenly on the question.

Importance. The importance of the issues in a case is a second criterion suggested by Rule 17, and it seems to be very useful in explaining the Court's screening decisions. It is reasonable for the justices to emphasize importance as a criterion; the best way for the Court to maximize its impact is to decide the cases which affect the most people and which include the most significant policy issues.

The criterion of importance eliminates from consideration a high proportion of the cases that come to the Court. Since 1980 the Court's rules have required that petitions for hearing list the "questions presented" by the case on the very first page, and a perusal of petitions makes it clear why the Court does so: in a great many cases the questions presented almost certainly are too narrow to merit some of the Court's limited attention. Yet even cases that seem to be of minor importance will be heard from time to time, particularly if four justices perceive a grave injustice in a lower court decision.

Cases that do contain issues of great importance have a good chance of being accepted by the Court. But there are numerous cases involving significant questions that the Court refuses to hear. Justices may vote against hearing such cases for a variety of reasons, including their satisfaction with the lower court decision in a case and their desire to delay before tackling a difficult issue. Seldom is a case so important that the Court is compelled to hear it. The Court may have had little choice but to decide the 1974 case concerning President Nixon's duty to surrender tape recordings of his conversations to a federal court, but that was a most extraordinary case.

Importance as a criterion is reflected in the propensity of the Court to hear cases in certain subject areas. Studies have shown that at least in some periods federalism issues and (in civil cases) civil liberties issues have served as "cues" that inclined the Court in favor of accepting cases.[40] Presumably these patterns reflect a belief by at least some justices that these are important areas of policy.

Policy Preferences. Rule 17 does not mention justices' personal values as a basis for case-screening decisions. But inevitably justices respond to petitions for hearing in part on the basis of their policy preferences. Because acceptance and rejection of cases is such an important part of the Court's policy making, members of the Court hardly could resist use of the agenda-setting process as a way to advance their policy goals.

The justices' concern with their policy goals might be manifested in several ways. Of these ways, seemingly the most common is a tendency for justices to vote to accept cases when they disagree with the policies adopted by a lower court. A justice who sees a court of appeals decision as wrong will be more likely to vote for acceptance of the case than is a colleague who views the court of appeals' judgment as correct. During the 1947-1956 terms, each justice was more likely to vote to reverse the lower court decision in cases that he had earlier voted to accept than in cases accepted over his dissent, and for several justices the tendency was fairly strong.[41] This relationship between the two votes indicates that disagreement with lower court decisions helps to induce justices to seek to review cases.

Of course, justices' evaluations of lower court decisions are not random but are based largely on their ideological positions. A liberal justice will be most skeptical of conservative lower court decisions. In the 1947-1956 terms, for instance, it was the Court's liberals who were the most likely to vote to hear criminal cases when the defendant had lost in the lower courts.[42] When dissents from certiorari denials are recorded, it usually is liberals who want to review conservative decisions in the lower courts, while conservatives want to review liberal decisions.

Because of this tendency, the ideological center of gravity on the Court influences the kinds of cases that the Court accepts. The conservative shift in the Court's membership in the 1970s and 1980s has made the Court more likely to accept cases in which the lower court reached a liberal result. This shift is particularly clear in criminal procedure cases. During Earl Warren's tenure as chief justice, about 90 percent of the cases accepted in this area were brought by defendants. By the late 1970s the figure had dropped to about 50 percent, and for cases decided in the 1982 term the figure was under 15 percent.[43]

A more complex manifestation of justices' policy preferences is a response to cases based on an estimate of what the Court would decide if a particular case were accepted. A justice who approves of a lower court decision may vote to hear a case if it is reasonable to expect the Court to affirm the decision, thus giving it nationwide application. Similarly, justices may vote to deny hearings in cases with decisions they dislike if they suspect that the Court would approve the undesired policy. As one member of the Court said, "I'd much prefer bad law to remain the law of the Eighth Circuit or the State of Michigan than to have it become the law of the land." [44]

This kind of concern probably will be most important to the members of the ideological minority at a given time, since they must be fearful of the Court's adopting policies with which they disagree. In the moderately conservative Burger Court it is the liberals, Justice Marshall and Justice Brennan, who seem most inclined to take into account the Court's likely decision when they vote whether to hear a case. One reporter indicated in 1975 that "the liberal Justices have an 'unwritten agreement' to try to keep many cases out of the hands of the Court so long as the conservatives have the five-vote majority needed to carry a decision." [45] Whether or not that report is accurate, the strategy it portrays is a reasonable one.

Clearly, policy preferences play a central role in the Court's screening of petitions for hearing, but their importance should not be exaggerated. A clear majority of all the screening decisions are unanimous denials; whatever justices' disagreements on policy, they generally view petitions similarly. Where policy preferences play their greatest part is in helping the justices choose from those petitions that have some merit, in which there are reasonable grounds for granting a hearing because of the importance of the issues or another characteristic. Preferences and ideological positions probably play a limited part in decisions as to whether a case should be put on the discuss list, but they may be the key to the disposition of cases which actually are discussed in conference.

Identity of the Petitioner. Some litigants and interest groups have enjoyed striking success in getting their cases heard by the Supreme Court. Such success may derive from several sources. One is simply the positions that these petitioners take. The NAACP's success has resulted in part from its espousal of civil rights toward which most recent justices have been sympathetic. A second source is the skills of some petitioners in developing litigation and presenting cases. Finally, some frequent litigants develop credibility with the Court, so that their support for a petition increases the attention that justices give to it. In interviews with justices, O'Connor and Epstein found that at least some are favorably disposed to hear cases brought by interest groups in whose work they have developed confidence. [46]

The one party whose identity has the greatest impact on the Court's responses to petitions for hearing is the federal government. Earlier in this chapter I discussed the government's behavior as a litigant; here I will look at its success in obtaining hearings. That success is impressive.

In the 1980 and 1981 terms, for instance, the Court accepted 74 percent of the federal government's petitions for certiorari, compared with 2 percent for the government's opponents. The Court also accepted 83 percent of the cases in which the government supported another party's petition for certiorari with an *amicus* brief.[47] No other category of cases is accepted at this rate.

The government's success should not be exaggerated. In policy areas of little interest to the Court a relatively low proportion of government petitions is accepted. Further, the government—like other litigants—does best when its arguments are ideologically acceptable to at least four justices. But the solicitor general's overall record is quite impressive.

The federal government's success can be ascribed to the fact that it is what Marc Galanter calls a "repeat player," a litigant engaged in many related cases over time.[48] The federal government has far more cases that it could take to the Supreme Court than does any other party. That situation provides at least three advantages to the government.

First, by bringing only a small minority of a large pool of cases to the Court, the solicitor general can select those whose characteristics make them most likely to be accepted. Almost any litigant who could be so selective would enjoy a fairly high rate of success in the Supreme Court.

Second, the solicitor general's selectivity earns some gratitude from the Court and builds credibility as well. If the federal government brought petitions at the high rates of other litigants, the Court's caseload problems would be aggravated considerably. Thus the solicitor general plays an important role in easing pressures on the Court. Almost inevitably, this help is reciprocated by the justices through a tendency to view the government's petitions in a favorable light. Further, the justices know that the government takes to the Court only the cases that its lawyers deem most worthy, so the justices too are inclined to view those cases as worthy.

Finally, the attorneys in the solicitor general's office who draft petitions for hearing handle a great many cases, so they can develop an unusual degree of expertise. Few other lawyers learn as much about how to appeal to the Court's interests. As a result, to the extent that cases can be made to appear. more attractive as candidates for decision on the merits, the government has an excellent opportunity to provide that appearance.

Avoiding Problematic Cases. Whatever their value in other respects, some cases will be rejected by the Court because of characteristics which make their acceptance inconvenient. These characteristics are of two types.

First, the facts of some cases may be inappropriate, particularly in relation to the decision which the justices expect to reach. The facts may be too muddled to allow a clear decision, or they may require justices to reach a decision on grounds different from the ones they would like to use. In other cases, the circumstances of a dispute or the identity of the litigants may cast an unfavorable light on the Court's likely decision.

It is quite common for the justices to select the "best" case on an issue after rejecting a large number of related cases because of their facts. For example, in 1961 the justices had resolved that they would establish the right of indigents to a free attorney in felony cases. Then, with their clerks, they searched for a case whose facts were appropriate for the establishment of that principle. A large number of cases were rejected before Clarence Gideon's petition was accepted. The *Gideon* case was ideal for the Court's purposes, in part because it involved the relatively minor felony of breaking and entering a poolroom with intent to commit a misdemeanor. A reversal of Gideon's conviction would be less likely to arouse public wrath than would reversal of a conviction for a violent offense.

Second, justices may seek to avoid issues altogether because of their controversial character and the damage that the Court might inflict upon itself by attempting to resolve them. One good example is the Court's refusal to rule on the constitutionality of American participation in the war in Vietnam. Few issues brought before the Court have ever been as important, but the Court refused to hear the cases that raised this question between 1967 and 1972. The Court's refusals to hear some other controversial cases in recent years have provoked suspicions that the justices were seeking to avoid being drawn into political conflicts. Indeed, in one 1978 case Justice Rehnquist criticized the Court for ducking a controversial issue by denying certiorari; Rehnquist complained that the Court should not use its power to deny hearings as "a sort of judicial storm cellar to which we may flee to escape from controversial or sensitive cases." [49]

This does not mean, of course, that the Court uniformly refuses to decide the most controversial issues. In its 1982 and 1983 terms the Court faced such issues as the constitutionality of city-sponsored nativity scenes, the status of home videotaping under the copyright laws (which was the heart of a major battle among industries), and the constitutionality of "legislative veto" provisions by which Congress seeks to control the executive branch.[50] But the justices mix courage with caution in deciding what to decide, and it is not surprising that they do so. The Supreme Court's power rests heavily on acceptance of its right to decide crucial questions. For that reason, members of the Court cannot help considering the impact of certain cases on that acceptance in deciding whether to hear these cases.

Conclusion. As this discussion suggests, the Court's decisions whether or not to hear cases are based upon a complex set of considerations. This complexity should not be surprising, given the variety of goals that justices are interested in advancing.

Of the criteria that I have discussed, two seem particularly significant. The importance of a case largely determines whether it receives serious consideration by the Court. Undoubtedly, most cases which fail to reach the discuss list are dismissed out of hand because of their lack of significance. For the cases which are given serious consideration, justices' policy preferences may be the dominant factor in determining their response. Since there are more worthy cases than the Court can hear, justices are likely to make the difficult choices among them in terms of their own policy goals.

It follows that the selection of cases to decide fully, like everything else that the Court does, is affected by the membership of the Court at a given time. There are many cases that are unlikely to be accepted no matter who is on the Court. But the composition of the few dozen that the Supreme Court actually does accept will be largely a function of who the justices are in a given term.

Caseload Growth and the Court's Burdens

The Growth in Caseload

The Process of Growth. Litigants brought 4,222 cases to the Supreme Court during the 1983 term. That figure reflects a massive increase in the number of filings during the 1950s and 1960s, followed by a more moderate increase in the 1970s and early 1980s. The growth in the Court's caseload is depicted in Figure 3-1, which shows that the Court's 1983 caseload was nearly double that of 1963 and more than four times that of 1943.

The growth in the Court's business has come disproportionately in certain areas.[51] Perhaps most important, the number of criminal cases has risen tremendously. Fifty years ago, the great majority of the Court's cases were civil. Since then, criminal cases have increased in number to the point that they constitute about half of a much larger docket.

Criminal cases usually involve issues of constitutional due process, and in that respect they comprise part of a general growth in civil liberties cases brought to the Court. Half a century ago, cases concerned with constitutional freedoms, other than those arising from regulation of business, were fairly rare. Now constitutional cases dominate the Court's docket, and the largest portion of these cases raise civil liberties issues. A typical case 50 years ago involved a disagreement between a taxpayer and the federal government over the interpretation of a tax statute. Today

Figure 3-1.   Cases filed in Supreme Court at five-year intervals, 1943-1983 terms

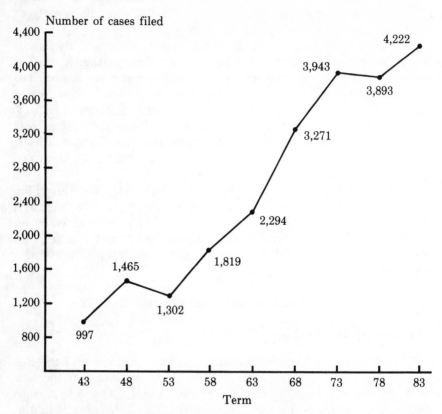

NOTE: The total for the 1973 term was adjusted by the Supreme Court Office of the Clerk to offset the unusual length of that term.

SOURCES: Gerhard Casper and Richard Posner, *The Workload of the Supreme Court* (Chicago: American Bar Foundation, 1976), 3; *United States Law Week* 48 (August 7, 1979): 3040, and 53 (July 24, 1984): 3028.

the typical case arises from a criminal defendant's claim that a due process right under the Fourteenth Amendment was violated during trial.

Explaining the Growth. The spectacular growth in the Court's caseload, with the attendant changes in the composition of that caseload, has stemmed from several sources. One of these sources is societal change. First of all, the population of the United States has doubled in the last 50 years, and that growth in population might produce a similar increase in litigation even if nothing else changed. Not just the Supreme Court but most other government institutions as well have been subject to an increasing volume of demands for action. During the same period, according to the best estimates, crime has increased far more rapidly than population. This increase inevitably has affected the Supreme Court's criminal caseload. Finally, there has been a general growth in "rights consciousness," in which Americans have shown an increased willingness to take action—including litigation—to protect what they see as their rights. The single most important example of increased rights consciousness is the black civil rights movement, which has been directly responsible for an impressive number of Supreme Court cases.

A second source of the growth is congressional action, particularly the adoption of legislation which creates new sources of litigation. The civil rights legislation of the 1960s and 1970s provided an important basis for legal action. So did economic legislation such as the Social Security Act of 1935, the environmental laws of the last two decades, and the considerable expansion of the federal criminal laws in the past few decades.

Finally, and perhaps most important, the Court itself has played a major role. Most clearly, its willingness to waive its ordinary requirements for the filing of cases has made possible the growth of the paupers' petitions so that they now constitute about half of the Court's caseload. The Court's establishment of the right to counsel for indigent criminal defendants and its elimination of the cost of the first appeal for indigent defendants have increased tremendously the opportunity to challenge convictions.

The Court's general policy direction also has spurred the growth of certain kinds of litigation. Since the 1940s the Court has shown considerable sympathy for challenges to government action which are based on alleged violations of civil liberties. This sympathy has encouraged those with civil liberties-related grievances to bring cases to the Court. The Court's support for civil liberties probably has had its greatest impact in two issue areas: criminal procedure, in which it has encouraged appeals by defendants through its tightening of due process requirements; and equality, in which its support for equality for racial minorities and other disadvantaged groups has spurred challenges to government action that allegedly violates equal protection of the laws.

In light of all these forces, the slower rate of growth in the Court's caseload over the last decade is of some interest. One relevant factor may be the Court's reduced sympathy for civil liberties claims in the 1970s and early 1980s, which probably has discouraged some potential litigants from coming to the Court. It also may be that some of the forces which brought about so much growth in the 1950s and 1960s had expended most of their energy by the 1970s. Without a clearer sense of its causes, it is difficult to predict whether this leveling trend will continue.

Responding to Caseload Growth

A Historical View. The growth in the Court's caseload in the last half century is not unprecedented. During most periods in the Court's history there has been a process of substantial growth in the number of cases brought to the Court.

At least since the late nineteenth century, increases in the Court's business have led to complaints by the justices that they were overburdened and unable to handle their work effectively. As a result, members of the Court and sympathetic observers have sought to provide it with greater control over its docket through an expansion in its discretion whether to hear cases. Congress has responded favorably in several instances. Two of these instances were particularly important. The first was the Court of Appeals Act of 1891, which created a new set of intermediate appellate courts and gave the Court discretionary jurisdiction over a large proportion of cases for the first time. The second was the Judiciary Act of 1925. This act provided that most cases would come to the Court as requests for writs of certiorari, which the Court could reject, rather than as mandatory appeals. The result was to expand considerably the Court's ability to choose the cases it would hear. The Supreme Court's jurisdiction has changed relatively little since that time.

The impact of the 1925 statute was tremendous. Its most obvious effect was to limit justices' workloads by allowing them to concentrate on a limited portion of the cases brought to them. More subtly, the Court obtained greater freedom to shape its own scope of activity, to determine the kinds of issues it would address and its role as a policy maker. The justices have used that freedom to concentrate on what they see as the most significant and worthy issues raised by the cases which come to the Court. As a result, according to one commentator, the Court has evolved from "a supreme corrector of errors" to "the effective arbiter of the federal form of government." [52]

Current Concerns. The 1925 law gave the Court freedom to determine which cases it would hear fully, but it could not prevent continued growth in the number of cases and legal issues brought to the Court. With that growth, justices and observers of the Court increasingly have argued that the Court is overburdened. The Court's burdens in turn are seen as creating problems for the Court itself and for the federal law.

For the Court itself, the basic problem is that the Court's capacity to do its job effectively is compromised. The Court is faced with more petitions for hearing to screen and more cases that seem to merit full consideration. As a result, the justices can give less careful consideration to their work, particularly to each case that they hear fully. Two legal scholars, for instance, argue that the Court's burdens have led to a "sleaziness of the opinions on the merits." [53] Some commentators also argue that increasing workloads and a resulting growth in the responsibilities of law clerks have weakened the Court by reducing the control that justices have over the Court's output.

For the federal law, the problem is one of uniformity and consistency. As the numbers of federal cases and judges have increased, so has the potential for conflicting interpretations of the law. But there is a limit to the number of cases that the Supreme Court can accept. Therefore, according to Justice White and others, the Court fails to resolve a good many conflicts in the law and thus leaves the law too unsettled.

Shortly after he came to the Court, Chief Justice Burger began to call attention to these problems, and in 1971 he created a Study Group on the Caseload of the Supreme Court to propose solutions. While some colleagues supported Burger's efforts, during the 1970s liberals on the Court such as Douglas and Brennan argued that Burger exaggerated the problems. Apparently the liberals feared that measures to reduce the Court's workload also would reduce its role as a protector of civil liberties.

By the early 1980s there was more of a consensus among the justices that the Court faced serious problems. In 1982 and 1983 a majority of the justices talked about workload issues in speeches. They differed in their diagnoses and prescriptions, but they agreed on the need to consider action to deal with the workload. Ironically, this increased consensus came while the volume of petitions for hearing was leveling off; one spur may have been a growing backlog of cases that were granted full hearings but had not yet been heard.

Proposals for Relief. The justices and others have made several kinds of proposals to attack workload problems.[54] The first involves internal procedural changes. The Court might adopt new procedures to improve efficiency, such as the use of panels of justices rather than the whole Court to make screening decisions. In 1982 Justice Stevens suggested that the Court could reduce the number of cases it hears by requiring five votes to grant a hearing.[55] The Court also might try to reduce the flow of petitions by increasing the costs of filing them.

The second kind of proposal involves jurisdictional change. The current justices agree that Congress should eliminate the remaining categories of cases that the Court is obliged to hear, because these cases create special burdens even though many are decided summarily. In 1978 and 1982 the justices wrote collectively to members of Congress to support this change. Chief Justice Burger also has supported elimination of the federal courts' diversity jurisdiction, which indirectly increases the number of cases brought to the Court.

The most sweeping proposals are for creation of one or more new courts above the federal courts of appeals and below the Supreme Court. Burger's study group produced one such proposal, and a commission created by Congress put forward a quite different proposal in 1975. More recently, some of the justices have offered variants of the earlier plans. Aside from details, the various proposals differ in the problems that they address. Some would give the new court responsibility to help the Supreme Court screen petitions for hearings or take over the screening function entirely, in order to reduce the Court's burdens. Others would have the new court decide cases involving legal conflicts between federal courts of appeals, in part to help the Court but primarily to address the need for uniformity of law.

The plan that has received the most attention recently was advocated by Burger in a 1983 speech.[56] The chief justice suggested that Congress create a temporary court as a panel of the specialized Court of Appeals for the Federal Circuit. The panel would draw members on a rotating basis from the federal courts of appeals. Its job would be to decide cases involving conflicts among courts of appeals and perhaps some category of statutory interpretation cases. After a set period, no more than five years, Congress could make the new court permanent or take some alternative action.

Debates and Prospects. This array of proposals has been the subject of considerable discussion, with much of the debate focusing on the idea of a new court. The growing consensus on the Court's workload problems has increased support for a new court, but some commentators are unsure that such a court would be effective in reducing those problems. Opponents of a new court have argued that it would create new problems. In general, people who support the Supreme Court's activism in the civil liberties area remain skeptical about an innovation that would transfer some of the Court's power to another tribunal. In addition, some argue that such a division of power would violate the constitutional mandate that there shall be "one supreme Court." [57] Proposals for a screening court have received special criticism on the ground that the Supreme Court must be able to set its own agenda in order to determine its role as a judicial policy maker.

The continued disagreement about the merits of proposals for a new court, both within the Supreme Court and elsewhere, reduces the chances that any such proposal will be adopted—although Congress is giving serious attention to the kind of court that Chief Justice Burger advocated. The proposal to eliminate the Court's remaining mandatory jurisdiction might be quicker to gain acceptance, but it would have only a moderate effect at best on the Court's workload. These realities give greater significance to measures that the Court itself might undertake.

The Court already has begun an apparent effort to provide financial disincentives for petitioners. As noted earlier, it has started to deny some litigants the right to file paupers' petitions. In 1983 the Court required an unsuccessful petitioner to pay $500 in legal expenses to his opponent,[58] and this seemingly unprecedented action may be the first sign of a concerted effort to discourage petitions that the Court deems to be frivolous. But the disagreement within the Court about these initiatives may limit their use in the future.

Some justices and observers also suggest that the Court could reduce its workload problems simply through a degree of self-restraint. It might accept fewer petitions, especially by refusing to hear cases of minor importance simply because four or more justices disagree with the lower court decision. Indeed, after accepting an unusually large number of petitions in the 1981 term, the Court showed considerably greater restraint in this respect in the next two terms. The justices also could curtail their growing propensity to write separate opinions that express marginal differences with other opinions. The recent record suggests that self-restraint in this area will be more difficult to achieve.

Conclusion

A central theme of this chapter has been the Supreme Court's capacity to set its own agenda. Congress and litigants play important parts in shaping the Court's agenda, but what the Court hears is largely under its own control. From a very broad range of legal and policy questions brought to the Court the justices can choose those few that they will address fully.

The justices have made effective use of their agenda-setting powers. Cases are selected and rejected on the basis of individual and collective goals, such as the avoidance of troublesome issues and the establishment of policies that the justices favor. Thus the process of selecting cases for full decision helps to determine the Court's role as a policy maker.

After the Court selects the cases to be decided fully, of course, it must actually decide those cases. Ultimately, its role depends on the decisions that it does reach. The next chapter will examine the process by which the Court makes its decisions.

Notes

1. J. Woodford Howard, Jr., *Courts of Appeals in the Federal Judicial System: A Study of the Second, Fifth, and District of Columbia Circuits* (Princeton: Princeton University Press, 1981), 63-64.
2. "Statistical Recap of Supreme Court's Workload During Last Three Terms," *U.S. Law Week* 53 (July 24, 1984): 3028.
3. *Young v. Town of Atlantic Beach* (1983). The case is described in Jim Mann, "Season of Lost Causes," *The American Lawyer* (November 1983): 112-113.

4. The case is *Regents of the University of California v. Bakke* (1978).
5. *Kolender v. Lawson* (1983). The case is described in Jim Mann, "A Vagrant Takes His Crusade to the Court," *The American Lawyer* (January 1983): 83, and William Carlsen, "How a 'Vagrant' Wound Up in the Supreme Court," *San Francisco Chronicle*, November 8, 1982, 4.
6. *Lynch v. Donnelly* (1984).
7. Jonathan D. Casper, *Lawyers Before the Warren Court: Civil Liberties and Civil Rights, 1957-66* (Urbana: University of Illinois Press, 1972), 167.
8. William O. Douglas, *The Court Years 1939-1975: The Autobiography of William O. Douglas* (New York: Random House, 1980), 183.
9. Federal Judicial Center, *Report of the Study Group on the Caseload of the Supreme Court* (Washington, D.C., 1972), 42.
10. Douglas, *The Court Years*, 178.
11. Bob Woodward and Scott Armstrong, *The Brethren: Inside the Supreme Court* (New York: Simon & Schuster, 1979), 79-81.
12. Karen O'Connor and Lee Epstein, "Amicus Curiae Participation in U.S. Supreme Court Litigation: An Appraisal of Hakman's 'Folklore,'" *Law & Society Review* 16 (1981-1982): 316.
13. Mary Frances Berry, *Stability, Security, and Continuity: Mr. Justice Burton and Decision-Making in the Supreme Court 1945-1958* (Westport, Conn.: Greenwood Press, 1978), 97.
14. This discussion draws from Karen O'Connor and Lee Epstein, "The Rise of Conservative Interest Group Litigation," *Journal of Politics* 45 (May 1983): 479-489.
15. O'Connor and Epstein, "Amicus Curiae Participation," 316; Karen O'Connor and Lee Epstein, "A Century of Conflict in the Court" (Paper delivered at the annual conference of the Midwest Political Science Association, Chicago, April 1983), Figure 1.
16. Stephen L. Wasby, "Interest Groups in Court: Race Relations Litigation," in *Interest Group Politics,* ed. Allan Cigler and Burdett Loomis (Washington, D.C.: CQ Press, 1983), 256.
17. This discussion of the Legal Defense Fund draws from Stephen Wasby's work on the organization, including "Interest Groups in Court."
18. Much of the information presented on the ACLU's activities is drawn from *Civil Liberties,* the organization's newsletter.
19. Ruth B. Cowan, "Women's Rights Through Litigation: An Examination of the American Civil Liberties Union Women's Rights Project, 1971-1976," *Columbia Human Rights Law Review* 8 (Spring-Summer 1976): 385. The case was *Weinberger v. Wiesenfeld* (1975).
20. *Annual Report of the Attorney General of the United States, 1982* (Washington, D.C.: Government Printing Office, 1984), 5, 7.
21. Erwin N. Griswold, "Rationing Justice—The Supreme Court's Caseload and What the Court Does Not Do," *Cornell Law Review* 60 (March 1975): 344.
22. "The Supreme Court, 1982 Term," *Harvard Law Review* 97 (November 1983): 299; "Statistical Recap of Supreme Court's Workload During Last Three Terms," *U.S. Law Week* 52 (July 1983): 3025.
23. *Board of Education of Rogers, Ark. v. McCluskey,* 458 U.S. 966, 972-973 (1982).

24. *Florida v. Meyers,* 80 L. Ed. 2d 381, 387 (1984).

25. David W. Rohde and Harold J. Spaeth, *Supreme Court Decision Making* (San Francisco: W. H. Freeman & Co., 1976), 120.

26. *Brown v. Herald Co., Inc.,* 78 L. Ed. 2d 301 (1983).

27. "Supreme Court, 1982 Term," 299; "Statistical Recap" (1983): 3025.

28. Doris Marie Provine, *Case Selection in the United States Supreme Court* (Chicago: University of Chicago Press, 1980), 28. I will refer to the 1947-1958 period several times. This was most of the period when Justice Harold Burton sat on the Court, and his papers provide the first available systematic data on justices' votes whether or not to hear cases. These data have been analyzed by Provine and by S. Sidney Ulmer, primarily for 1947-1958.

29. The case was *Robinson v. California* (1962), in which the Court applied the constitutional prohibition against cruel and unusual punishments to the states.

30. William J. Brennan, Jr., "The National Court of Appeals: Another Dissent," *University of Chicago Law Review* 40 (Spring 1973): 480.

31. Provine, *Case Selection in the Supreme Court,* 32; John Paul Stevens, "The Life Span of a Judge-Made Rule," *New York University Law Review* 58 (April 1983): 17; Brennan, "National Court of Appeals," 481-482.

32. Provine, *Case Selection in the Supreme Court,* 32.

33. Ibid., 22.

34. John Paul Stevens, "Some Thoughts on Judicial Restraint," *Judicature* 66 (November 1982): 179.

35. J. Harvie Wilkinson III, *Serving Justice: A Supreme Court Clerk's View* (New York: Charterhouse, 1974), 18-19.

36. *United States v. Villamonte-Marquez* (1983); *Iron Arrow Honor Society v. Heckler* (1983).

37. Commission on Revision of the Federal Court Appellate System, *Structure and Internal Procedures: Recommendations for Change* (Washington, D.C., 1975), 101.

38. "The Supreme Court: Deciding Whether to Decide," *Time Magazine,* December 11, 1972, 72.

39. See Arthur D. Hellman, "The Supreme Court, the National Law, and the Selection of Cases for the Plenary Docket," *University of Pittsburgh Law Review* 44 (Spring 1983): 614.

40. Joseph Tanenhaus, Marvin Schick, Matthew Muraskin, and Daniel Rosen, "The Supreme Court's Certiorari Jurisdiction: Cue Theory," in *Judicial Decision-Making,* ed. Glendon Schubert (New York: Free Press, 1963), 125; Provine, *Case Selection in the Supreme Court,* ch. 3; Stuart H. Teger and Douglas Kosinski, "The Cue Theory of Supreme Court Certiorari Jurisdiction: A Reconsideration," *Journal of Politics* 42 (August 1980): 834-846.

41. S. Sidney Ulmer, "The Decision to Grant Certiorari as an Indicator to Decision 'On the Merits,'" *Polity* 4 (1972): 429-447.

42. S. Sidney Ulmer, "Supreme Court Justices as Strict and Not-so-Strict Constructionists: Some Implications," *Law & Society Review* 8 (Fall 1973): 13-32.

43. Except for the 1982 term, figures are taken from Hellman, "Supreme Court, National Law," 549.

44. "Supreme Court: Deciding Whether to Decide," 77.
45. Nina Totenberg, "Behind the Marble, Beneath the Robes," *New York Times Magazine*, March 16, 1975, 60.
46. Karen O'Connor and Lee Epstein provided this information to me from their research in progress.
47. *Annual Report of the Attorney General, 1982*, 7.
48. Marc Galanter, "Why the 'Haves' Come Out Ahead: Speculations on the Limits of Legal Change," *Law & Society Review* 9 (Fall 1974): 97-125.
49. *Ratchford v. Gay Lib*, 434 U.S. 1080, 1081 (1978).
50. The cases were, respectively, *Lynch v. Donnelly* (1984); *Sony Corporation of America v. Universal City Studios, Inc.* (1984); and *Immigration and Naturalization Service v. Chadha* (1983).
51. This discussion draws from material in Gerhard Casper and Richard A. Posner, "A Study of the Supreme Court's Caseload," *Journal of Legal Studies* 3 (1974): 339-362.
52. Eugene Gressman, "Much Ado About Certiorari," *Georgetown Law Journal* 52 (1964): 756, 762.
53. Philip B. Kurland and Dennis J. Hutchinson, "The Business of the Supreme Court, O.T. 1982," *University of Chicago Law Review* 50 (Spring 1983): 648.
54. The discussion of proposals draws from Note, "Of High Designs: A Compendium of Proposals to Reduce the Workload of the Supreme Court," *Harvard Law Review* 97 (November 1983): 307-325.
55. Stevens, "Life Span of a Rule," 14-21.
56. Warren E. Burger, "Annual Report on the State of the Judiciary," *American Bar Association Journal* 69 (April 1983): 442-447.
57. U.S. Constitution, Art. 3, sec. 1.
58. *Tatum v. Regents of the University of Nebraska-Lincoln* (1983).

Decision Making 4

While much of the Supreme Court's work involves the selection of cases for full decision on the merits, the heart of its work is actually deciding these cases. For it is in that select group of cases that the Court explicitly and directly makes policy. Thus it is important to understand how and why the Court chooses its decisions on the merits. That is the subject of this chapter.

In the first section of the chapter, I will discuss briefly the character of the Court's decisions and the procedural steps that a case takes from its acceptance by the Court to the Court's ultimate decision. In the remaining sections I will turn to the primary concern of the chapter, the factors that shape the Court's decisions on the merits. The discussion of these factors is intended to provide a sense of the reasons for the Court's choices among alternative policies.

Decisions and the Decisional Process

The Court's Dual Decision

A full decision by the Supreme Court has several levels. We may examine those levels in terms of two components: the Court's treatment of the parties to the case and its establishment of a position on the legal and policy issues raised by the case.

First, cases come to the Court as disputes between contending parties with specific interests in the case. The parties that bring cases to the Court may have broad policy concerns, but at the most basic level they are asking the Court simply to upset a ruling against them in a lower court. A person convicted of a crime wants the Court to overturn the conviction. A litigant who was denied a monetary award by a lower court wants the Court to grant the award.

The Court's task is to decide whether and in what ways to change the lower court's allocation of benefits and burdens between the parties. It may affirm the lower court, leaving undisturbed that court's treatment of the parties. Alternatively, it may modify or reverse the lower court decision, changing the judgment in some way. The terms *modify* and *reverse* are imprecise. Reversal generally refers to a fairly complete overturning of the lower court's decision, while modification is a more limited, partial overturning. The Court also may "vacate" (make void) the lower court decision; the effect is similar to that of reversal.

In some cases, the parties are so important that what happens to them specifically is crucial. In *United States v. Nixon* (1974), for instance, the Court's determination that President Nixon must yield certain tape recordings to the courts helped to ensure his resignation from office. More often, the Court's treatment of the parties has little impact on the nation as a whole. Nonetheless, the Court's decisions in such cases may be very important because of their second component, the statement of general principles of law on which the Court bases its treatment of the parties.

The statement of general principles comes in the Court's opinion. In every case that the Court decides fully, the decision is accompanied by an opinion that explains the decision. Generally at least five justices subscribe to this opinion, so that it constitutes an authoritative statement for the Court.

The opinion serves several functions. First, it is an effort to justify the Court's decision. When the Court overturns a criminal conviction, it can explain the principles that led it to that decision and thus seek to convince its audiences that its decision was correct. Second, if the Supreme Court modifies or reverses a lower court decision, the case usually will be sent back, "remanded," to the lower court to be reexamined; the Court's opinion provides directions for that reexamination. If a court of appeals has refused to issue an injunction in a freedom of speech case and the Supreme Court overturns its refusal, the Court's opinion can express the principles of interpretation for the First Amendment that the court of appeals should follow in rehearing the case.

Finally, and most important, the opinion lays down general principles of law that are applicable to other cases, principles that theoretically are binding on lower court judges whenever they are relevant. Together, the principles that the Court establishes in an issue area constitute its policies in that area.

The importance of the opinion as a source of law and policy is illustrated by the Court's opinion in *Immigration and Naturalization Service v. Chadha* (1983). In this case the House of Representatives acted under a "legislative veto" provision to overrule an administrative ruling and require that Jagdish Rai Chadha leave the United States. The Supreme Court ultimately ruled that Chadha must be allowed to remain in the country. In its opinion the Court's majority based that ruling on the unconstitutionality of the legislative veto provision that Congress used, and its reasoning indicated that a variety of other legislative veto provisions in federal law also were unconstitutional. Without this opinion, the Court's decision would have been of great importance to Chadha personally but of little significance to the nation as a whole. With the opinion, the *Chadha* decision had a tremendous potential impact on the legal and policy relationships between Congress and the executive branch on issues as important as the commitment of troops to combat.

Just as the Court can choose which party to favor in its decision, so it can choose the basis on which its decision rests. A particular treatment of the parties may be justified on a variety of different grounds, and which ground the Court adopts will help to determine the long-term impact of its decision. If the Court overturns the death penalty for a particular defendant, it might rest that decision on a whole range of possible grounds—from the existence of a specific error in that defendant's trial to the unconstitutionality of the death penalty under all circumstances. Obviously, a decision based on the first ground will have a good deal less impact than one based on the second ground.

The Decision-Making Process

Presentation of Cases to the Court. When a case is accepted for decision on the merits with full treatment by the Court, the parties already have submitted written briefs concerning the desirability of hearing the case. After acceptance, attorneys for the parties submit new briefs that directly argue the merits of the case, as well as reply briefs in response to the opposition's arguments. As noted in Chapter 3, in many cases individuals and groups other than the parties submit *amicus curiae* briefs to supplement the arguments of the parties.

The primary material in these briefs generally is an argument on the legal issues in the case. The parties muster evidence to support their interpretations of relevant constitutional provisions and statutes. Some briefs offer policy arguments as well, seeking to convince the justices that support for their position constitutes not only good law but also good public policy. In a sense, this practice was made legitimate by the Court in a 1908 decision, *Muller v. Oregon*. That case concerned the constitutionality of a state law limiting the number of hours that women could work. In upholding the law, the Court praised a lengthy analysis of sociological data presented by attorney Louis Brandeis—who later became a justice—in support of the policy that underlay the law. A brief that addresses sociological issues sometimes is referred to as a "Brandeis brief."

Material in briefs is supplemented by attorneys' presentations in oral argument before the Court. Oral argument is strictly limited in time. At present, each side generally is provided half an hour for argument to the Court. Attorneys for the parties to the case nearly always participate in the argument. Occasionally they are joined by representatives of other individuals and groups, most often the federal government.

Oral argument provides an opportunity for attorneys to supplement the material in their briefs. More important, perhaps, it provides the justices with a chance to probe issues that concern them. Presentations by lawyers are interrupted frequently by questions and comments from members of the Court, typically more than 100 times in an hour of argument on a case. In one 1981 argument the justices became so intent on pursuing their concerns that the argument extended for half an hour beyond the scheduled hour, and altogether the justices made more than 200 interruptions.[1]

Occasionally an oral argument becomes a forum for disagreements between justices, as it did in a clash between William Rehnquist and Thurgood Marshall in a 1981 death penalty case. After Rehnquist pressed the point that it would be cheaper to execute a prisoner than to imprison him for a long period, Marshall interjected, "Well, it would be cheaper just to shoot him when you arrested him, wouldn't it." [2] The disagreements, like the justices' questions, sometimes descend from high legal issues to more trivial matters; in a 1982 session Rehnquist and John Paul Stevens differed on the position played by Hall of Fame baseball player Kiki Cuyler.[3]

Tentative Decisions. After oral argument on a case is held, the Court discusses it in one of its conferences later in the same week. This conference marks the starting point for the Court's decision on the merits of a case.

The conference is held in a closed session from which all people other than the justices are barred. The chief justice presides at the conference. The chief opens discussion on each case. The other justices follow, from the most senior member (in service on the Court, not in age) to the most junior.

The character of the discussion depends in part on the chief justice's style of leadership. The most striking contrast during this century was between Charles Evans Hughes and Harlan Stone. Chief Justice Hughes controlled discussion tightly, limiting the time devoted to each case in order to dispose of the Court's business quickly. This approach helped to limit strains on the Court, but it may also have prevented the justices from giving each case full consideration. Stone, who succeeded Hughes in 1941, preferred a more open discussion. Under Stone, conferences were longer and more acrimonious, and the Court had more difficulty disposing of its business. However, Stone's willingness to tolerate open discussion may have improved the Court's ability to confront fully the issues in cases. To some degree, of course, the style of leadership that a chief justice adopts will be dictated by the preferences of the other justices.

At one time the discussion was followed by a formal vote on the treatment of the parties, with the junior justice voting first and the chief justice last. Today the Court often dispenses with the formal vote, because the justices make their positions clear as they discuss the case. But their task remains the same: they must choose between two or more alternative dispositions of the case. In an antitrust case, for instance, they may be deciding whether or not a lower court decision allowing two firms to merge should be upheld.

After the Court reaches its tentative decision, its opinion in the case is assigned to a justice. An assignment is made even when the decision is to be announced through an unsigned *per curiam* opinion, as occasionally occurs even if cases are given full treatment by the Court. The chief justice assigns the opinion whenever the chief is in the majority. Because so many cases are unanimous or nearly unanimous, the chief justice usually is in the majority. In other cases the most senior justice in the majority makes the assignment. When there is no tentative majority because some justices wish to reserve judgment or because the Court is deeply split, the chief justice assigns the opinion. The power to assign the opinion is very important, because it may help to determine not only the grounds on which the Court's decision rests but also the ultimate size of the majority. I will discuss the ways in which the assignment power is used later in this chapter in connection with the chief justice's role.

Reaching Final Decisions. Following the conference the justice who was assigned the opinion begins work, drafting an initial version of the opinion. This justice will be guided by the views expressed in conference concerning the appropriate rationale for the Court's decision. Other justices also may work on the case, reconsidering their positions and— particularly if they voted with the minority—writing alternative opinions. During this process views of the case may change even before the assigned opinion is produced in draft form.

Once that opinion is completed and circulated, it often becomes a focus of negotiation. Ordinarily the assigned justice wishes to obtain the support of as many colleagues as possible for the opinion. The writer will seek to convince justices who were originally in the minority to change positions, and it also may be necessary to discourage allies in conference from leaving the fold. At the very least, the assigned justice will wish to maintain the original majority for the outcome supported by the opinion and a majority in support of the rationale expressed in the opinion, so that the opinion becomes the official statement for the Court. The justice may fail in this task, so that another justice's opinion reaching the same outcome or a different one becomes the opinion of the Court.

The negotiation that occurs during this period focuses on the wording of the opinion. The assigned justice and rival opinion writers may be willing to change arguments or the ways in which they are expressed in order to satisfy other justices and thus to enlist their support. When the Court is deeply divided, this process may be quite complex and difficult, and the result often is an opinion that lacks clarity and coherence because of the need to appeal to other justices.

Occasionally no opinion gains the support of five justices. In this situation the original opinion may retain its official status, but no opinion will have the authority of a majority. This phenomenon has been fairly common in the 1970s and 1980s; in the 1969-1980 terms, by one count, there were 78 decisions without majority opinions, about 5 percent of the cases fully decided.[4] Among the major cases without majority opinions since 1970 are *Furman v. Georgia* (1972), in which the Court struck down existing capital punishment laws; *New York Times Co. v. United States* (1971), in which the Court allowed publication of the "Pentagon Papers" on the Vietnam war; and *Regents v. Bakke* (1978), in which the Court ruled on the constitutionality of affirmative action programs for medical school admissions. In *Bakke* four members of the 5-4 majority supported one opinion, while the fifth (Justice Powell) announced the Court's judgment and offered a very different basis for his vote in a separate opinion. In *Furman* and *New York Times* each member of the majority wrote a separate opinion.

A case without a majority opinion is unfortunate in the sense that there is no authoritative statement of the Court's position on the legal issues in the case. Sometimes the Court reduces confusion with a brief *per curiam* opinion that indicates the points for which majority support exists. This was done in *Arizona Governing Committee v. Norris* (1983), a case involving pension plans that gave reduced benefits to women, in which no five justices agreed even on the outcome of the specific case; a *per curiam* opinion pulled together the rules that received majority support. Without such a *per curiam* opinion—or even with it—the Court may leave its position on some important issues murky. In this situation, lower court judges and other observers can attempt to discern a "least common denominator" from the positions of the justices on the majority side, but this task may be difficult. In *Furman* the five justices in the majority expressed quite different reasons for concluding that the existing death penalty laws were unconstitutional. As a result, legislators and others concerned with the decision had difficulty determining just what kinds of death penalty laws—if any—were acceptable in the Court's collective view.

Concurring and Dissenting Opinions. A single opinion does obtain majority support in the preponderance of cases, as I have noted, but most of the time it lacks unanimous support. In the 1982 term, more than 75 percent of all fully decided cases included dissenting opinions, concurring opinions, or both. Concurring and dissenting opinions lack legal force but serve other functions; these functions and the general character of both types of opinions should be made clear.

The dissenting opinion expresses disagreement with the result reached by the Court as it affects the parties to a case. If a conviction is reversed, for instance, the dissenter believes that it should have been affirmed. A dissent need not be accompanied by an opinion. Ordinarily there is a dissenting opinion, however, because the opinion provides the justice with a way to justify disagreement. Further, as Chief Justice Hughes said,

> A dissent . . . is an appeal to the brooding spirit of the law, to the intelligence of a future day, when a later decision may possibly correct the error into which the dissenting judge believes the court to have been betrayed.[5]

Indeed, there have been several instances in which a dissenting view on an issue later became the majority position of the Court. One famous example is Justice Black's dissent in *Betts v. Brady* (1942), in which he argued that indigent criminal defendants had the right to a free attorney. The Court reversed itself 21 years later in *Gideon v. Wainwright,* and Black had the rare satisfaction of writing the Court's opinion that turned his long-standing position into the law of the land.

Dissenters often include in their opinions the expression "I respectfully dissent." Justice Powell opened a 1983 dissent by saying, "The Court's opinion addresses the several questions presented in this case with commendable thoroughness." [6] But some dissenting opinions express their disagreements with the majority in strong and even nasty terms, as the examples in Table 4-1 indicate.

When more than one justice dissents, all the dissenters may join in a single opinion. Alternatively, they may write multiple opinions. In such instances dissenters may express agreement with each other's opinions.

A concurring opinion agrees with the result reached by the Court but offers its own statement on the decision. Most concurring opinions express full or partial disagreement with the rationale provided by the Court's opinion. For instance, in *United States v. Place* (1983), the Court overturned a conviction for possession of narcotics after a luggage search in an airport. Justice O'Connor's majority opinion held that the temporary detention of luggage was acceptable under the Fourth Amendment but that the length of the detention in this case was constitutionally unacceptable. Justice Brennan's concurring opinion agreed that the conviction should be overturned, but he disagreed with O'Connor by arguing that under the circumstances of this case even the temporary detention of luggage was unacceptable.

Table 4-1.　Excerpts from selected dissenting opinions, 1982-1984

"This remarkable result is the product of an equally remarkable misapplication of the ancient doctrine of sovereign immunity."

> Justice John Paul Stevens in *Pennhurst State School & Hospital v. Halderman,* 1984

"The issue actually presented is an important one, and there may be arguments supportive of the instruction. The Court, however, chooses to present none. Instead, it approves the Briggs Instruction by substituting an intellectual sleight of hand for legal analysis."

> Justice Harry A. Blackmun in *California v. Ramos,* 1983

"In approaching this statutory construction question the Court quite adeptly avoids the statute it is construing. This I am sure is no accident, for there is nothing in the language of § 501(c)(3) that supports the result obtained by the Court."

> Justice William H. Rehnquist in *Bob Jones University v. United States,* 1983

"The majority's decision is apparently based on a cursory examination of Illinois statutes. . . . This reasoning has no basis in Illinois law and appears to derive from nothing more than judicial intuition."

> Justice Thurgood Marshall in *Lane v. Williams,* 1982

"The Court's analysis is completely result-oriented, and represents a noteworthy exercise in the very judicial activism that the Court so deprecates in other contexts. . . . The Court has now begun to furnish its house of cards—and the furniture is as jerry-built as the house itself. . . . The Court justifies its results today with several additional reasons—or, rather, sentiments in reasons' clothing."

> Justice William J. Brennan in *Engle v. Isaac,* 1982

Sometimes a concurring opinion is written to "interpret" the majority opinion in a particular way. For instance, a justice may join in the majority opinion but write a separate opinion indicating that "I join the Court's opinion on the understanding that it" has a particular meaning.[7] A justice may even write a concurring opinion to take issue with a dissenting opinion.

Concurring opinions sometimes are frowned upon as sources of confusion, and some observers regard the unprecedented numbers of concurring opinions since 1970 as a sign of weakness in the Court. This criticism may be valid. But occasional use of concurring opinions is inevitable, because the Court's position on legal issues is at least as important as its treatment of the litigants.

Frequently, an opinion will be labeled as "concurring and dissenting." Such an opinion agrees with the Court's treatment of the parties in part, but disagrees with some aspect of that treatment.

Announcing the Decision. The process of decision making in a case ends when all the opinions are written and all justices have determined which opinion they will join. At this time the decision will be announced in open court.

The justices sometimes read the entirety of their opinions in court, but more often they summarize them. Occasionally justices engage in outbursts of anger in reporting their opinions. The most famous of those outbursts came in a 1935 decision in which the Court supported a New Deal law. In dissent, Justice James McReynolds cried, "This is Nero at his worst. The Constitution is gone!" [8]

The Court suffers from relatively few "leaks" of decisions prior to their formal announcement. One exception occurred in 1979, when a television news reporter obtained advance information on two decisions. Chief Justice Burger responded by requesting transfer of a typesetter who was suspected of responsibility for the leak. In 1982 Justice O'Connor suggested a change in a federal jurisdictional rule during congressional testimony on the Supreme Court budget, and some people inferred from her suggestion what both her position and the Court's decision in a pending case on the rule would be; their inferences, as it turned out, were basically correct. [9] Burger has been especially vigilant about maintaining secrecy for the Court's work, and some observers of the Court argue that his vigilance interferes with effective reporting on Court decisions.

The Court's announcement of its decision completes the major stages of processing for a case. The length of time required for the case to go through these stages can vary a good deal, depending chiefly on the backlog of cases scheduled for oral argument and the time that the justices take to settle on a decision and set of opinions. Table 4-2 illustrates this variation with the timetable for two cases decided on the same day in July 1983.

Influences on Decisions: Introduction

The remaining sections of this chapter will be concerned with explanation of the choices made by the Supreme Court and by its individual members in reaching decisions. As I have indicated, these choices have two components: the treatment of the parties to the case and the Court's position on the general legal and policy issues in the case. From the perspective of the individual member of the Court, we need to explain justices' votes on the outcome of the specific case and the content of the opinions to which they subscribe.

Explanation of policy choices anywhere in government is difficult. Policy makers are influenced by a broad range of considerations that interact in a complex way. We hardly can say that a particular policy chosen by a legislature or an administrative agency resulted from a specific set of influences and specify the importance of each influence

Table 4-2. Timetable for processing of two Supreme Court cases

Action	Ruckelshaus v. Sierra Club	Guardians Assn. v. Civil Service Comm.
Case filed	August 11, 1982	August 31, 1981
Certiorari granted	October 18, 1982	January 11, 1982
Oral argument	April 25, 1983	November 1, 1982
Decision announced	July 1, 1983	July 1, 1983
Time from filing to decision	10½ months	22 months

with precision. We can, however, point to the general kinds of factors that do shape policy choices in significant ways.

The factors that affect decisions of the Supreme Court can be placed in four general categories: (1) the state of the body of law that is applicable to a case; (2) the external environment of the Court, including other policy makers, interest groups, and public opinion; (3) the personal values of the justices concerning the desirability of alternative decisions and policies; and (4) interaction among members of the Court.

Each of the following four sections of the chapter will examine one of these categories: its significance as an influence on the Court's decisions and the ways in which it operates. Together, these sections should provide a sense of the bases for the decisions that the Court reaches.

The State of the Law

It should be clear by now that the Supreme Court makes its policy choices in a legal context. Like all other courts and most administrative agencies, the Court selects among alternative policies in the form of interpreting provisions of law. Accordingly, an examination of influences on the Court's decisions must begin with a look at the law that the Court interprets and a discussion of the law's significance in determining what the Court does.

Means of Interpretation

The law that the Supreme Court interprets comes primarily from the United States Constitution and from federal statutes. In deciding cases, members of the Court must exercise their judgment as to the meaning of one or more provisions of the Constitution, of statutes, or both. They can utilize several time-honored judicial techniques to make their interpretations.

"Plain Meaning." One of these techniques is an analysis of the literal meaning of the words in question. In some cases the plain meaning of a provision of law will be sufficiently clear to resolve the controversy. For instance, the Twenty-second Amendment to the Constitution states, "No person shall be elected to the office of the President more than twice." The Supreme Court would have little difficulty in rejecting a claim that a twice-elected person could run for a third term.

But the Court seldom faces such easy cases, because the justices see little purpose in reviewing a lower court judgment that has reached an obvious result. Most of the Court's decisions involve ambiguous provisions such as the Fourteenth Amendment's protection of "due process of law," for which there is no plain meaning.

Moreover, the plain meaning of some provisions may be a matter of dispute. The First Amendment states that "Congress shall make no law . . . abridging the freedom of speech." Justice Black read these words to mean that Congress could not restrict speech in any way. But other commentators have argued that in the context of the period when the First Amendment was written, "freedom of speech" meant only a limited protection for speech from government control.[10]

Legislative Intent. A second means of interpretation is an effort to ascertain the intentions of those who write a provision into the law. For statutes, this effort may concentrate on reading the "legislative history" of the act, particularly the committee reports that attempt to convey congressional intentions authoritatively. In interpreting the Constitution justices make use of records of the Constitutional Convention and the congressional debates that preceded the adoption of amendments.

Unfortunately, the intent of the convention or Congress often is quite murky. Statements of purpose may be absent or contradictory, so that their analysis fails to resolve a disagreement over interpretation. For instance, scholars and justices have not been able to agree on congressional intent in proposing the Fourteenth Amendment after the Civil War. Some argue that the amendment was designed to make all the prohibitions of the Bill of Rights applicable to state governments, while others believe that Congress did not intend that result.[11] This disagreement is particularly important because the Fourteenth Amendment is the primary constitutional basis for protection of civil liberties at the state and local level, but it is far from unique.

At times there will be no legislative intent relevant to an issue faced by the Court. For instance, a legal provision may have to be applied to a situation that did not exist when the provision was written. Wiretapping became technologically possible more than a century after the Fourth Amendment's requirements for searches and seizures were written, so the writers of that amendment could have had no intent concerning the legal status of wiretapping. In this kind of situation, the justices may rely upon "purposive" interpretation, in which they seek to apply the goal that underlies a provision to the new issue.

This kind of interpretation may be used in dealing with "old" issues as well. Capital punishment existed when the Eighth Amendment's prohibition on cruel and unusual punishments was written, and the Congress that proposed the amendment surely did not intend to eliminate capital punishment. But a justice can argue that the underlying purpose of the Eighth Amendment was to prohibit punishment that is inconsistent with dominant standards of decency, and if those standards eventually made capital punishment unacceptable to most people, it would follow the "real intent" of the framers of the Constitution for the

Supreme Court to prohibit it. Purposive interpretation, of course, gives tremendous discretion to justices in applying a provision of law.

Precedent. A third means of interpretation is analysis of the Supreme Court's own past decisions, its precedents. In a sense, judicial precedents constitute a separate body of law in themselves. Indeed, in some traditional areas of law such as property and contracts, English and American law first developed primarily through the aggregation of judicial decisions rather than through constitutions or statutes, and the only law to be interpreted was precedent. Seldom is this the case for the Supreme Court today, but precedents remain very important for the Court's interpretation of statutes and of the Constitution.

Precedents are important first of all because a basic doctrine of the law is *stare decisis* ("let the decision stand"), under which a court is bound by its own precedents and those of courts above it in the judicial hierarchy. Judges are expected generally to follow the interpretations of constitutions and statutes that already have been established in other cases. Aside from legal doctrine, precedents have a practical value. The following of precedent allows a judge to rely on past practice rather than to take new and perhaps dangerous directions in legal interpretation; more generally, it eases the task of decision making.

Technically, a court is bound to follow not everything stated in a relevant precedent but only the rule of law that was necessary for decision in that case, what is called the *ratio decidendi*. Other statements, called *obiter dicta* or simply *dicta,* have no legal force. In *Jones v. Barnes* (1983), the Supreme Court held that a defendant's constitutional right to counsel was not violated when the assigned counsel did not raise all the issues urged by the client in appealing a conviction. Chief Justice Burger's opinion for the Court laid down rules on the obligations of appointed counsel in appeals; because the decision was based on these rules, they may be considered the *ratio* of the decision. The opinion also stated, "There is, of course, no constitutional right to an appeal";[12] because that judgment was unnecessary to decide the case, it may be considered *dictum.* In this case the distinction between *ratio* and *dictum* is fairly clear, but often it is difficult to discern the distinction. This difficulty gives a court some freedom to choose what it will regard as binding in a precedent.

In any case, the rule of precedent hardly eliminates all ambiguity in legal interpretation. Most cases before the Supreme Court involve issues that are at least marginally different from those decided in past cases, so precedent seldom determines a decision in a strict way. The precedents that are relevant to a case are likely to point in more than one direction; it is an old adage that precedents generally can be found to support both sides of a case. Furthermore, because the Court is not absolutely bound to follow precedent, in a given case the justices must consider whether a departure from past interpretations of the law would be desirable.

The Significance of the Law in Shaping Decisions

To what extent are the Supreme Court's decisions determined by the state of the applicable law? Some justices and legal scholars have argued that the law is the key factor in determining what the Court does. This argument probably was best expressed by Justice Owen Roberts in a 1936 decision for which he knew the Court would be criticized heavily. Seeking to turn back such criticism, Roberts wrote as follows:

> It is sometimes said that the court assumes a power to overrule or control the action of the people's representatives. This is a misconception.... When an act of Congress is appropriately challenged in the courts as not conforming to the constitutional mandate the judicial branch of the Government has only one duty,—to lay the article of the Constitution which is invoked beside the statute which is challenged and to decide whether the latter squares with the former. All the court does, or can do, is to announce its considered judgment upon the question. The only power it has, if such it may be called, is the power of judgment.[13]

The discussion thus far should make clear the weakness of Roberts's argument. Even if members of the Supreme Court wished to do no more than follow the law, the state of the law seldom is sufficiently certain to allow that passive approach. Most of the time, justices' conclusions about the meaning of the law must be supplemented with other bases for judgment. In this respect the Court differs from the appellate courts that must hear most of the cases brought to them. Judges on these courts commonly indicate that most of their cases can be decided only one way under the law. But the Supreme Court ordinarily hears only cases involving truly disputed interpretations of the law. As a result, the justices have no choice but to exercise discretion.

Moreover, few justices would be content to take a passive approach even if it were possible. Justices frequently have strong reasons for preferring one policy to another, and they wish to see their preferences reflected in the Court's decisions. Accordingly, they will not only accept the freedom provided by the law's ambiguity but will seek to extend it.

This attitude is reflected in a willingness to overturn a precedent where no other mechanism exists to change a policy in disfavor. That willingness has increased in the last quarter century. According to one count, the Court overruled prior decisions in 75 decisions between 1961 and 1980, in contrast with a total of 96 overrulings during the Court's entire history through 1960.[14] Often the Court overturns a precedent from an earlier and very different era. This was true when *Brown v. Board of*

Education (1954) overruled an 1896 decision (*Plessy v. Ferguson*) that had held that the states could give blacks and whites "separate but equal" treatment. But sometimes, especially in recent years, overturnings have come more quickly. In 1977 and 1978 the Court overruled two decisions that were three and four years old.[15] Viewing this record, one scholar concluded that "if a majority of the Warren or Burger Court has considered a case wrongly decided, no constitutional precedent—new or old—has been safe." [16]

Even without overturning precedents, the Court can "distinguish" them from the facts of later cases in order to narrow their impact and allow the Court to change its direction. One good example is *Solem v. Helm* (1983), in which the Court held that a South Dakota sentence of life imprisonment without possible parole for a seventh nonviolent felony conviction constituted cruel and unusual punishment. Only three years earlier the Court had reached the opposite result in a fairly similar case, but the majority opinion cited differences between the cases—especially possible parole in the earlier case—that justified a shift. Writing an opinion for four dissenters, Chief Justice Burger complained that "today's holding cannot rationally be reconciled" with the earlier decision,[17] but the majority rejected his argument. More broadly, in the 1970s and 1980s the Burger Court majority made narrow interpretations of some Warren Court decisions that had supported the rights of criminal defendants, so as to blunt their force and minimize their effects.

The justices' desire to use their freedom in interpreting the law is reflected in other practices as well. Sometimes the Court reaches a decision that seems contrary to the plain meaning of the law but which it justifies on other bases. Article I, section 10 of the Constitution prohibits the states from adopting laws "impairing the obligation of contracts." But in *Home Building & Loan Assn. v. Blaisdell* (1934), the Supreme Court upheld a Minnesota law that postponed payments on home and farm mortgages in order to prevent wholesale foreclosures during the Depression. Chief Justice Hughes's opinion in that case employed circuitous logic to justify a decision that the majority wished to reach despite the actual wording of the Constitution.

The Court also has adopted major legal doctrines that seem to have little basis in any mode of interpretation of the Constitution. Perhaps the classic example is the establishment of a new constitutional right to privacy in *Griswold v. Connecticut* (1965). In that decision seven of the justices agreed that a state law which prohibited the use of birth control devices violated a constitutional liberty, but they could not agree on the provisions that provided a source for this liberty. Decisions such as *Griswold* underline the Court's partial freedom from constraint by the state of the law.

It would be a mistake, however, to dismiss the law altogether as a factor in Supreme Court decisions. Several related forces cause justices to see their jobs in terms of legal interpretation rather than simply as independent policy making. Members of the Court are trained in a tradition that emphasizes the law as a basis for judicial decision. They are judged by a legal audience largely in terms of their adherence to what are regarded as good legal principles. Perhaps most important, they work in the language of the law, and scholars such as John Brigham and Timothy O'Neill have emphasized that this language channels judges' thinking and constrains their choices.[18]

Because justices approach decisions partly in legal terms, certain potential policies that cannot easily be justified in those terms are eliminated from consideration. The Supreme Court's effective range of alternatives often will be narrowed because of the state of the law as it stands. Even among the policies that could be justified legally, for one or more justices the weight of the applicable law may lie so heavily on the other side as to move them away from a policy that they prefer personally. Occasionally, justices will note that their decisions do not reflect their personal views. Harry Blackmun and Potter Stewart both voted to uphold capital punishment laws. But Blackmun expressed his "distaste, antipathy, and, indeed, abhorrence, for the death penalty," and Stewart said, "If I were a legislator, I wouldn't ever vote for it." [19] In 1982 Chief Justice Burger wrote in an opinion that a policy to deny education to illegal aliens was "senseless," "folly," and "wrong," but nonetheless he dissented from a decision overturning that policy.[20]

The state of the law, then, serves as one element in the decisional process. Seldom, if ever, does it force the Court to adopt a particular policy, but it may exert a subtle force in channeling the Court's choices. As C. Herman Pritchett has said, "Judges make choices, but they are not the 'free' choices of congressmen." [21] The considerable freedom that justices do possess requires that other factors be employed to explain their decisions.

The Court's Environment

Public policy makers are subject to influence from at least four elements of their environments: the mass public; relevant elite groups in the population; those who bring demands to them, especially interest groups; and other governmental institutions. Certainly congressional behavior reflects influence from each of these sources. Indeed, some commentators argue that the decisions of members of Congress can be explained chiefly by their desire to appeal to public opinion in their constituencies in order to ensure reelection. Similarly, the policies of some administrative agencies, such as the independent regulatory commissions of the federal government, have been ascribed primarily to their relationships with the private groups that are most concerned with their decisions.

Courts are not immune to influence from their environments, but most courts do possess a degree of freedom that distinguishes them from most other policy makers. The freedom of the Supreme Court is particularly great, and it helps to make the Court a rather different kind of institution from, say, Congress. As Justice Harold Burton replied when he was asked about his move from Congress to the Court, "Have you ever gone direct from a circus to a monastery?" [22]

The Court's insulation has several sources, some of which are common to other courts.[23] The most important source of the Court's freedom from influence is the lifetime term, which reduces tremendously justices' dependence upon public opinion and upon other policy makers. Formal and practical constraints on interest group activity in the judiciary augment the Court's freedom. Finally, the Court's status as the highest judicial body eliminates the review by judicial superiors that limits the autonomy of lower courts.

Nonetheless, each element of the environment that I have listed exerts a meaningful influence on the Court. Collectively, they have a significant impact on the Court's decisions. The specific impact of each merits examination.

Mass Public Opinion

Legislators may wish to act in accordance with public opinion for two general reasons. Most important, they wish to maintain public support in order to secure reelection or political advancement. In addition, they may feel some responsibility to represent their constituents' views in order to serve their district effectively. Both of these motives are relatively weak in the Supreme Court. Justices do not depend on public opinion to keep their positions, and few are interested in other positions. Moreover, the Court is not intended to be a representative body. The limited significance of public opinion for the Court is reflected in its adoption of some highly unpopular policies. The Court's decisions prohibiting organized prayers in public schools and promoting busing of students for racial desegregation have been supported by a relatively small minority of the public and opposed strongly by large segments of that public. Its support for the rights of criminal defendants, particularly during the 1960s, has been equally unpopular.

Yet the opinion of the general public has some effect on the Court's decisions, for several reasons. Perhaps most important, justices know that the impact of their decisions depends in part on acceptance of individual decisions and of the Court's authority as an institution by the mass public. Presumably, the more favorably people view the Court and its work, the more likely they are to carry out the Court's policies rather than to impede them.

This concern is likely to have a subtle effect on some decisions involving controversial issues. Occasionally the effect is fairly clear, as in the Court's implementation decision in *Brown v. Board of Education* (1955). The Court chose to establish an indefinite timetable for school desegregation in the South rather than demanding quick action. This choice was based in part on a calculation that flexibility by the Court would help to obtain Southern acceptance of the general principle of desegregation. The desire to maintain public support for the Court also affects the ways in which some decisions are presented. Traditionally the chief justice writes the Court's opinion in major cases when the Court wishes to lend the chief's prestige to its decision. Chief Justice Earl Warren authored the opinion in *Brown v. Board of Education* (1954), Chief Justice Warren Burger in *United States v. Nixon* (1974). Occasionally justices take special pains to make their opinions persuasive in an effort to forestall public criticism. One example may be Chief Justice Burger's opinion for the Court in a 1980 decision that had the effect of increasing the salaries of the justices (*United States v. Will*). Apparently recognizing the Court's vulnerability, Burger stressed reasons why the Court needed to decide a case that had a direct monetary impact on its members.

Aside from the Court's institutional needs, at least some justices have a personal interest in the popularity of their actions. This concern may arise simply from the desire to be liked, but in rare instances it may stem from an interest in future elective office. William Douglas apparently had some ambition for the presidency, and some of his colleagues believed that this ambition affected his decisions.[24] Sandra Day O'Connor has received attention as a potential presidential candidate, and there is some speculation that this possibility might influence her course as a justice.

Finally, public opinion is regarded as a legitimate basis for interpretation of some constitutional provisions. The best example is the Eighth Amendment prohibition of "cruel and unusual punishments." Justices have made their judgments as to what this provision means in part on the basis of current public views. In the Court's Eighth Amendment decisions on capital punishment, such as *Gregg v. Georgia* (1976), justices on both sides have cited public opinion surveys in support of their interpretations.

Elite Opinion: The Mass Media and the Legal Community

Along with general public opinion, the opinion of narrower groups may have some effect on the Supreme Court. Two groups whose opinions potentially are relevant to all justices are the mass media and the legal community. Ordinarily, neither is likely to exert more than a subtle influence on the Court, but even that subtle influence may be significant under some conditions.

The mass media are important because they link the Court to the general public and to other policy makers, communicating and evaluating what the Court does. The media also are significant in themselves because they serve as visible reviewers of the Court's work. Justices have shown some sensitivity to criticism in the press, and Potter Stewart once wrote a letter to the *Wall Street Journal* to refute the *Journal's* criticism of a decision.[25]

Media criticism may have had considerable impact on a 1980 decision. In *Gannett v. De Pasquale* (1979), the Court held that judges could bar the public—including the press—from pretrial proceedings, and it implied that the First Amendment does not provide the public with a right of access to trials. The decision was attacked a good deal in the press, which was very concerned with its own access to court proceedings, and four justices took the unusual step of making public statements about the decision and its meaning. Only a year later, in *Richmond Newspapers v. Virginia* (1980), the Court "retreated" by holding that the First Amendment does guarantee the public a right of access to most trials. "Without *Gannett,* and the critical reaction it aroused," wrote the journalist Anthony Lewis, "I doubt that the Supreme Court would soon have found in the First Amendment a public right to know about public institutions." [26]

The legal community is important as a professional reference group. Justices draw many of their acquaintances from this community, and most of them continue to interact a good deal with lawyers and lower court judges after they join the Court. The legal community also serves as the primary source of expert evaluation of the Court, particularly in the law reviews published by law schools and edited by their students. As I suggested earlier, the legal community helps to make legal considerations important to the Court's decisions. Where a particular view of legal issues is dominant in the bar or in a segment of the bar relevant to a justice, that view may affect the one that the justice adopts.

The law reviews can have another kind of impact as well. As cited in briefs and read by justices and clerks, law review articles constitute an important source of the information about legal questions that enters into decisions. Justices frequently cite law review articles in support of their positions, and on occasion articles may help to determine the positions themselves.

Of course, a justice may take cues and information from a wide range of specialized groups. Undoubtedly, some justices are influenced by their own friends and acquaintances—whether or not they are attorneys.

Justice Harry Blackmun once served as counsel for the Mayo Clinic, and he has drawn a good deal from medical scholarship for some of his opinions. Justice Tom Clark once telephoned J. Edgar Hoover to ask for information relevant to a case.[27]

Litigants and Interest Groups

The roles of litigants and groups in bringing cases to the Supreme Court were discussed in Chapter 3. In this section I will examine their influence over the judgments that the Court reaches in the cases accepted for full decision.

Certainly litigants and the groups that support them make the most direct efforts to influence Supreme Court decisions. As I have noted, however, their influence is severely limited by characteristics of the Court as an institution. Although individual litigants and groups play a crucial role in bringing cases to the Court, it is difficult for them to achieve influence over the Court's decisions on those cases.

The most important basis for influence is effective advocacy in written briefs and oral arguments. In the Court, as in the other branches of government, group representatives seek to shape policy makers' perceptions of the choices that they face. The impact of these efforts may be limited by the requirement that communications go through formal legal channels; groups have a greater opportunity for influence in the other branches, where they often deal directly with policy makers. But the quality of representation for particular policy positions affects the Court's response to cases at least occasionally. Justice Harlan said that oral argument "may in many cases make the difference between winning and losing." [28] The expertise of the experienced advocates in the solicitor general's office helps to explain the federal government's success in decisions on the merits, just as it helps the government in getting its petitions for hearings accepted by the Court. The same is true of other lawyers with skills in Supreme Court advocacy, including some who frequently write briefs or participate in oral argument on behalf of interest groups.

The impact of advocacy should not be exaggerated. The Court is not totally dependent upon litigants for information and arguments, and justices may approach cases with very strong predispositions. Occasionally, the Court will adopt a policy that none of the parties to the case suggested. Often justices' attitudes will be sufficiently well formed that even the best or worst advocacy can have little effect on the outcome. In the famous *Gideon* case on counsel for indigent criminal defendants, future justice Abe Fortas employed his own considerable skills and the services of a large law firm on behalf of Gideon, while his opponent was a young and inexperienced attorney who developed his case virtually alone and part time. Yet the disparity between the two sides probably had no effect on the Court's decision, because most justices already had decided to adopt the policy supported by Fortas even before they accepted Gideon's case. As legal scholar Bernard Schwartz wrote, "The Fortas eloquence was only the battering of an open door." [29]

It follows that the effect of argumentation on the Court varies a good deal with the type of case. John Frank, a former law clerk, suggests that in many cases justices are not really open to persuasion; this is especially true in cases on which they have strong feelings. "On the other hand, in a very large number of cases the Justices are pursuing no special enthusiasms and invoking no sentiments. In those cases the function of counsel may be controlling." [30] Thus in the Court, as in Congress, interested parties have the greatest impact when policy makers feel least strongly about the issues before them.

Congress, the President, and Other Policy Makers

Several sets of policy-making institutions are important to the Court. Lower courts and some administrative agencies are responsible for implementation of the Court's decisions. The president plays some role in enforcement of decisions, helps to shape public attitudes toward the Court, and may have close personal relations with some justices. Congress holds crucial powers over the Court as an institution as well as power to change Court-made policies.

Understandably, members of the Court make some effort to achieve good relations with each of these institutions. For instance, individual justices sometimes seek to develop friendly contacts with lower court judges. The Court's expressions of deference to administrative expertise in its opinions also may reflect a desire for support from other policy makers. Most important, an interest in maintaining the support of other policy makers may exert an impact on the substance of the Court's decisions.

Congress and the president probably are the policy makers that affect the Court's decisions most. The potential influence that Congress gains through its powers over the Court deserves relatively lengthy discussion here. I will discuss the influence of the president more briefly; some of the most significant forms of presidential influence already have been considered, and another is linked to congressional powers.

Congressional Powers. The array of congressional powers over matters important to the Court is impressive. First, Congress largely controls the structure and powers of the Court. It can limit the Court's appellate jurisdiction—its power to hear cases—as it did in 1868 to prevent the Court from ruling on the constitutionality of Reconstruction-era legislation. It can set the justices' salaries, although those salaries cannot be reduced; at times Congress has expressed its displeasure with the Court by holding salaries constant during times of inflation. Congress also sets the number of justices and has changed that number several times, although the current number of nine has become so well established that it would be difficult to alter.

Further, congressional legislation on substantive matters can be important to the Court. The establishment of new legal rights can increase the Court's caseload. Statutes may strengthen or overturn the policies that the Court makes in particular areas of law, and congressional overturning of a Court policy may be intended as a rebuke to the Court. These substantive powers, in combination with congressional control over the Court as an institution, make Congress very relevant to the Court.

The Court's Behavior. Members of the Supreme Court hardly can be unconcerned with the relevant actions of Congress. Occasionally justices directly lobby Congress for or against legislation. Chief Justice Taft worked hard to obtain the Judiciary Act of 1925, the statute which gave the Court its broad discretionary jurisdiction. Some members of the Court intervened to help defeat Franklin Roosevelt's "Court-packing plan" in 1937. Chief Justice Burger has been an active advocate on legislation that concerns him, particularly laws affecting federal court structure and jurisdiction.

More important, the Court's policies may be affected by a desire to deter Congress from enacting legislation that attacks the Court in some way. During several periods in the Court's history justices seemed to be motivated by the goal of avoiding decisions that would arouse—or aggravate—the displeasure of Congress. At the beginning of the nineteenth century John Marshall's Court faced congressional attacks because of its activist policies, and Marshall was careful to limit the occasions on which the Court reached decisions that would further anger its opponents. After the Civil War the Court retreated from conflict with the Radical Republicans in Congress, primarily through its acceptance of a statute that removed its jurisdiction over the Reconstruction laws while it considered a case involving those laws. Probably the most striking instance of the Court's efforts to avoid congressional attack was its shift from opposition to support of New Deal legislation in 1937 while Congress was considering President Roosevelt's Court-packing plan; this episode was discussed at greater length in Chapter 1.

A more recent episode with some drama occurred in the late 1950s. From 1954 to 1957 the Court adopted libertarian policies in several areas and thereby aroused a good deal of displeasure in Congress and the country at large. Members of Congress introduced bills to attack the Court's policies and to limit its jurisdiction, and a few of the bills received serious consideration. Meanwhile, in 1958 and 1959 the Court handed down some decisions in which it retreated from policies that had displeased Congress, including a virtual reversal of its position on congressional investigation of subversive activities. This shift seems to have constituted what one commentator called "a tactical withdrawal," [31] and it helped to quiet congressional attacks on the Court.

No dramatic events like these have taken place since the 1950s, and it is difficult to point to recent decisions that were influenced by congressional pressure. Yet the pressure itself has existed. The Court has been attacked in Congress for its position on a variety of civil liberties issues, including school desegregation, legislative reapportionment, abortion, and school prayer. On each of these issues efforts have been made to overturn the Court's decisions, to limit its jurisdiction, or both.

The Court has adhered to some of its disfavored policies, and its continued support for school busing in the face of strong congressional opposition is striking. In other areas it has altered its positions. While most of the alterations seem best explained by other factors, a desire to reduce conflict with Congress may have played a part in some.

Church-state issues are interesting in this respect. As of 1984 the Court had not backed down from its opposition to organized school prayer, but it reached decisions on some other issues in this area that avoided aggravating its problems in Congress. Of particular interest is the Court's 1984 decision allowing a government-sponsored nativity scene (*Lynch v. Donnelly*). Presumably by coincidence, that decision was announced on the day that the Senate began debate on a constitutional amendment to allow school prayer exercises; a decision in the opposite direction probably would have increased interest in attacking the Court on church-state issues through support of the amendment.

Conclusions. The impact of Congress on the Court should not be exaggerated. The instances in which congressional attacks have affected Supreme Court policies are significant, but they hardly constitute all of the Court's history. Only occasionally has the Court faced a serious possibility of adverse action by Congress, and even at these times conflict between Congress and the Court has involved only a limited set of issues. Nor does the Court always retreat under pressure. In recent years the Court has maintained very liberal policies on several civil liberties issues despite considerable criticism from Congress.

But we also should be careful not to assume that Congress is irrelevant to the Court most of the time. Undoubtedly most justices are constantly aware of Congress as well as other elements of their environment. All else being equal, justices would prefer to take actions that please their audiences, and concern with congressional reaction may exert influence on their decisions from time to time that is too subtle for outsiders to recognize.

The President. Presidents have multifaceted relationships with the Supreme Court, and these relationships provide several sources of potential influence. First, the president helps to shape government litigation policy through appointment of the solicitor general and occasional intervention in specific cases. This role is significant in light of the government's frequent participation in Court cases.

Second, the president helps to shape responses of other institutions to the Court. The president can support anti-Court action in Congress, as Franklin Roosevelt and Reagan have done, or defend the Court against such action. Presidents can aid the Court in obtaining implementation of its policies or refuse to help. Thus justices have reason to keep the peace with the president just as they do with Congress.

Third are the personal relationships between justices and presidents. Some members of the Court were close associates of presidents who later selected them, and both they and other justices may interact with presidents while serving on the bench. Some, such as Abe Fortas, have been frequent visitors to the White House for advisory or social purposes. Such relationships hardly compel justices to support the president's position in decisions, but they may exert a subtle impact on a justice's responses to cases with which the president is concerned.

.   The appointment power should be considered another form of influence over the Court. Indeed, it probably is the most potent external influence on the Court. At any given time, the direction of the Court is determined largely by the presidents who appointed its members. Other institutions and the public can have a meaningful impact on what justices do, but the president has the advantage in determining who those justices are.

Justices' Values

The Role of Policy Preferences

Preferences and Decisions. The members of the Supreme Court are people with active interests in political issues. Inevitably, they have strong views about most of the policy questions that the Court is called upon to decide. A justice who comes to the Court without an opinion on a particular judicial issue is likely to develop one as the Court confronts cases which raise that issue.

In the traditional conception of judicial decision making espoused by Justice Roberts, judges' policy preferences have no impact on their decisions because decisions are dictated by the state of the law. As I have indicated, this conception is fallacious—particularly for the Supreme Court. Seldom is the law so clear on the issues faced by the Court that it dictates a particular decision. Choices among legally acceptable alternative policies must be based on other factors, and the justices' conceptions of good policy certainly are among these other factors. Like other policy makers, members of the Supreme Court respond to policy choices largely in terms of their personal attitudes about policy.

Indeed, policy preferences may play a larger role in the Court than in legislatures and administrative agencies. While justices' policy choices are constrained by the state of the law, this constraint may be more than counterbalanced by the Court's relative freedom from environmental pressures. In any case, it can be argued that justices' policy preferences are the most important of the factors that affect Supreme Court decisions.

The significance of preferences in decisions is suggested by the writings of justices such as William Douglas, which express the same views about policy that their decisions support. Similarly, some biographies of individual justices trace the ways in which their attitudes toward policy issues are reflected in their behavior on the Court. Another kind of evidence is the consistency that most justices show in the positions that they take on particular sets of issues, not only from case to case but also from year to year. Justice Brennan's regular support for civil liberties from the mid-1950s through the mid-1980s is difficult to explain except in terms of a strong personal commitment to those liberties.

Whatever their importance in explaining decisions generally, policy preferences almost certainly provide the best explanation for differences among the justices in decisional behavior. This is true because no other factor varies so much from one justice to another. Most efforts by scholars to examine the effects of preferences on decisions have focused on differences among justices, using the assumption that differences in their voting behavior generally reflect differences in personal views about policy issues.[32] This procedure is reasonable so long as we avoid assuming that *all* Supreme Court behavior is based solely on policy preferences. In the remainder of this section I will use comparisons among justices to probe the role of their policy preferences in the Court's decisions.

The Sources of Preferences. The views of Supreme Court justices on policy issues, of course, derive from the same general sources as political attitudes generally. Family socialization is a key element in the development of attitudes. Other institutions such as schools and the mass media also are important. Finally, career experiences can help to shape justices' attitudes.

Some observers of the Supreme Court have sought to explain justices' preferences, and thus their behavior, in terms of certain specific "background" characteristics such as religious affiliation.[33] Certainly these characteristics do help to shape attitudes. The views of justices Pierce Butler and Frank Murphy on some issues before the Court, for instance, have been ascribed to their Catholicism.[34] But the relationship between specific characteristics and attitudes is a complex one, and a judge's attitudes cannot be explained completely in terms of those characteristics. Certainly justices whose backgrounds were rather similar in many respects have behaved quite differently as members of the Supreme Court.

The Ideological Dimension

The pattern of a justice's preferences on the various issues addressed by the Supreme Court is not random. Rather, the attitudes that each justice holds tend to be interrelated in a fairly logical way. As Benjamin Cardozo wrote before he reached the Court,

> There is in each of us a stream of tendency, whether you choose to call it philosophy or not, which gives coherence and direction to thought and action. Judges cannot escape that current any more than other mortals.[35]

In this respect, of course, judges are similar to others with active interests in political issues.

Liberalism and Conservatism. The coherence that exists in the attitudes of Supreme Court justices and other people can be understood in terms of liberalism and conservatism. In the United States one set of preferences on a wide range of issues is labeled liberal, while the opposing preferences are called conservative. Most of the issues that come to the Supreme Court involve conflicts between liberal and conservative positions. As described by David Rohde and Harold Spaeth, those issues can be placed in three general categories.[36]

The first category is called "freedom." It includes civil liberties issues involving procedural rights, such as the rights of criminal defendants, as well as substantive rights such as freedom of expression and freedom of religion. The liberal position is favorable to these rights. The conservative position gives relatively great weight to values that compete with these rights, such as the capacity to fight crime effectively.

The second category is labeled "equality," and it includes issues that derive from claims of discriminatory treatment under the Fourteenth Amendment and other provisions of law. The liberal position tends to support these claims, while the conservative position is less sympathetic.

The third category has been called "New Dealism," though it might also be called economic regulation. This category contains issues of governmental regulation of the economy, an activity associated with the New Deal. The liberal position on regulatory issues is somewhat complex, though it generally is favorable to regulation. One important element of the liberal position is support for regulatory activity which is favorable to labor and unfavorable to business.

This categorization may suggest too neat a picture of the issues that come to the Court. Some cases, such as disputes between states over water rights, do not have a clear ideological content. Other cases present conflicts between values that stand on the same side of the ideological spectrum, such as the conflict between two "freedom" values in clashes between freedom of the press and the right of criminal defendants to a fair trial. With these important cautions, however, it is useful to consider cases in terms of the three categories of ideological issues that I described.

Ideology and Decisions. Liberalism and conservatism provide important organizing principles for people's views on policy issues. Most policy makers stand at about the same positions on the liberal-conservative continuum on most issues. If a senator is a conservative on public welfare, the senator's positions on national defense are likely to be conservative as well.

The same is true of Supreme Court justices. Over the course of their careers, most justices establish fairly consistent positions on the ideological spectrum, across the broad range of issues that the Court decides. This is particularly true of justices at either end of the spectrum. There is no difficulty in characterizing Justices Brennan and Marshall as liberals or Chief Justice Burger and Justice Rehnquist as conservatives.

This does not mean that a justice will be equally liberal or conservative on all issues, and some justices have deviated considerably from that pattern. Justice White, for instance, has been more liberal in his decisions on issues in the equality category than on issues in the freedom category. While some justices are considered moderates because they take middle-of-the-road positions on most issues, others appear to be moderates because of a combination of liberal positions on some issues and conservative positions on others. Ideological consistency across issues is a strong tendency but not an absolute rule.

There is a higher level of consistency within each of the three categories identified by Rohde and Spaeth. This consistency is illustrated by the voting patterns in 38 nonunanimous decisions that the Court reached in the Freedom area in the 1982 term. These patterns are depicted in the "scalogram" in Figure 4-1. In a scalogram, justices and cases are ranked according to the number of liberal votes, in order to determine how consistently the overall rankings of justices are reflected in individual cases.

Figure 4-1 shows, first of all, that the justices varied considerably in their support for liberal outcomes, from Marshall at the liberal end of the spectrum to Rehnquist at the conservative end. For the most part, the divisions in individual cases followed the same lines as the overall rankings of justices. For instance, when the Court divided 5-4 in a conservative direction, in eight of nine cases it was the four justices with the most lib-

Figure 4-1 Scalogram of justices' votes in cases involving "freedom" issues, 1982 term

Cases[a]	Justices[b]									Liberal votes
	Ma	Br	St	Bl	Po	Wh	Bu	O'C	Re	
74 - 297	+	+	+	+	+	+	+	+	−	8
75 - 295	+	+	+	+	+	+	+	+	−	8
75 - 903	+	+	+	+	+	−	+	+	−	7
74 - 430	+	+	−	+	+	+	+	−	+	7
74 - 250	+	+	−	+	+	+	+	−	−	6
76 - 687	+	+	+	+	+	−	−	−	−	6
77 - 180	+	+	+	+	−	+	+	−	−	6
75 - 229	+	+	+	−	+	+	−	−	−	5
74 - 823	+	+	+	+	−	+	−	−	−	5
77 - 637	+	+	+	+	+	−	−	−	−	5
75 - 547	+	+	+	+	−	−	+	−	−	5
74 - 646	+	+	+	+	−	−	−	−	−	4
74 - 675	+	+	+	+	−	−	−	−	−	4
75 - 708	+	+	+	+	−	−	−	−	−	4
76 - 733	+	+	+	+	−	−	−	−	−	4
77 - 694	+	+	+	+	−	−	−	−	−	4
77 - 721	+	+	+	+	−	−	−	−	−	4
77 - 405	+	+	+	+	−	−	−	−	−	4
77 - 1171	+	+	+	+	−	−	−	−	−	4
74 - 794	+	+	+	−	+	−	−	−	−	4
74 - 3	+	+	+	−	−	−	−	−	−	3
75 - 813	+	+	+	−	−	−	−	−	−	3
76 - 527	+	+	+	−	−	−	−	−	−	3
77 - 22	+	+	+	−	−	−	−	−	−	3
77 - 1003	+	+	+	−	−	−	−	−	−	3
77 - 1019	+	+	+	−	−	−	−	−	−	3
77 - 1201	+	+	+	−	−	−	−	−	−	3
77 - 1267	+	+	+	−	−	−	−	−	−	3
77 - 1275	+	+	+	−	−	−	−	−	−	3
77 - 614	+	−	−	+	−	+	−	−	−	3
77 - 1090	+	+	−	+	−	−	−	−	−	3
77 - 1134	+	+	−	+	−	−	−	−	−	3
77 - 987	+	+	−	−	−	−	−	−	−	2
74 - 748	+	−	+	−	−	−	−	−	−	2
74 - 535	+	−	+	−	−	−	−	−	−	2
74 - 12	+	−	−	−	−	−	−	−	−	1
74 - 21	+	−	−	−	−	−	−	−	−	1
76 - 143	−	−	+	−	−	−	−	−	−	1
Liberal votes	37	32	30	21	9	8	8	3	1	

[a] Numbers are volumes and pages of cases citations in *Supreme Court Reports, Lawyers' Edition*.

[b] Ma = Marshall, Br = Brennan, St = Stevens, Bl = Blackmun, Po = Powell, Wh = White, Bu = Burger, O'C = O'Connor, Re = Rehnquist.

NOTE: Cases were included if the Court decided issues of procedural due process or substantive civil liberties, except equal protection, by nonunanimous vote; cases dealing with remedies for rights violations are excluded. Liberal votes are designated +; conservative votes, −. Boldface line divides justices into two groups according to conventional rules of scalogram analysis; − signs to left of line and + signs to right may be interpreted as votes inconsistent with ideological ordering of justices.

eral overall records who dissented. There were many exceptions to perfect ideological consistency, but most were moderate rather than extreme. For instance, there were no cases in which Rehnquist or O'Connor cast the only liberal vote.

This pattern is similar to that found in other issue categories and other years. It suggests that within a broad category of cases justices divide primarily on the basis of a single ideological dimension. Not only are justices' policy preferences largely responsible for differences in their decisional behavior, but to a considerable degree those preferences are expressed in a moderately simple ideological form.

Patterns of Agreement. Another perspective on the Court's ideological divisions can be obtained by examining the patterns of agreement among justices. Figure 4-2 shows the mean proportions of cases in which each pair of justices supported the same opinion during the 1981 and 1982 terms. This figure, unlike Figure 4-1, includes cases in all issue categories. As the figure shows, some pairs of justices agreed with each other a good deal more than other pairs, though the differences are not as sharp as we might have expected.

Figure 4-2. Median percentages of cases in which pairs of justices supported the same opinion, 1981-1982 terms

	Br	Bl	St	Wh	Po	Bu	O'C	Re
Marshall	87	71	61	58	48	47	44	39
Brennan		75	65	59	52	51	52	42
Blackmun			64	66	58	60	59	53
Stevens				56	55	53	56	52
White					68	73	67	71
Powell						80	76	78
Burger							79	81
O'Connor								84
Rehnquist								

NOTE: Numbers are medians, for the two terms, of the percentages of cases in each term in which a pair of justices agreed. Both unanimous and nonunanimous cases are included.

SOURCE: "The Supreme Court, 1982 Term," *Harvard Law Review* 97 (November 1983): 304.

Not surprisingly, levels of agreement are highest for the justices whose ideological positions in Court decisions are closest. Brennan and Marshall supported the same opinion in nearly nine of every 10 cases. Among the four most conservative members of the Court (Rehnquist, O'Connor, Burger, and Powell), each pair agreed more than 75 percent of the time. By the same token, the lowest rates of agreement were between the most "distant" justices ideologically; Marshall supported the same opinion as Rehnquist only about two-fifths of the time. Of the justices who are considered by some to populate the ideological center of the Court, White agreed more with the four most conservative justices and Stevens and Blackmun with the two most liberal. These patterns suggest that White occupied something of a pivotal position in the center of the Court, and to a considerable extent that was the case; of the 33 decisions with 5-4 votes in the 1982 term, 17 found White allied either with the four most liberal members or with the four most conservative members.[37]

We should be careful not to make too much of these patterns. First, as some of the votes in Figure 4-1 suggest, the justices do not always line up in expected ways. Indeed, in cases which lack clear-cut ideological conflicts, rather unusual alliances may appear. This was true in two well-publicized cases decided by 5-4 votes in 1984. In *Silkwood v. Kerr-McGee Corporation,* the dissenters who thought that a suit could not be brought over Karen Silkwood's death were Blackmun, Marshall, Powell, and Burger. In *Sony Corporation v. Universal City Studios,* the dissenters who thought that sale of home videotape recorders violated the copyright laws were Blackmun, Marshall, Powell, and Rehnquist.

Second, we should not assume that patterns of agreement reflect self-conscious alliances or blocs of justices. To some degree justices who hold similar policy preferences work together to achieve favorable outcomes, and members of the Court are aware of general patterns of agreement among themselves. But it is their shared preferences, not the existence of concerted action, that best explain the tendency for certain justices to support the same opinion.

Preferences and Policy Change

The process of policy change on the Supreme Court is a complex one, because the issues before the Court constantly are changing. If the Court reduces its support for the rights of criminal defendants, that shift might reflect a change in the Court's approach to defendants' rights or simply a change in the kinds of defendants' rights cases that reach the Court, and it is not always easy to distinguish between the two. Still, at times it is clear that the Court's collective approach to a policy area or a set of policy areas (such as civil liberties) has changed.

Such changes can occur for a variety of reasons. But the discussion of policy preferences in this section suggests that a primary source of policy change on the Court must be changes in the preferences of the justices as a group. Such changes can come in two ways: from changes in the views of people already serving on the Court and from change in the Court's membership. In practice, both kinds of change are significant.

Changes in Views. We would expect the preferences of Supreme Court justices on major policy issues to be relatively stable. Fundamental values will be very well formed by the time that an individual reaches the Court. As a result, these preferences should be rather impervious to change.

In general, this appears to be the case. If we measure a justice's preferences by a pattern of statements in opinions or by bloc membership, the primary pattern is one of stability. A justice who begins as a liberal generally remains a liberal. Sometimes a justice's relative position on the Court will change because the Court's ideological center of gravity shifts. Justice Stewart, for instance, moved toward the liberal side of the Court in the 1970s as new appointments made the Court as a whole more conservative. But this shift probably did not represent a fundamental change in Stewart's own views.

Occasionally such a fundamental shift does appear to occur. Probably the best recent example is Justice Harry Blackmun. Blackmun came to the Court in 1970 as a Nixon appointee, and early in his career he aligned himself chiefly with the other conservative justices. He and Chief Justice Burger, boyhood friends from Minnesota, were dubbed the "Minnesota Twins." But gradually Blackmun moved toward the center of the Court, and by the 1980 term he was joining Justice Brennan in opinions more often than he joined Burger. In an interview published in 1983, he indicated that one personal goal was to prevent the Court "from plunging rapidly to the right." Blackmun also referred obliquely to his changed views: " . . . I think, clearly, this is an educational process—and I would hope that one matures as the years go by." [38] Then Blackmun further confounded observers by taking a distinctly more conservative stance in the 1983 term. The only clear conclusion from his record was that he defied the general rule of stability in a justice's ideological position.

More common than individual ideological shifts are changes in the views of the justices as a group on particular issues. Major external events such as wars and the development of social movements influence public opinion generally, and members of the Supreme Court are not immune to this influence. For instance, the onset of the cold war with the Soviet Union in the late 1940s caused many Americans to conclude that the Communist Party in the United States was a threat to national security.

The Court's opinions in cases involving conflicts between free expression and national security showed that most justices had come to share this feeling; the opinion affirming the criminal convictions of Communist Party leaders in *Dennis v. United States* (1950) is especially clear in this respect. Similarly, the development of the black civil rights movement in the 1950s and 1960s helped to increase public support for the goals of black citizens, and the sympathies of most justices undoubtedly were enlisted by the movement. The extraordinary willingness of the Court to overturn convictions of civil rights demonstrators who had been arrested attests to this enlistment of sympathies.

Issues concerning the legal status of women offer an unusually clear example of the impact of external events. The Warren Court gave unprecedented support to equality under the law, but it did not attack legal provisions that treated women and men differently. Its successor, a more conservative Court on most issues, nonetheless handed down a series of decisions promoting legal equality for the sexes. This seemingly anomalous pattern can be explained primarily by the impact of the women's liberation movement on justices' views about women's social roles. As a result of the movement, even conservative justices in the 1970s were more supportive of sexual equality than liberal justices in the 1960s. The impact of the women's movement, like that of the civil rights movement and of the cold war, might be classified as an example of an environmental influence on the Court's decisions. In any case, it demonstrates that significant changes in justices' attitudes toward particular policy issues do indeed take place.

Membership Change. Although shifts in the positions of sitting justices can produce major policy changes on the Court, more often such changes result from new appointments to the Court. Membership change is probably the primary source of policy change on the Court, rivaled only by fundamental changes in the Court's environment. Indeed, the importance of appointments should be evident from the discussion thus far: if Supreme Court policies are primarily a product of the justices' preferences, and if those preferences tend to be stable, then change will come most easily through the replacement of one justice with a successor who has a different set of policy preferences.

The Court's history since the 1950s demonstrates the significance of membership change. The early Warren Court was closely divided between liberals and conservatives, and from 1958 until 1961 there was a relatively stable division between a four-member liberal bloc and a moderate to conservative bloc of five. By the standards of the 1920s and 1930s the Court's policies were fairly liberal, but on major civil liberties controversies the results were mixed.

In 1962 President Kennedy made two appointments to the Court. The moderate Byron White replaced conservative Charles Whittaker, and the liberal Arthur Goldberg replaced Felix Frankfurter. On a closely divided Court, these appointments were sufficient to change the general direction of policy. Their effects were reinforced by the selection of Thurgood Marshall in 1967 to replace Tom Clark. (In 1965, Goldberg was replaced by another liberal, Abe Fortas.) The period from 1962 to 1969 probably was the most liberal in the Court's history. The Court established strikingly liberal positions in a variety of policy areas.

Between 1969 and 1971, President Nixon was able to fill four vacancies on the Court, and he used these opportunities to move the Court in a conservative direction. Liberals Warren and Fortas, along with Harlan and Black, were replaced by four justices who ranged from moderately conservative (Powell and Blackmun) to strongly conservative (Burger and Rehnquist) in their views. Later the very liberal Douglas was succeeded by the moderate-to-liberal Stevens (in 1975) and the moderate Stewart was succeeded by the conservative O'Connor (in 1981). These changes made the Court still more conservative, though they were balanced somewhat by Blackmun's move in a liberal direction.

As noted in Chapter 1, the impact of this membership change has been somewhat ambiguous. The Court's policies in the 1970s and early 1980s were characterized by both continuity and change.[39] On the one hand, the Court adhered to some policies of the Warren Court and even took some new liberal directions on issues such as abortion. Yet the Burger Court generally was less supportive of civil liberties than its predecessor had been, and it also adopted new conservative positions on some issues concerning government regulation of the economy. On the whole, its policies were a good deal more conservative than those established by the Court in the 1960s.

The limits on the Supreme Court's policy shift in the 1970s and 1980s caution against exaggerating the impact of membership change. But the change in policies that did occur is noteworthy. Certainly it suggests that the appointment process is the most important mechanism by which the Court's policies may be altered, at least in the short run.

Role Values

Role Values on the Court. Thus far the discussion of justices' values has been limited to their policy preferences. But these are not the only kinds of values that may affect the Court's decisions. The choices that justices make also may be influenced by their role values, their views about what constitutes appropriate behavior for the Supreme Court and its members.

Several sets of role values can affect justices' decisions. Their views about the legitimacy of dissenting opinions will help to determine the frequency of unanimous decisions. Their attitudes concerning the desirability of judicial activism may be important in their decisions whether to overturn acts of Congress. Their views concerning the bases on which decisions should be reached also may be important. For instance, justices who believe that the Court should not take public opinion into account may be especially willing to adopt unpopular positions on policy issues. Similarly, some justices may feel more constrained to follow the state of the law as they perceive it than do others.

Attitudes toward activism and the law as a constraint both were expressed in the quite different ways that Oliver Wendell Holmes and Hugo Black summarized their roles on the Court. Once, when bidden by a friend to "do justice," Holmes replied, "That is not my job. My job is to play the game according to the rules." [40] In contrast, when Black was asked what he conceived his basic task to be, "His eyes blazed, his right hand shot into the air, and without hesitation he fervently said, 'To do justice!' " [41] While both statements oversimplify the views of the justices who made them, they reflect real and significant differences in role conceptions.

It is difficult to reach firm conclusions about the impact of role values on justices' behavior, and observers of the Court differ in their judgments. In one sense, role values are fundamental: everything that justices do is shaped by the ways in which they perceive their jobs. Yet justices could be expected to adopt role values that are consistent with their policy goals, either deliberately or unconsciously, so that these role values might exert little independent effect on decisional behavior.

On the whole, I think that the evidence suggests a limited impact for role values. The general policy positions that most justices adopt appear to be rather consistent with their personal policy preferences. Thus it is their conceptions of good public policy that seem most responsible for their policy choices.

This conclusion is supported by the history of the debate over judicial activism and restraint in this century. During the 1920s and early 1930s, activist Supreme Court policies generally involved attacks on government regulation of the economy. Conservative justices took the most activist positions, while liberals on the Court and elsewhere argued for judicial restraint. Since the 1940s, however, activism has meant primarily support for civil liberties against legislative and executive action. In this context it is liberals who have given the most support to Supreme Court activism, while conservatives have argued for judicial restraint. This history suggests that positions on activism and restraint have served chiefly as justifications of policy choices rather than determining those choices themselves.

The Case of Justice Frankfurter. Certainly it is possible that role values have been the major driving force behind the decisions of some justices. The justice who is suggested most often as fitting this description is Felix Frankfurter. As a liberal law professor in the 1920s and 1930s, Frankfurter argued strongly for judicial restraint. After joining the Court in 1939, he supported restraint not only on issues of economic regulation but also on civil liberties questions. As civil liberties issues became more important in the Court's work, Frankfurter stood out for his opposition to decisions that overturned government policies on civil liberties grounds.

This pattern of behavior suggests that the primary factor influencing Frankfurter's decisions was his conception of the Court's role in government. Frankfurter himself took this position, stating in several opinions that he supported conservative results despite his liberal policy preferences because of his belief in judicial restraint.

Expressions such as these did not persuade all observers of the Court. Some have argued that Frankfurter really was a conservative on civil liberties issues. In their view, his arguments for restraint were intended to veil a lack of personal support for constitutional freedoms. Others, however, have accepted Frankfurter's explanation of his decisions. In their view, his work demonstrates that a justice can subordinate personal preferences to a role value.[42]

The debate about Frankfurter's motives is difficult to resolve. But this debate should not obscure the fact that Frankfurter is, at most, an exceptional case. If his behavior was determined primarily by his role values, he stands out among justices whose role values seemed to have only a limited effect on their decisions. For the justices as a group, policy preferences are the most important values that contribute to their decisions.

Group Interaction

A Quasi-Collegial Body

The Supreme Court's decisions are made both individually and collectively. The justices do most of their work within their own offices, with the help of their law clerks and in isolation from their colleagues. As Justice Powell has written, "for the most part, perhaps as much as 90 percent of our total time, we function as nine small, independent law firms." [43] But there also is an important group element to the Court's decision making. Part of the decisional process occurs in the group setting of the Court's conferences. Beyond this important fact, justices have incentives to interact and work together on decisions outside of conference. Justices who feel strongly about cases often work to persuade colleagues to their points of view, and there may be a good deal of competition between opposing sides to win crucial votes in a close case. In addition, the desire to achieve as much consensus as possible gives justices reason to work together to reach agreement on outcomes and opinions in cases. The Court may be called a quasi-collegial body, one in which group processes play a limited but significant role in decisions.

Interaction among justices affects the Court's ultimate policies a good deal. Most frequently, the Court's opinion is shaped through negotiation between the assigned justice and other members of the Court. Indeed, the final opinion sometimes is fundamentally different from its first draft, even when the official author is the same. This apparently was the case in *United States v. Nixon* (1974), in which Chief Justice Burger's original opinion was found unsatisfactory by several colleagues. Reportedly they worked together to produce a more acceptable final opinion, which nonetheless was issued in Burger's name.[44]

Group interaction also accounts for much of what J. Woodford Howard called "the fluidity of judicial choice," [45] the shifting of individual votes and collective decisions after tentative decisions in conference. A justice may change a position independently after further study of a case, but frequently it is input from colleagues that spurs reconsideration of an initial position. Certainly group interaction was crucial in the single most famous instance of fluidity, the process by which a Court that had been closely divided eventually produced a unanimous decision in *Brown v. Board of Education*.[46] Histories of the Court offer other accounts of cases in which persuasion within the Court shifted votes and sometimes majorities.

A more systematic picture of decisional fluidity is provided by Saul Brenner's comparisons of justices' votes at conference and their final votes in the same cases. In the 1956-1967 period 10 percent of the individual votes shifted from one side to the other during the decisional process, and at least one shift occurred in about half of the cases. Most of the vote changes increased the size of the original majority, as the Court worked toward consensus. But in 85 cases during those 11 years, about 9 percent of the total, an initial minority became a majority as a result of vote shifts or shifts between participation and nonparticipation in the vote.[47]

These findings do not give a perfect indication of group impact on decisions. Not all vote shifts stem from group influences, and group influences may be reflected in initial conference votes as well as shifts later in the process. But the findings nonetheless are noteworthy. On the one hand, they suggest that group processes do make a difference. Perhaps more important, the stability of most votes cast in conference suggests that there are limits to the impact of colleagues on the positions that justices take. Individual policy preferences appear to be considerably more important than group processes in shaping the Court's decisions.

Of course, the two factors are not necessarily opposing forces. Interaction among like-minded justices may reinforce the expression of their shared ideological positions. For instance, a liberal justice who votes tentatively for a conservative position in a case may be persuaded by liberal colleagues to support the position more consistent with their basic views.

The group life of the Court may have an effect on its decisions that is broader and more subtle than shifts of position in individual cases. A Court may have patterns of influence that give special weight to the positions of some justices in determining the Court's policies. The Court's ability to reach consensus may depend on the extent of conflict among its members. In the remainder of this section I will examine those two issues and through them look in more detail at the characteristics of the Court as a group.

Patterns of Influence

Sources of Influence. Except for the chief justice, all members of the Supreme Court are essentially equal in their formal powers. Each has one vote. In a sense, then, the justices begin with equal opportunities for influence over their colleagues.

As in other groups, however, members of the Supreme Court differ in what they make of these opportunities. In part, these differences result from variation in the desire for influence. Justice Douglas wrote that "Most judges content themselves with making up their own minds," but Stone, Black, and Frankfurter "were evangelists," "active proselytizers." [48] Douglas himself was an extreme case of a justice who is uninterested in exerting influence; one colleague reported, presumably with some overstatement, that "Bill Douglas is positively embarrassed if anyone on the court agrees with him." [49]

In addition, justices differ in qualities that help to determine interpersonal influence on the Court. One crucial quality is skill in legal reasoning and argumentation. Ultimately, policy positions must be justified within the Court and to its audiences as good law and good policy. For this reason a justice who can make very strong arguments for personal positions will have disproportionate influence. A good example might be John Harlan, a conservative on the distinctly liberal Warren Court. Despite his minority position, Harlan seemed to have considerable influence with his colleagues because of his extraordinary skills as a legal craftsman. On the current Court Lewis Powell may hold special influence because of his widely acknowledged strengths as a legal scholar. On the other side, justices with clearly limited skills are likely to hold relatively little influence in the decisional process.

A second relevant quality is a justice's personality. Supreme Court justices, like other people, vary in their likability and their skills in personal relations, and these characteristics inevitably will affect their influence. Justice James McReynolds, who alienated his colleagues with his unpleasantness, was not likely to have much impact on their decisions. Certainly he did not improve his chances of changing his colleagues' positions with his practice of noting on drafts of opinions, "This statement makes me sick." [50] In contrast, a person who gets along well with colleagues—as William Rehnquist, for instance, appears to do—is likely to gain in influence as a result.

In this respect, as in so many others, Felix Frankfurter is an interesting case. Frankfurter came to the Court in 1939 expecting to play a major leadership role, and he made great efforts to influence his colleagues. He gave special energy to courting new colleagues. But these efforts suffered from his arrogance and his tendency to lecture to his colleagues. His messages to other justices during the decision-making process included an abundance of statements like the following: "And so please, Mr. Jackson, do find time to read, if you have not already read, the chapter on Presumption in J. B. Thayer's Preliminary Treatise." "I would like to ask you to read or reread in cold blood the following cases." [51] He also reacted sarcastically to opinions with which he disagreed. Frankfurter unintentionally alienated several colleagues with his behavior, and his influence within the Court was fairly limited.

In the operation of influence among justices, subgroups within the Court may be important in two respects. First, an individual justice may exert much more influence over some colleagues than over others, because of general ideological agreement or personal ties. Second, two or more justices who share a viewpoint on most Court issues may work together to influence the Court as a whole. In practice these two factors can meld together, with a subgroup leader working through like-minded colleagues to influence the Court as a whole. Thus Chief Justice Taft held occasional Sunday afternoon sessions with other conservative justices so that they could "present a united front to the rest of the Court." [52] More recently, Justice Brennan seems to have played an important leadership role for the Court's liberals in their efforts to influence the Court's direction.

Equality of Influence. It is important not to exaggerate the influence—or lack of influence—of individual justices. First of all, it is doubtful that a single member of the Court could become totally dominant under today's conditions, because other justices also will care deeply about the issues on which they rule and will seek to avoid complete subordination to a single leader. Chief Justice John Marshall exerted tremendous control over the Court in the early nineteenth century, and he actually wrote the Court's opinion in a majority of cases. But his capacity to do so resulted from conditions that no longer exist, including the very close contact among the justices throughout their time in Washington. No contemporary justice could hope to come close to Marshall's position.

Further, the fact that each justice holds a single vote does provide an important equalizing force. No matter how limited a justice's skills or how weak a justice's personality, that member still has the power to vote to affirm or reverse, to support one opinion or another. Particularly on a closely divided Court, every justice has the capacity to secure changes in opinions to meet objections. When Justice Stewart joined an ideologically split Court in 1958, he reportedly was "wooed" by the competing factions "in much the manner of an uncommitted delegate at a political convention." [53] Stewart's colleagues could have known little about his professional and personal qualities at that time, but his mere presence on the Court as a potentially pivotal member gave him real influence.

The Chief Justice

In efforts to exert influence over the Court the chief justice is in an unusually strong position. The chief holds several formal powers that provide a special capacity for influence, and the prestige of the chief justice's position augments the influence of its occupant. But these advantages in themselves do not guarantee leadership. A chief who does not make effective use of the position's formal and informal powers may carry little more weight than any associate justice. Thus the chief's position is an ambiguous one.

The Chief Justice's Powers. Perhaps the most important power attached to the position of the chief justice is that of presiding over the Court in oral argument and in conference. In presiding over conference, the chief can direct discussion and frame alternatives, thus helping to shape the outcome of the discussion. It is especially important that the chief is the first to speak on a case in conference.

Two other powers are quite important. The first is the chief's part in creating the "discuss list," the set of petitions for hearing that the Court will give full consideration. The chief, aided by clerks, makes up the initial version of the discuss list. This task gives the chief the largest role in determining which cases are set aside without group judgment. The second is the power of opinion assignment, which merits discussion in some detail.

Opinion Assignment. By custom, the chief justice assigns the Court's opinion whenever the chief is in the majority on the initial vote in conference. Because of this rule, the chief may vote "insincerely" with the majority in order to assign the Court's opinion. Chief Justice Burger apparently has done so on occasion. He also reportedly refrains from expressing a judgment about some cases at the beginning of discussion in order to remain free to join the majority that emerges from the discussion. According to Bob Woodward and Scott Armstrong, Justice Stewart once drew a tombstone for Burger that was inscribed with the words, "I'll Pass for The Moment." [54] Even without these strategems, however, the chief justice will be the primary assigner of opinions. For instance, Chief Justice Warren assigned more than 80 percent of the opinions during his tenure.[55]

The significance of the assignment power should be underlined. First of all, the selection of the opinion writer may determine whether the initial majority stands up and what its ultimate size will be, since different justices may produce opinions with different effects on their colleagues. More directly, the policy proclaimed by the Court may depend in large part on who writes the opinion—if the selected writer can maintain the support of at least four colleagues for the opinion. In addition, the assignment power allows the chief to reward and punish colleagues and thus provides an extra degree of leverage over them.

To some extent, patterns in opinion assignment are dictated by organizational needs.[56] The chief justice needs to assign a relatively equal number of opinions to the justices in order to spread out the workload, and recent chiefs have adhered rather closely to an equality principle. Further, a justice who does not receive a reasonable share of desirable opinions—such as those in important cases—may become dissatisfied, and ordinarily a chief will seek to avoid dissatisfaction.

But these principles still leave the chief with considerable room to make opinion assignments in such a way as to advance personal policy goals. The chief may assign the opinion in a case to the most "moderate" member of the majority, to maximize the likely appeal of the opinion to other justices and thus to strengthen the original majority. Alternatively, the chief may choose to write the opinion or give it to an ideological ally in order to obtain the legal position that the chief favors. In practice, there is a tendency for the chief justice to follow this latter strategy in the more important cases, with justices who are ideologically distant from the chief getting most of their opinions in cases less important to the chief justice.

Other factors are involved in assignment decisions. As noted earlier, the chief justice is especially likely to write the opinion in very important cases. On the average, the chief justices from Taft to Burger have been twice as likely to assign cases to themselves on major constitutional questions as on other issues. On another level, the chief may assign most cases in a particular area of law to a member with some expertise in that area. Because so many factors contribute to chief justices' opinion assignment decisions, the pattern of assignments is rather complex. But the most important factors almost surely are the need to equalize workload and the chief's interest in obtaining desired results in cases.

Variation in Leadership. What particular chief justices make of these formal powers and of the prestige of their position will vary with their interest in exerting leadership, their skill as leaders, and the general willingness of the associate justices to accept such leadership.

For these reasons, the roles of chief justices have differed greatly. Hughes was a very powerful leader, one who held rather tight control over the Court's decision-making process. In conference, as one scholar has put it, Hughes was both the task leader and the social leader.[57] Taft was a moderately influential leader on the Court who played a large role in such external matters as the selection of justices and the enactment of legislation that concerned the judiciary. Stone did not seek and did not achieve a major leadership role on the Court.

The last two chiefs, Earl Warren and Warren Burger, are of particular interest. Their tenure is too recent for us to have obtained a clear picture of their roles. Still, it is possible to sketch out their positions generally.

Earl Warren did not have outstanding legal skills, and he could not compete with some colleagues as a scholar. He faced a Court with several skillful and strong-minded members, such as Black, Douglas, and Frankfurter, and the Court was closely divided between liberals and conservatives during most of his tenure. These conditions would have made it very difficult for Warren to establish himself as the dominant leader of the Court, and he did not.

But Warren did have some major assets. Most important, he had leadership skills that included a great capacity to produce consensus. This capacity was demonstrated at the beginning of his career on the Court. He came to the Court in 1953 during the deliberation over the school desegregation cases, which had divided the Court sharply. Chiefly through what Justice Douglas called "a brilliant diplomatic process which Warren had engineered," [58] the Court handed down a unanimous decision in *Brown v. Board of Education* at the end of his first term. Warren was able to play a major leadership role on the Court, albeit one that was shared with and contested by some colleagues.

Warren Burger is an especially interesting case. He has considerable ambition for leadership; in effect, he has sought to combine Hughes's position within the Court with Taft's influence outside the Court. Within the Court his efforts to lead are reflected in several procedural innovations, such as changes in the treatment of paupers' petitions (see Chapter 3). Elsewhere, he has appeared regularly before bar association conventions and at other forums to argue for a wide range of changes in the legal system, and he has sought to influence the course of some legislation on legal issues.

There is evidence, however, that Burger's efforts at leadership have not been very successful. Outside the Court he has achieved only limited success in his goals for legal reform. Indeed, his attempts to influence the legislative process have aroused some hostility in Congress, particularly in a 1978 dispute over a bankruptcy bill that the chief justice opposed. Within the Court he has not established himself as a leader comparable to Hughes or, it seems, even to Warren. One apparent reason for his limited success is an absence of the skills needed for effective persuasion. A former clerk for Justice Powell has said that Burger "does not have the gift of leadership or conciliation." [59] Burger is accused of bullying the Court and of attempting to control decisions illegitimately, and at least some colleagues have reacted negatively to his efforts.

Any assessment of Burger's leadership must take into account the difficulties he has faced. His ambitious goals for change in the legal system are inherently difficult to achieve. It may also be true that any chief justice with Burger's personal conservatism would have had difficulty in leading the Court during the 1970s and early 1980s, because he stands near one end of an ideologically diverse group of justices. In any case, his example demonstrates that a concerted campaign to exercise leadership as chief justice does not guarantee success.

Harmony and Conflict

The Supreme Court is an institution in which disagreement about policy is inevitable. At any time the Court will include members with very different views about policy, and much of the time their differences will be expressed publicly in the Court's decisions. The existence of frequent dissents and concurring opinions no longer is noteworthy; rather, it is expected.

Disagreements about policy need not lead to personal conflict among justices, but the potential for personal animosity is considerable. Given the intensity of feelings that justices have on policy questions, clashes on issues are likely to spill over into personal relations. The pressures of Court work also tend to promote conflict. For these reasons, reports of personal friction within the Court should not be surprising.

But the extent of such conflict seems to have varied a good deal over time. In some periods the Court has been a fairly harmonious body, whose members could work well together despite their differences. At other times, however, the Court has been severely divided on a personal level, with considerable antagonism among its members.

The extent of conflict on the Court is an interesting matter in itself, but it also can affect the functioning of the Court. A harmonious Court probably will be able to maximize consensus in decisions, because members can work easily with each other and are willing to compromise. Such a Court also could be expected to function most efficiently, because good interpersonal relations speed the process of reaching decisions and resolving internal problems.

For these reasons, in virtually any Court justices will make some effort to achieve friendly relationships and to avoid conflict. Even where justices are unhappy with their colleagues' behavior, they often try to avoid open conflict that leads to permanent bitterness. A reporter asked a member of the Burger Court why he did not complain about an alleged violation of norms by the chief justice; the justice replied, "You don't have to live here for the rest of your life." [60]

Despite these efforts, justices will not always be successful in achieving harmony. Where the combination of policy disagreements and personality clashes is too potent, the Court may become the scene of considerable conflict. Perhaps the most conflictual Court of this century was that of the late 1940s. Hugo Black and Robert Jackson engaged in an open feud that included a letter from Jackson to the Senate Judiciary Committee attacking Black's behavior on the Court. The papers of the justices who served during that time document the bitterness and distrust that existed between other pairs of justices as well. Felix Frankfurter, for instance, complained that his colleague Harold Burton was too naive and "hasn't the remotest idea how malignant men like Black and Douglas not only can be, but are." [61]

In the Warren Court fundamental policy differences among the justices were reflected in some serious conflicts. The most visible was the dispute between Warren and Frankfurter that surfaced in Court sessions during the late 1950s and early 1960s. But the general tone of personal relations on that Court is not yet clear.

It is also difficult to reach judgments about personal relations on the Burger Court, although there are some signs of personal conflict. Published accounts of personal relations on the Court suggest that there is considerable animosity among some justices. The bitterness of the language in some opinions, such as the dissents quoted in Table 4-1, is noteworthy. Also significant are the open disagreements among justices on procedural matters, such as admissions of attorneys to practice before the Supreme Court, eligibility to file paupers' petitions, and even the length of an appendix to a legal brief that a litigant can submit. Personal conflicts may well be reflected in the proliferation of separate opinions, including an unprecedented number of concurring opinions; this proliferation suggests an inability or unwillingness of the justices to work out differences in their views of cases. But these signs probably exaggerate the depth of conflict, and the current Court may not be especially conflictual by historical standards.

A Final Note

This discussion of the Court as a group suggests that it is similar to other governmental institutions in its internal dynamics. Members negotiate over cases as members of Congress do over legislation. Justices engage in feuds just as administrators do, and these feuds may affect the disposition of policy questions in the same way.

These characteristics of the Court's group life disturb some observers, particularly those who see the Court as standing outside "politics." Yet it is difficult to imagine how the Court could avoid them. Some people regard a process of judicial decisions through negotiation as illegitimate or undesirable. But that process is necessitated by the goal of obtaining consensus on cases and encouraged by justices' interest in securing policies with which they agree. Conflict among justices may not be desirable, but it is inevitable at some times because of conflicts over policy and the pressures involved in reaching decisions. However it may differ from other institutions, the Court necessarily functions much like most other groups that make important decisions.

Conclusion

The discussions of the major factors in Supreme Court decisions suggest that the Court's policy choices cannot be explained in simple terms. Forces as different as the state of the applicable law and the relationships among the justices help to determine what the Court decides.

Of these forces, however, one seems preeminent. This is the policy preferences of the justices. Because the law usually is ambiguous and environmental constraints generally are weak, the justices are largely free to choose positions in accordance with their own conceptions of good policy. The law and the environment undoubtedly limit the meaningful options for the Court at a given time on a particular issue. Within those limits, the justices can follow the lines of policy that they prefer.

For this reason the process of selecting members of the Supreme Court is central to the Court's policy direction. Some observers view the change from a liberal Court in the 1960s to a moderate Court in the 1970s and 1980s as an inevitable product of the need to slow down the Court's role in social change. But there was little of an inevitable nature about the Court's change in direction. Rather, that change resulted primarily from the appointment of conservative justices by President Nixon. Thus, one can ascribe the policies of the Court in the 1970s and 1980s largely to the events that allowed Nixon to win a narrow victory in 1968. Had Hubert Humphrey been a slightly more effective campaigner—or a little luckier—that Court might have been an extension of the Warren Court rather than a contrast to it.

If justices' preferences explain a great deal, of course they do not explain everything. A Court labeled as conservative can make strikingly liberal decisions in important cases. The force of precedent can slow policy change in any direction. Effective leadership by the chief justice can help to marshal the Court behind a particular policy. One who seeks to understand why the Court does what it does must accept the complexity of the process by which the Court reaches its decisions.

Notes

1. The case was *Plyler v. Doe* (1982).
2. Fred Barbash, "Brennan, Marshall Keep Vigil Against Death Penalty," *Washington Post,* December 5, 1983, A10. The case was *Eddings v. Oklahoma* (1982).
3. Jim Mann, "Year-End Salute," *The American Lawyer* (September 1983): 94. The case was *Morris v. Slappy* (1983).
4. Michael F. Altfeld, David W. Rohde, and Harold J. Spaeth, "When the Court Can't Decide, Who's to Blame?" (Paper delivered at the annual conference of the Midwest Political Science Association, Chicago, April 1984), 3.
5. Charles Evans Hughes, *The Supreme Court of the United States* (New York: Columbia University Press, 1928), 68.
6. *Container Corporation v. Franchise Tax Board,* 77 L. Ed. 2d 545, 574 (1983).
7. The quoted language is taken from Justice Brennan's opinion in *Nevada v. United States,* 77 L. Ed. 2d 509, 534 (1983).
8. Henry J. Abraham, *The Judicial Process,* 4th ed. (New York: Oxford University Press, 1980), 234.
9. Fred Barbash, "O'Connor, Breaking Unwritten Rule, Speaks Publicly on a Pending Matter," *Washington Post,* March 10, 1982, A2. The case was *Patsy v. Florida Board of Regents* (1982).
10. Black's view is expressed in his opinions in *New York Times Co. v. Sullivan,* 376 U.S. 254, 293-297 (1964); and *New York Times Co. v. United States,* 403 U.S. 713, 714-720 (1971). The opposing view is expressed in Leonard W. Levy, *Legacy of Suppression: Freedom of Speech and Press in Early American History* (Cambridge: Harvard University Press, 1960).
11. See the opinions in *Adamson v. California* (1947).
12. *Jones v. Barnes,* 77 L. Ed. 2d 987, 993 (1983).
13. *United States v. Butler,* 297 U.S. 1, 62-63 (1936).
14. Congressional Research Service, *The Constitution of the United States of America: Analysis and Interpretation* (Washington, D.C.: Government Printing Office, 1973 and 1982).
15. The overruling decisions were *Oregon ex rel. State Land Board v. Corvallis Sand & Gravel Co.* (1977) and *United States v. Scott* (1978).
16. Earl M. Maltz, "Some Thoughts on the Death of Stare Decisis in Constitutional Law," *Wisconsin Law Review* (1980): 467.
17. *Solem v. Helm,* 77 L. Ed. 2d 637, 658 (1983).

18. John Brigham, *Constitutional Language: An Interpretation of Judicial Decision* (Westport, Conn.: Greenwood Press, 1978); Timothy J. O'Neill, "The Language of Equality in a Democratic Order," *American Political Science Review* 75 (September 1981): 626-635.
19. Blackmun: *Furman v. Georgia,* 308 U.S. 238, 405 (1972); Stewart: Barbara Reynolds, "It's Best to Be a Judge—Not a Philosopher," *USA Today,* January 10, 1984, 9A.
20. *Plyler v. Doe,* 457 U.S. 202, 242 (1982).
21. C. Herman Pritchett, "The Development of Judicial Research," in *Frontiers of Judicial Research,* ed. Joel B. Grossman and Joseph Tanenhaus (New York: John Wiley & Sons, 1969), 42.
22. Mary Frances Berry, *Stability, Security, and Continuity: Mr. Justice Burton and Decision-Making in the Supreme Court 1945-1958* (Westport, Conn.: Greenwood Press, 1978), 27.
23. The discussion in this paragraph draws much from David W. Rohde and Harold J. Spaeth, *Supreme Court Decision Making* (San Francisco: W. H. Freeman & Co., 1976), 72.
24. Joseph P. Lash, ed., *From the Diaries of Felix Frankfurter* (New York: W. W. Norton & Co., 1975), 77, 155, 182, 229-230, 339-340.
25. "Justice Stewart Dissents," *Wall Street Journal,* July 3, 1968, 6.
26. Anthony Lewis, "A Public Right to Know About Public Institutions: The First Amendment as Sword," in *The Supreme Court Review 1980,* ed. Philip B. Kurland and Gerhard Casper (Chicago: University of Chicago Press, 1981), 2.
27. Bernard Schwartz, *Super Chief: Earl Warren and His Supreme Court—A Judicial Biography* (New York: New York University Press, 1983), 311.
28. Anthony Lewis, *Gideon's Trumpet* (New York: Random House, 1964), 162.
29. Schwartz, *Super Chief,* 459-460.
30. John P. Frank, *Marble Palace: The Supreme Court in American Life* (New York: Alfred A. Knopf, 1958), 98.
31. Walter F. Murphy, *Congress and the Court* (Chicago: University of Chicago Press, 1962), 246.
32. Examples of this work include Glendon Schubert, *The Judicial Mind Revisited* (New York: Oxford University Press, 1974); and Rohde and Spaeth, *Supreme Court Decision Making.*
33. See C. Neal Tate, "Personal Attribute Models of the Voting Behavior of U.S. Supreme Court Justices: Liberalism in Civil Liberties and Economics Decisions, 1946-1978," *American Political Science Review* 75 (June 1981): 355-367.
34. David J. Danelski, *A Supreme Court Justice is Appointed* (New York: Random House, 1964), 189-190; J. Woodford Howard, Jr., *Mr. Justice Murphy: A Political Biography* (Princeton: Princeton University Press, 1968), 324.
35. Benjamin N. Cardozo, *The Nature of the Judicial Process* (New Haven: Yale University Press, 1921), 12.
36. Rohde and Spaeth, *Supreme Court Decision Making,* 138.
37. "The Supreme Court, 1982 Term," *Harvard Law Review* 97 (November 1983): 298.

38. John A. Jenkins, "A Candid Talk with Justice Blackmun," *New York Times Magazine,* February 20, 1983, 20.
39. The term is borrowed from Stephen L. Wasby, *Continuity and Change: From the Warren Court to the Burger Court* (Pacific Palisades, Calif.: Goodyear Publishing Co., 1976).
40. Charles P. Curtis, *Law as Large as Life* (New York: Simon & Schuster, 1959), 156-157.
41. Arthur Selwyn Miller, *Toward Increased Judicial Activism: The Political Role of the Supreme Court* (Westport, Conn.: Greenwood Press, 1982), 127.
42. See, respectively, Harold J. Spaeth, "The Judicial Restraint of Mr. Justice Frankfurter—Myth or Reality?" *Midwest Journal of Political Science* 8 (February 1964): 22-38; and Wallace Mendelson, *Justices Black and Frankfurter: Conflict in the Court* (Chicago: University of Chicago Press, 1961).
43. "What the Justices are Saying . . ." *American Bar Association Journal* 62 (November 1976): 1454.
44. Bob Woodward and Scott Armstrong, *The Brethren: Inside the Supreme Court* (New York: Simon & Schuster, 1979), 310-347.
45. J. Woodford Howard, Jr., "On the Fluidity of Judicial Choice," *American Political Science Review* 62 (March 1968): 43-56.
46. Richard Kluger, *Simple Justice: The History of Brown v. Board of Education and Black America's Struggle for Equality* (New York: Alfred A. Knopf, 1976), 582-699.
47. Saul Brenner, "Fluidity on the Supreme Court: 1956-1967," *American Journal of Political Science* 26 (May 1982): 388-390.
48. William O. Douglas, *The Court Years 1939-1975: The Autobiography of William O. Douglas* (New York: Random House, 1980), 18.
49. "The Court's Uncompromising Libertarian," *Time Magazine,* November 24, 1975, 69.
50. Merlo J. Pusey, *Charles Evans Hughes* (New York: Macmillan, 1951), 2:671.
51. H. N. Hirsch, *The Enigma of Felix Frankfurter* (New York: Basic Books, Inc., 1981), 160-161.
52. Walter F. Murphy, *Elements of Judicial Strategy* (Chicago: University of Chicago Press, 1964), 79.
53. James F. Simon, *In His Own Image: The Supreme Court in Richard Nixon's America* (New York: David McKay Co., 1973), 176.
54. Woodward and Armstrong, *The Brethren,* 413.
55. Rohde and Spaeth, *Supreme Court Decision Making,* 177.
56. The discussion of patterns in opinion assignment that follows draws heavily from the data in Elliot E. Slotnick, "Who Speaks for the Court? Majority Opinion Assignment from Taft to Burger," *American Journal of Political Science* 23 (February 1979): 60-77.
57. David J. Danelski, "The Influence of the Chief Justice in the Decisional Process of the Supreme Court," in *American Court Systems: Readings in Judicial Process and Behavior,* ed. Sheldon Goldman and Austin Sarat (San Francisco: W. H. Freeman & Co., 1978), 509-513.
58. Douglas, *The Court Years,* 115.
59. "Inside the High Court," *Time Magazine,* November 5, 1979, 63.
60. Nina Totenberg, appearing on CBS television program "60 Minutes," March 26, 1979.
61. Lash, *Diaries of Frankfurter,* 343.

Policy Outputs   5

In the book so far, one underlying concern has been the policies that the Supreme Court makes. This chapter will focus directly on those policies, looking at the substance of what the Court does. I will examine the Court's policy outputs—what it decides—from several perspectives. These discussions will help to provide an understanding of the Court's role in the making of public policy.

The first section of the chapter will deal with the Court's work as a policy maker in terms of the fields of policy in which the Court is most involved. The second and third sections will discuss what the Court actually decides in its fields of major activity, focusing on the extent of its activism and on the direction of its policies. In the final section I will seek to explain patterns in the Court's policy-making role.

Areas of Activity

In Chapter 3 I examined the process by which the Supreme Court's agenda is set. Through the actions of Congress, litigants, and, most important, the Court itself, a select group of fewer than 200 cases is chosen each term for full decision on the merits. In this section I will explore the substance of that agenda, the composition of the cases heard and decided fully by the Court. In order to provide a broader perspective on what the Court does today, I will be comparing its current agenda with those of other policy-making institutions and with the Court's own past agendas.

The Court's Current Activity

The Emphases. The Court's decisions always have dealt with a considerable range of subjects, and this certainly has been true in recent years. During any term the Court adjudicates a variety of issues in fields as different as antitrust, environmental protection, and freedom of speech. In this sense the Court's agenda is a highly diverse one, and the

Court has an opportunity to contribute to the development of public policy in a great many fields. This diversity does not mean that the Court gives equal attention to a large number of policy areas. Most of its efforts are concentrated on a fairly narrow range of cases. In this sense, the Court may be viewed as a specialist.

The Court's concentration on certain fields may be examined on the basis of the distribution of cases it decides with full opinions. Of course, the number of cases that the Court decides in a field does not always indicate the significance of its work in that field. A single major decision such as the Court's 1983 ruling on the legislative veto of executive-branch decisions (*Immigration and Naturalization Service v. Chadha*) may be more important than several dozen "little" decisions in another policy area. But the distribution of cases provides a fairly good sense of the Court's specialization. That specialization has several aspects.

First, the overwhelming majority of cases that the Court decides involve disputes that arise out of government activity. In the 1978 through 1982 terms, 78 percent of all the Court's decisions involved at least one government agency as a party.[1] Moreover, most of the disputes between private parties were based fairly directly on government policy, such as the regulation of labor-management relations and the awarding of patent rights. In traditional legal terms, the Supreme Court is predominantly a public law court rather than a private law court.

Within the public law category, the Court's primary area of activity is civil liberties. The term civil liberties may be given a variety of definitions. In the current era it is perhaps best defined as encompassing three general types of rights: procedural rights of criminal defendants and other people in governmental proceedings; the right of disadvantaged groups to equal treatment by government; and certain "substantive" rights, the most important of which are freedom of expression and freedom of religion. During the 1978 through 1982 terms, according to one calculation, 50 percent of the Court's decisions fell in those three civil liberties areas.[2] Although civil liberties cases are a diverse lot, the fact that half of the Court's decisions involve this single kind of issue is an indication of its specialization.

Related to the Court's civil liberties emphasis is an interest in criminal law and procedure. A significant proportion of the Court's business arises out of criminal prosecutions. In the 1978-1982 period, 22 percent of the Court's decisions came in criminal appeals or other actions by prisoners to challenge their convictions. Some of the criminal cases involve statutory interpretation, but in a large majority of cases the issues concern constitutional due process rights.

Civil liberties comprises the largest field of the Court's business by far, but it does not dominate the Court's agenda entirely. About half of the cases fall into other fields of policy. These other cases, like civil liberties cases, generally arise from government policy. However, they tend to involve issues of statutory interpretation rather than the constitutional issues that predominate in civil liberties cases.

A high proportion of the non-civil liberties cases involve economic issues, most commonly government regulation of economic activity. In the 1978-1982 terms, by one count, about 32 percent of the Court's cases dealt with economic regulation.[3] Within this category, the largest number of cases concerned labor-management relations. Other large categories include antitrust, securities regulation, and environmental protection.

Another major subject of Court activity is federalism. Issues of federal and state powers are involved in a significant minority of cases, cases that arise in a broad range of substantive contexts. Criminal cases from the states sometimes raise issues about the relationship between federal and state courts. *Silkwood v. Kerr-McGee Corporation* (1984) concerned the allocation of regulatory power over the nuclear industry between federal and state governments. As these examples suggest, federalism overlaps with other issues and Court concerns.

The 1983 Term. Both the diversity and the specialization of the Court's business may be understood better through a look at the agenda in a single year, the 1983 term. It will be useful to begin by describing the issues in a fairly representative sample of cases decided during that term.

—Whether a defendant is placed in double jeopardy when retried after, in the original trial, the jury failed to agree on guilt and the judge declared a mistrial. (*Richardson v. United States,* 1984)

—Whether Title VII of the Civil Rights Act of 1964 applies to a decision by a law firm about awarding partnership to an attorney with the firm. (*Hishon v. King & Spalding,* 1984)

—Whether a company and its wholly owned subsidiary can be charged with conspiring with each other under the Sherman Antitrust Act. (*Copperweld Corp. v. Independence Tube Corp.,* 1984)

—Whether a police officer must read a suspect *Miranda* warnings before asking questions about the location of a gun that might pose a danger to public safety. (*New York v. Quarles,* 1984)

—Whether a state court decision awarding custody of a child to the father because the mother had married a man of another race violates the equal protection clause of the Fourteenth Amendment. (*Palmore v. Sidoti,* 1984)

—Whether a state's regulation of casino industry union officials is preempted by the federal National Labor Relations Act. (*Brown v. Hotel and Restaurant Employees and Bartenders International Union,* 1984)

—Whether interest-free demand loans between family members are subject to the federal gift tax. (*Dickman v. Commissioner of Internal Revenue,* 1984)

—Whether a city ordinance that prohibits the posting of signs on public property, as applied to signs supporting political candidates, violates the constitutional protection of freedom of expression. (*City Council v. Taxpayers for Vincent,* 1984)

—Whether officers of a private company involved in a federal block grant program are "public officials" subject to prosecution under the federal bribery statute. (*Dixson v. United States,* 1984)

—Whether the doctrine of collateral estoppel prevents the federal government from relitigating an issue already litigated against the same party in another case involving virtually identical facts. (*United States v. Stauffer Chemical Co.,* 1984)

As these examples indicate, in the 1983 term the Court addressed a wide variety of policy questions. But the examples also suggest the extent of the Court's specialization. That suggestion is confirmed by statistics on the 152 cases fully decided by the Court during the term (Table 5-1).

Perhaps the most noteworthy characteristic of these cases is that a government party was present in nearly 85 percent of them. Moreover, most of the cases that included only private parties arose under programs of the federal government. In other words, the Court was concerned overwhelmingly with public law rather than private law.

Table 5-1.   Characteristics of cases decided by Supreme Court with full opinions in 1983 term[a]

Total number of decisions	152	100%
Cases from lower federal courts	121	80
Cases from state courts	28	18
Original cases	3	2
Federal government party[b]	64	42
State or local government party[b]	64	42
No government party	24	16
Constitutional issue present	83	55
No constitutional issue	69	45
Civil liberties issue present	80	53
No civil liberties issue	72	47
Criminal cases[c]	41	27
Civil cases	111	73

[a] Based on listings of cases in *United States Law Week.* Consolidated cases decided with one set of opinions were counted once and categorized according to the characteristics of the first case listed.
[b] Cases with both federal government and another government party were listed as federal government. Government as party includes agencies and individuals representing agencies.
[c] Includes actions brought by prisoners to challenge the legality of their convictions but excludes cases involving rights of prisoners.

The other characteristics of the Court's agenda in recent years also were reflected in the business of the 1983 term. A bit more than half contained civil liberties issues, and a slightly larger majority included constitutional issues. Criminal cases, in most of which the constitutional rights of defendants were in question, comprised more than one-quarter of the agenda. The other civil liberties cases were diverse, arising under a number of constitutional provisions as well as recent and long-standing federal statutes protecting civil rights.

Non-civil liberties cases also were quite diverse. Many arose from federal regulation of private economic activities in areas such as labor-management relations and banking. Others involved issues of federalism, particularly potential conflicts between state regulations of economic activity and related federal laws. The primacy of civil liberties and the secondary place of economic regulation, like most other characteristics of the 1983 agenda, were typical of the Court's work in the current era.

Change in the Court's Agenda

The subject matter of the Supreme Court agenda, of course, is not constant. Some variation in the distribution of cases, much of it random, occurs from one year to the next. More important, the agenda undergoes systematic changes. The Court's attention to specific categories of cases may rise and decline over relatively short periods of five or ten years. Over longer periods the Court's agenda as a whole undergoes fundamental changes. We can gain a sense of change in the agenda by taking both short-term and long-term perspectives.[4]

Short-Term Change. When a particular category of cases becomes more or less prominent on the agenda, a variety of factors may be responsible. Some of these factors are internal to the Court. As the collective interests of the justices change, perhaps because of a change in the Court's membership, they may decide to devote more attention to an area or to shift away from an area. Sometimes the Court in effect opens up a policy area with a major decision that requires further action or closes up an area with a decision that settles issues.

Agenda change also can be spurred by elements of the Court's environment. Most often, a new federal statute brings cases to the Court and requires interpretation by the Court. Nonstatutory policy changes such as a shift in federal administrative activity also can have an effect. Social changes may bring more cases of a particular type to the Court and increase the Court's interest in that area.

In the past two decades the Court has orchestrated changes in its own agenda in several areas. It opened up libel as an agenda item with a 1964 decision (*New York Times v. Sullivan*) that created rules for libel suits by public officials, and since that time it has heard a moderate number of libel cases. On the other side, the Court's 1973 obscenity decisions signaled a desire to leave this field,[5] and in the ensuing decade the Court has heard fewer obscenity cases. The area of legislative apportionment has seen both a rise and a decline since the early 1960s. The Court's decision in *Baker v. Carr* (1962) held that federal courts could deal with apportionment issues. The Court then plunged into this area, hearing 27 cases in the next dozen terms.[6] Having resolved most of the major issues in the area, the Court has heard fewer apportionment cases since the mid-1970s.

Since the 1960s new statutes have increased the Court's activity in several policy areas. The Court's attention to environmental policy issues was negligible until Congress adopted the National Environmental Policy Act of 1969 and a succession of other statutes in this area; as a result, environmental cases have been a staple of the agenda in the 1970s and 1980s. Title VII of the Civil Rights Act of 1964 and other legislation opened up employment discrimination as an area of Court activity, and the Court decided 70 cases in this area in the 1973-1982 terms. Adoption of the Freedom of Information Act in 1966 created a small new area of activity for the Court by the late 1970s.

Sex discrimination cases illustrate the complex effects of social change on the Court's agenda. The Court heard virtually no cases in this area until 1970. But in the 1973-1982 terms the agenda included 46 sex discrimination cases. The most fundamental reasons for the change were the development of the women's movement and the associated change in people's attitudes toward the roles of women. More directly, several things happened: a much larger number of cases in this area was brought to the Court, new federal laws on sex discrimination produced legal issues to resolve, and the justices themselves became more interested in this area.

During any given era, then, the detailed agenda of the Court changes a good deal. Particular subjects rise and fall in importance, even appear and disappear. The general composition of the Court's business, its primary emphases, tend to change more slowly. Thus, fundamental changes in the Supreme Court agenda are best viewed from a long-term perspective.

Long-Term Change. The Supreme Court agenda in its 1933 term bears some resemblance to the agenda 50 years later. In 1933 about two-thirds of the cases that the Court heard included government parties. The vast majority raised public law issues.

But in other characteristics the Court's 1933 business was quite different from its business in recent terms. Although no single field of policy dominated, nearly 90 percent of the cases could be classified as economic. More than 20 percent involved disputes over federal or state taxes. Challenges to government regulations of business and private disputes over economic rights also were common.

In contrast, the types of civil liberties issues that fill much of the Court's agenda today were barely visible in 1933. Only a few cases raised questions of procedural rights for criminal defendants. Issues of freedom of expression and equality for disadvantaged groups simply did not appear. The Court did decide a number of cases under civil liberties provisions of the Constitution, but these cases generally were brought by businesses that complained of unfair treatment by government.

The differences between the 1933 and 1983 terms highlight the changes that have occurred in the Court's agenda over the past half century. The Supreme Court has evolved from an institution concerned primarily with economic issues to one that gives primary attention to the civil liberties of individuals. Economic questions remain important, but less so, and some specific kinds of economic cases have become far less prominent in the Court's work.

This change process is documented by some of the findings from Richard Pacelle's study of the agenda, shown in Table 5-2. This table shows the growth of civil liberties cases generally and the equally striking growth in two types of civil liberties issues. It also depicts the decline in some types of economic cases. Perhaps most interesting is the major drop in federal tax cases during an era in which the number of people subject to the income tax and the complexity of the tax code both have increased.

How might we explain these long-term changes? All the factors that help to explain short-term changes are relevant. The rise in civil liberties cases might be traced to such factors as the activities of interest groups such as the NAACP and ACLU, the increased number of criminal prosecutions, and congressional legislation on civil rights. The most important factor may be the interests of the justices themselves: they hear more civil liberties cases because they *want* to do so. As I will show in the next section, the Court of the past 40 years generally has been quite supportive of civil liberties in the cases that it decides; undoubtedly that support and the growth of civil liberties as an agenda item share some roots. The decline in some kinds of economic cases may result largely from their being "crowded out" by civil liberties cases. The Court's increased acceptance of the broad outlines of government economic policy after the mid-1930s also has played a part in that decline.

As Table 5-2 suggests, there has been a slight reversal of the post-1933 trends in the last decade. Civil liberties cases have declined as a proportion of the agenda and to a lesser extent in absolute numbers. At the same time, the Court's attention to economic regulation and federalism has grown. These changes may represent the beginnings of a new set of trends; whether those trends develop further will depend in large part on the membership of the Court.

Table 5-2.   Proportions of Supreme Court agenda devoted to selected issue areas, selected five-year periods between 1933 and 1983[a]

	Terms			
Issue area	*1933-1937*	*1948-1952*	*1968-1972*	*1978-1982*
Civil liberties[b]	7.8%	27.8%	59.1%	49.8%
Racial equality[c]	0.3	2.0	6.6	5.0
Criminal procedure[c]	3.4	12.0	24.1	18.9
Federal taxation	17.8	6.5	3.6	2.5
Bankruptcy	6.0	1.6	0.5	0.6

[a] Cases decided with full opinion.
[b] Includes due process, equality, and substantive rights such as freedom of expression and freedom of religion.
[c] Included within civil liberties category.

SOURCE: Richard Pacelle, "The Supreme Court Agenda Across Time: Dynamics and Determinants of Change" (Ph.D. dissertation, Ohio State University, forthcoming), ch. 3. Used by permission of Richard Pacelle.

Comparison with Other Institutions

If the Court's current agenda differs from those of past Courts, it also differs from those of other policy makers. The subjects of the Court's work may be compared with the work of lower appellate courts, Congress, and the president.

Lower Courts. The two sets of lower courts most comparable with the Supreme Court are the federal courts of appeals and the state supreme courts. The courts of appeals stand directly below the Supreme Court, and a great majority of the cases decided by the Supreme Court come to it from the courts of appeals. The state supreme courts share with the U.S. Supreme Court a position at the top of their judicial systems, and about two-thirds share the Court's discretionary jurisdiction.

But neither level is fully comparable with the Supreme Court. The courts of appeals have a more limited control over their agendas, and the state supreme courts deal primarily with state legal issues rather than federal issues. As a result, the agendas of these lower courts differ from that of the Supreme Court in two important respects.[7]

First, private parties and private law are more important below the Supreme Court level. This is particularly true in the state supreme courts. There, about half of the decisions concern essentially private disputes involving such matters as contracts, property, personal injuries, and family relations. These are areas that the Supreme Court scarcely touches in its decisions, chiefly because they generally involve only state law.

Second, civil liberties issues are rather uncommon except in criminal cases. In the courts of appeals, more than one-quarter of the criminal cases involve civil liberties issues, but in other cases these issues are rare. Very few decisions address issues of constitutional equality or freedom of expression. Similarly, one study of the state supreme courts classified only 2 percent of the cases, other than criminal litigation, as civil liberties cases.[8]

Thus, the mix of subject matter on the Supreme Court's agenda is unique in some important respects. The private law issues that dominate the work of state courts are largely absent, while the Supreme Court stands alone in its emphasis on civil liberties. As a court, the Supreme Court has a set of concerns that distinguish it from every other court in the United States.

The President. The president's agenda is very different from that of the Supreme Court.[9] If the current Court is a specialist in civil liberties, most recent presidents have been specialists in foreign policy and management of the economy.

The president is preeminent in the making of foreign policy decisions. Moreover, foreign policy probably consumes the largest share of the time and energy that most presidents devote to policy making. This emphasis is in sharp contrast to the role of the Court, which makes few decisions that involve any questions of foreign policy.

Particularly during periods when the economy is functioning poorly, management of the economy is another central concern of the president. Presidents seek to maintain the nation's economic health by acting and proposing actions on matters such as the federal budget, control of the money supply, and regulation of energy supplies and allocations. While the Court makes a great many decisions involving government economic activity, the current Court has barely touched the function of general economic management to which presidents are so devoted.

Like the Supreme Court, presidents deal with a variety of policy issues outside their areas of specialization. For instance, the civil liberties field on which the Court focuses is occasionally an area of presidential concern, and for some presidents it has been fairly important. But in general the overlap between the areas of presidential interest and the fields of Supreme Court interest is relatively limited.

Congress. Congress differs from both the president and the Supreme Court in the range of issues to which it devotes significant attention.[10] As an institution Congress is something of a generalist.

Congress plays an active role in the issue areas that concern the Supreme Court most. Certainly it makes important policy on government regulation of the economy. Civil liberties, broadly defined, is also a major focus of congressional activity.

But Congress also devotes itself to a variety of issues that the Supreme Court deals with rather little, in addition to foreign policy and management of the economy. Many of these issues involve various kinds of government benefits to sectors of society, such as agricultural programs and natural resources projects. Even where the concerns of Congress and Court overlap, relative emphases often differ. Issues of environmental quality, for instance, have been more important in Congress than in the Court. By the same token, the civil liberties issues on which the Court focuses its attention are less important in congressional policy making.

Conclusion: The Court's Position

These comparisons between the Supreme Court and other policy makers provide a useful perspective on the Court's role. Most important, they make clear the limited range of the Court's work. The Court's jurisdiction is very broad, but the bulk of its decisions are made in a few policy areas. Certainly it is appropriate to consider the Court a specialist.

The Court's concentration on a few policy areas, particularly civil liberties, has important implications for its potential role. Even in civil liberties, the Court can address only a small proportion of the policy issues that arise. But by deciding as many cases as it does in this area, the Court maximizes its opportunities to shape law and public policy on civil liberties.

In contrast, the Court's lack of activity in several major areas of policy ensures that its impact in those fields will be limited at most. The Court hardly can have much effect on development of the law in private law fields such as contracts and torts. The current Court has little effect on government management of the economy and even less on foreign policy, and many people would consider these the two most important areas of government policy.

This fact should give pause to those who believe that the Supreme Court is the most important policy maker in the United States. The Court's significance is indisputable. But how can it be regarded as preeminent when the range of its activities is so limited? The Court could not possibly be dominant as a policy maker except in civil liberties and some limited areas of economic policy. As I will suggest in Chapter 6, even here the Court's dominance is not at all certain.

Supreme Court Activism: Judicial Review

The preceding section has sketched out the areas in which the Court's work is concentrated. The next two sections will examine the policies that the Court makes in its major fields of activity. In this section

I will discuss these policies in terms of their activism. The section that follows will discuss their ideological and political direction.

As noted in Chapter 1, there are many aspects to judicial activism. Here I will concentrate on the element of activism that concerns the Court's relations with the other branches of government. To what extent has the Court made decisions that conflict with the policies of Congress, the executive branch, and state and local governments? Investigation of the frequency and importance of such decisions can help in understanding the Court's position in the policy-making process.

The Court's activism in this sense often is gauged by its use of judicial review, the power to overturn acts of other policy makers on grounds that they violate the Constitution. Judicial review is not the only basis for activist policies; the Court may come into conflict with the policies of the other branches through its interpretations of statutes. But the Court intervenes in the policy-making process most directly and most clearly through its use of judicial review. For this reason I will focus on judicial review in this section, though I will give some attention to statutory interpretation as well.

Voiding Acts of Congress

The most familiar use of judicial review is over federal statutes. This form of judicial review also represents a striking assertion of power by the Court. When the Court overturns a federal law on constitutional grounds, implicitly it substitutes its judgment for that of the other branches of the federal government.

The Court first held an act of Congress unconstitutional in 1803, in *Marbury v. Madison*. Through 1983, by one count, it had overturned 114 federal laws, in whole or in part.[11] This number in itself is significant. On the one hand, it indicates that the Court has made fairly frequent use of its review power—on the average, more than once every two years. On the other hand, the laws struck down by the Court constitute a minute fraction of the more than 60,000 laws that have been adopted by Congress. But to understand the significance of the Court's decisions overturning federal laws we must take a closer look at these decisions.[12]

One question is the importance of the provisions that the Court has overturned. The Court has struck down some statutes of major significance. Among these were the Missouri Compromise of 1820, concerning slavery in the territories, which the Court declared unconstitutional in the *Dred Scott* case in 1857; the child labor laws that the Court struck down in 1918 and 1922; and the New Deal legislation that the Court overturned in 1935 and 1936.[13] But a good many of the Court's decisions declaring measures unconstitutional, perhaps a majority, were rather unimportant to the policy goals of Congress and the president. Some of the statutes involved were minor. In other instances the Court struck down relatively unimportant provisions of statutes or declared them unconstitutional only as applied to particular circumstances. In *United States v. Grace* (1983), the Court struck down a statute that prohibited picketing or leafletting on Supreme Court grounds, insofar as that statute applied to public sidewalks; it is doubtful that this very narrow decision attracted much attention in the other branches.

A related question is the timing of the Court's use of judicial review. Much of the time the Court has struck down legislation many years after its enactment. As of 1982, 61 percent of all decisions voiding legislation came more than four years after enactment, 28 percent after more than 12 years.[14] When legislation has been in effect for several years before the Court overturns it, the overturning is unlikely to arouse much congressional wrath. This is particularly true when the majority in support of the policy in question has disappeared in the intervening time.

For these reasons, the Court's fairly frequent use of its power to review congressional acts is somewhat misleading. Any decision that strikes down a federal statute might seem to involve a major conflict between Court and Congress, but such decisions actually may attract little congressional or public notice. Generally speaking, the Court's voiding of acts of Congress is most significant when the acts themselves are important and they are overturned rather quickly. Only a minority of cases meet these criteria.

Another aspect of timing is the historical patterns of judicial review. As Table 5-3 shows, the Court has not overturned federal statutes at a regular pace. It voided only two statutes prior to 1865. In the following eight years the Court overturned eight laws, and for the next half century the Court attacked acts of Congress at a rate of more than one in every two years. Then the Court's use of this form of judicial review accelerated: 15 times during the 1920s, and 12 times in the three years from 1934 to 1936. Over the next quarter century the Court employed this power sparingly. But in the 21 years from 1963 through 1983, it overturned 43 statutes, a record number for that short a period and more than one-third of the total for the Court's entire history.

On the basis of these patterns it is possible to identify periods in which the Court has been in major conflict with Congress as a legislator. The most conflictual period lasted from 1918 to 1936. During that period the Court overturned 29 laws. More important, much of the legislation voided by the Court was significant. Between 1918 and 1928 the Court struck down two child labor laws and a minimum wage law, along with several less important statutes. This was a minor irritant. Then, between 1933 and 1936, a majority of the Court engaged in what can only be called a frontal attack on the New Deal program, an attack that abated with the Court's retreat in 1937.

Table 5-3. Provisions of federal law held unconstitutional by Supreme Court, by decade

Period	No.	Period	No.
1790-99	0	1890-99	5
1800-09	1	1900-09	9
1810-19	0	1910-19	5
1820-29	0	1920-29	15
1830-39	0	1930-39	13
1840-49	0	1940-49	2
1850-59	1	1950-59	4
1860-69	4	1960-69	16
1870-79	8	1970-79	19
1880-89	4	1980-83	8
		Total	114

SOURCE: Congressional Research Service, *The Constitution of the United States of America: Analysis and Interpretation* (Washington, D.C.: Government Printing Office, 1973 and 1982), updated by the author.

The Court overturned legislation with even greater frequency during the period from 1963 to 1983. But few of the Court's decisions overturned major laws, and much of the legislation that the Court voided was rather old. A typical overturning decision in this period struck down a minor law or an unessential provision of a major law.

There were a few clear exceptions to this pattern. One was *Buckley v. Valeo* (1976), which held invalid some important provisions of the Federal Election Campaign Act concerning campaign financing. Another was *Northern Pipeline Construction Co. v. Marathon Pipe Line Company* (1982), which overturned the bankruptcy court system that Congress had established in 1978. *Immigration and Naturalization Service v. Chadha* (1983) struck down a relatively minor provision of immigration law, but its ruling against a legislative veto provision suggested the invalidity of some much more important federal laws. (Indeed, the Court struck down two other legislative veto provisions soon afterward.) In general, however, the legislation overturned by the Court since 1963 has not been nearly as significant as the economic legislation that the Court struck down in the 1930s.

During periods other than those two, the Court made decisions that voided major pieces of legislation. But these decisions were sporadic, and they constituted even more limited policy interventions than in the current period. Only in a single period, then, has the Court's power to review federal legislation been used to disturb a major line of federal policy.

The Court and Presidential Decisions

The Court passes on the legality of presidential orders as well as legislation. Decisions by the president may be challenged on grounds that they conflict with statutes, with the Constitution, or both. In ruling on such challenges, the Court can overturn presidential policies just as it can overturn congressional policies.

The Court occasionally has invalidated major presidential actions. In *Ex parte Milligan* (1866), the Court held that President Lincoln had lacked the power to suspend the writ of habeas corpus for military prisoners. *Youngstown Sheet and Tube Co. v. Sawyer* (1952) declared that it was illegal for President Truman to order the federal government to seize major steel mills during a wartime strike. Most recently, in *Train v. City of New York* (1975), the Court limited the power of the president to refuse to spend money appropriated by Congress. This practice, known as impoundment, had been used by President Nixon to reduce or eliminate programs with which he disagreed.

These examples stand out because there are few other examples of significant presidential action that the Court has overturned. Indeed, the Court seldom has invalidated even minor decisions. A review by Glendon Schubert in 1957 found only 14 cases in which the Court had ruled that presidential actions were illegal. In about half these cases the Court's decision was based on the Constitution.[15] The Court's intervention in presidential policy, like its intervention in congressional policy, has been fairly sporadic.

Voiding State and Local Policies

The Supreme Court has used its power of judicial review far more frequently at the state and local level than at the federal level. One measure of the difference is the number of laws declared unconstitutional. By the end of 1983, by one count, the Court had overturned 1,088 state statutes and local ordinances, on the grounds that they directly violated the Constitution or that they were superseded by federal law under the constitutional principle of federal supremacy. In contrast, it will be recalled, the Court had struck down only 114 federal laws. The disparity is even greater than these figures suggest, because many of the Court's overturnings of state and local laws indirectly affected laws that were not involved in the cases. For instance, in 1973 *Roe v. Wade* and *Doe v. Bolton* directly struck down the abortion laws of only two states, but implicitly they invalidated similar laws in nearly all other states.

A similar disparity seems to exist in the Court's use of judicial review to strike down nonstatutory policies. A decision that declares unconstitutional the practices of an administrative body or a lower court may be as significant as the overturning of a statute. At least in the current era, the Court holds administrative and judicial policies at the state and local levels unconstitutional far more often than it does at the federal level. The most important area of such activity is criminal procedure, in which the Court often has found police or trial-court practices in violation of the Fourteenth Amendment rights of defendants.

As measured by the numbers of laws overturned per decade, shown in Table 5-4, the Court's voiding of state and local laws has increased tremendously over time. Four-fifths of all the laws struck down have been overturned since 1910. The Court's use of this form of judicial review has peaked in the last quarter century; between 1960 and 1983 it declared unconstitutional an average of 17 state and local laws per year.

Prior to 1860 the Court struck down relatively few state and local laws, but its decisions during that period played an important role in limiting state powers under the Constitution. For instance, under John Marshall the Court weakened the states' role with decisions such as *McCulloch v. Maryland* (1819), which denied the states power to tax federal agencies, and *Gibbons v. Ogden* (1824), which narrowed state power to regulate commerce.

Table 5-4. Provisions of state laws and local ordinances held unconstitutional by Supreme Court, by decade

Period	No.	Period	No.
1790-99	0	1890-99	36
1800-09	1	1900-09	40
1810-19	7	1910-19	118
1820-29	8	1920-29	139
1830-39	3	1930-39	93
1840-49	9	1940-49	58
1850-59	7	1950-59	68
1860-69	23	1960-69	140
1870-79	37	1970-79	193
1880-89	45	1980-83	63
		Total	1,088

SOURCE: Congressional Research Service, *The Constitution of the United States of America: Analysis and Interpretation* (Washington, D.C.: Government Printing Office, 1973 and 1982), updated by the author.

The laws overturned by the Court in more recent periods have been a mixture of the important and the minor. In the aggregate the Court's decisions have been sufficiently important to give it a significant role in shaping state policy. During the late nineteenth century and the first third of the twentieth century, the Court struck down a great deal of important state economic legislation, including numerous regulations of commercial practices and of labor-management relations. The net effect, as with the New Deal, was to turn back much of a major tide of public policy.

The Court's decisions over the last three decades also have impinged upon important elements of state policy. A series of rulings helped to break down the legal basis for racial segregation and discrimination in Southern states. The Court's decisions in the 1960s struck down the prevailing pattern for apportionment of state legislative seats and required the redrawing of districts for nearly all the state legislatures. The Court imposed upon the states a new set of rules for the processing of criminal cases and the treatment of defendants. More subtly, through a series of decisions the Court has limited state powers of economic regulation in areas that Congress has preempted under its constitutional supremacy.

The Court's significance in relation to state and local governments should not be exaggerated. Its decisions have affected only a small proportion of all public policies in the states. But the contrast between its use of judicial review at the national level and the state and local levels is striking.

Judicial Review: The General Picture

The Supreme Court's use of judicial review is difficult to characterize because of the variation in the record. Historically, the extent of the Court's activism has changed over time. In general, the level of activism seems to have increased over the Court's history.

Even more notable is the variation among levels of government. The Court has been considerably more willing to overturn state and local policies than to overturn federal policies. With the exception of the New Deal period and some isolated decisions in other periods, the Court has not resisted major elements of national policy. The Court has done much more to limit the freedom of action of state and local governments on issues of central importance.

The Court's record as a whole can be viewed from two very different perspectives. On the one hand, the justices clearly have made meaningful use of the judicial review power as an instrument of policy making. By striking down government decisions the Supreme Court has played an important role in some parts of the policy process.

At the same time, the impact of this power is limited. The great majority of public policies at all levels of government have continued in operation without interference by the Court. As noted in the previous section, at any given time the Court is active in only a limited number of policy areas. Even within those areas, the Court's use of judicial review has been selective. Certainly the Court has not made itself the dominant participant in the policy-making process through judicial review.

Statutory Interpretation

The Court's use of judicial review, of course, is not the only important element of its policy making. Although it is appropriate to focus on judicial review as a mode of activism, statutory interpretation merits some attention as well. Even today about half of the Court's decisions are statutory rather than constitutional, and these statutory decisions often have activist components.

First, the Court's interpretations of statutes sometimes overturn policies of the federal executive branch. I have noted the rare occasions on which the Court strikes down presidential actions as unauthorized by statute. The Court regularly strikes down policies of federal administrative agencies on that ground or because the agency failed to follow proper procedures in reaching its decision. The Court overruled some important policy initiatives of the Reagan administration on these bases, including the administration's extension of tax benefits to private schools that discriminate by race and its rescinding of a rule requiring passive restraints such as airbags in new cars.[16]

In addition, the Court's statutory decisions often do much to shape federal policy within the general outlines established by Congress. The Warren Court broadened the range of business conduct prohibited by the antitrust laws, while the Burger Court has narrowed that range. The Court has established a series of principles for analysis of employment discrimination within the rather vague terms of the Civil Rights Act of 1964. Occasionally the Court's interpretation of a statute brings it into direct conflict with Congress, where the Court has departed from the interpretation generally accepted by members of Congress. But even when no such conflict arises, the Court often is asserting itself as an independent policy maker through its treatment of statutory language.

Judicial review remains the mechanism by which the Court takes an activist position most directly. The pattern of the Court's use of judicial review to strike down government policies probably is the best indicator of the Court's activism and the limits on its activism. But a general assessment of the Court's significance as a policy maker must take into account all aspects of its work.

The Direction of Policy

I have examined the Supreme Court's policies in terms of the Court's relationship with other public policy makers. Those policies also may be examined in terms of their ideological and political direction. In conflicts between liberal and conservative views of policy, where has the Court positioned itself? What groups in society have benefited from its policies?

My discussion of these questions in this section will focus on the last century. Since the 1880s the Court's policies have taken two rather different directions in successive periods. A comparison of those periods will help in understanding variation in the Court's policies as well as the forces that determine their direction.

The 1880s to the 1930s

Protecting Business from Government. The Court's agenda in its 1933 term was fairly typical of its work throughout the previous five decades. During that period the Court's primary concern was government policy that affected the activities of private businesses. The largest part of the Court's work in this area involved regulation of business practices toward consumers and workers. The Court also dealt with other areas of business-government relations, particularly taxation.

As earlier discussions of this period have indicated, the major theme of the Court's decisions on legislation affecting business was protection for business enterprises. The Court declared unconstitutional a great deal of legislation that limited business freedom, including some very important regulatory laws. The Court also limited the operation of some statutes by interpreting them narrowly. This was its response to two major federal laws: the Interstate Commerce Act of 1887, which was an effort to regulate the railroads, and the Sherman Antitrust Act of 1890, which was an effort to combat monopolies and anticompetitive practices.[17]

The strength of this theme should not be overemphasized. The Court did not invalidate a majority of laws concerning business that came before it. Moreover, in some areas it interpreted government regulatory powers rather broadly.

But the negative element was strong throughout this period, and it gradually grew stronger. In the first half of the period the Court's reaction to laws limiting business freedom could be characterized as mixed. By the 1920s the negative theme had become dominant, and it remained dominant through 1936. The growth of the Court's opposition to government policy toward business is reflected in the number of laws involving economic issues that it overturned in successive decades: 44 from 1900 to 1909, 111 from 1910-1919, and 133 from 1920 to 1929.[18]

Constitutional Doctrines. In any period the Court's perspective on major issues will be reflected in the doctrines that it adopts to interpret constitutional provisions. Between the 1880s and the 1930s most justices accepted a series of doctrines that limited government power over the private economy.

At the national level the powers of the federal government to regulate commerce and to tax were interpreted narrowly. In this way the Court limited the use of these powers as mechanisms to control business activities. In contrast the Tenth Amendment's general limitation on federal power was read broadly to prohibit some federal action on grounds that it interfered with state prerogatives.

At the state level the Court interpreted the Fourteenth Amendment as limiting government power to regulate business. In a decision of great importance symbolically as well as practically, the Court held in *Santa Clara County v. Southern Pacific Railroad Co.* (1886) that corporations were "persons" whose rights were protected by the Fourteenth Amendment. The Court also established the doctrine of "substantive due process." The due process clause of the Fourteenth Amendment seems only to require that the government follow proper procedures—that it provide the "due process of law"—in making decisions. But in the late nineteenth century the Court interpreted this amendment as creating an absolute prohibition against regulation of business that interfered unduly with the liberty and property rights of corporations. In other words, certain kinds of laws would be held to violate "due process" no matter how proper the procedures under which they were adopted and carried out. Moreover, the Court interpreted the corporate rights protected by the due process clause very broadly, to include such matters as the capacity of a public utility to make what the Court deemed an adequate profit.[19]

These doctrines were important as mechanisms by which the Court could strike down legislation that affected business. They also make clear the Court's collective view of policy during this period. Given tremendous discretion in interpreting the Constitution, most justices chose interpretations that protected business from government.

The Court's Beneficiaries. Broadly speaking, the business community in general benefited from the Court's policies during this period. But major corporations benefited the most. Much of the regulatory legislation that the Court overturned or limited was aimed primarily at the activities of the largest businesses, which were viewed by legislators as abusing their great economic power. The railroads were the most prominent example; in the decade from 1910 to 1919, the Court overturned 41 state laws in cases brought by railroad companies. Thus major corporations such as railroads might be considered the "clientele" of the Court in that half century.

Large corporations did not simply benefit from the Court's decisions; they helped to bring about the Court's favorable policies.[20] Beginning in the late nineteenth century, the corporate community employed much of the best legal talent in the United States to challenge the validity of regulatory statutes. Doctrines such as substantive due process were formulated and urged upon the Court by attorneys representing corporations. The justices would not have accepted these doctrines had they not been basically sympathetic toward business interests. But effective advocacy by corporate attorneys certainly helped to lay the groundwork for the Court's policies toward business.

The corporate interests that brought their claims to the Supreme Court focused their attention on the judiciary because of their defeats elsewhere in government. Congress and the state legislatures were not uniformly unfriendly to business interests, but there was strong legislative support for regulation of private enterprise. In accepting the business position so frequently, the Court served as a "court of last resort" for corporations in a political sense as well as the legal sense.

Civil Liberties: A Limited Concern. Civil liberties as I have defined them were only a minor concern of the Court between 1880 and the mid-1930s. When the Court did address civil liberties issues, it was generally not sympathetic to claims that government action violated civil liberties.

One subject that the Court addressed was the civil rights of black citizens in the South. In the *Civil Rights Cases* (1883) and other decisions, the Court interpreted narrowly the power of the federal government to protect black rights. In *Plessy v. Ferguson* (1896), the Court upheld the legitimacy of racial segregation by establishing the "separate but equal" doctrine. Other decisions were more favorable to blacks, but they did not have the significance of these two lines of doctrine.

In the early twentieth century the Court began to determine how the Fourteenth Amendment affected state criminal proceedings. To what extent did the due process clause require that a state provide procedural rights specified by the Bill of Rights, such as the protection against compulsory self-incrimination? In *Twining v. New Jersey* (1908), the Court viewed the clause as "incorporating" only a select sample of these rights. This narrow interpretation of the due process clause contrasted with the Court's very broad interpretation of its protections for business enterprises.

The Court did interpret the due process clause favorably for civil liberties in the area of freedom of expression. In a series of decisions from 1925 to 1931, the Court held that the clause protected freedom of speech and freedom of the press from state violations.[21] This was an interpretation seemingly as illogical as the doctrine of substantive due process, and its adoption by the Court reflected some sympathy for freedom of expression. But in the most significant set of conflicts involving this freedom the Court gave limited support to it. In *Schenck v. United States* (1917) and later cases the Court held that the First Amendment allowed the federal government to prosecute persons whose expressions allegedly endangered military recruitment and other national security interests.

Overview. In ideological terms, the Court of this period clearly was conservative. It interpreted the law so as to protect advantaged interests in society: business corporations. At the same time it did little to protect disadvantaged groups such as blacks.

This conservatism was not new; much of the Court's work in earlier periods also had a conservative slant. Particularly under John Marshall's leadership, the Court exhibited considerable support for the rights of property holders. Support for liberal values such as civil liberties was far less common.

Thus an observer of the Supreme Court in the mid-1930s had good reason to conclude that the Court was a fundamentally conservative institution. Indeed, this was the position of two distinguished observers as late as the early 1940s. According to Henry Steele Commager in 1943, the Court's record

> discloses not a single case, in a century and a half, where the Supreme Court has protected freedom of speech, press, assembly, petition, or religion against Congressional attack. It reveals no instance [with one possible exception] where the court has intervened on behalf of the underprivileged—the Negro, the alien, women, children, workers, tenant-farmers. It reveals, on the contrary, that the Court has effectively intervened, again and again, to defeat Congressional attempts to free the slave, to guarantee civil rights to Negroes, to protect workingmen, to outlaw child labor, to assist hard-pressed farmers, and to democratize the tax system. From this analysis the Congress, and not the courts, emerges as the instrument for the realization of the guarantees of the Bill of Rights.[22]

Attorney General Robert Jackson, soon to join the Court, put the matter more simply in 1941: "never in its entire history can the Supreme Court be said to have for a single hour been representative of anything except the relatively conservative forces of its day." [23]

The 1930s to the Present

As of the late 1930s, the Court's long history of conservatism might have suggested that major change in its stance was unlikely. Yet, within a few years after its confrontation with the New Deal, the Court changed its ideological position drastically. That change was reflected both in its treatment of economic issues and in its positions on civil liberties questions.

Acceptance of Government Economic Policy. Beginning in 1937, it will be recalled, the Court shifted its position on government economic powers. In a series of decisions, majorities accepted the constitutional power of government—particularly the federal government—to regulate and to manage the economy. The Court abandoned altogether the anti-regulatory spirit that had developed over the previous half century.

The Court's collective change of heart proved to be long-standing. Since the late 1930s the Court has been fairly consistent in viewing government economic power broadly. This position is reflected in its treatment of federal legislation. Between 1937 and 1983 the Court struck down only seven federal laws dealing with regulation of the economy and of business enterprises.[24] Two of these laws involved civil liberties issues concerning inspections of businesses, three concerned the separation of powers within the federal government, and none affected basic powers over the economy. The Court has continued to monitor state economic legislation for its consistency with federal powers, and the Court has struck down a good many state laws on grounds that they were preempted by federal statutes. But in other respects state governments have been given more freedom to make economic policy. The Court's position in the current era is illustrated by *Hawaii Housing Authority v. Midkiff* (1984), in which it unanimously upheld a state law that required large landholders in effect to sell portions of their land to people who own homes on that land. That kind of law probably would not have survived the Court's scrutiny in the early twentieth century.

The current Court also addresses nonconstitutional economic issues that arise from decisions of federal regulatory agencies such as the Interstate Commerce Commission and the National Labor Relations Board. The Court has deferred to decisions of federal agencies in some instances, while in others it has intervened to hold that agency policies are contrary to statute. Some of the Court's interventions have been significant. But the Court has not challenged the basic economic programs of the federal government.

Support for Civil Liberties. When the Court renounced its opposition to government economic policies, it began to adopt a new activist position in support of civil liberties. That position was signaled in Justice Harlan Stone's opinion for the Court in *United States v. Carolene Products Co.* (1938). This case was simply one of many in which the Court upheld federal economic policies. But in what has become a famous footnote, Stone argued that the Court was justified in taking a tolerant view of government economic policies, while it gave "more exacting judicial scrutiny" to policies that infringed on civil liberties.

The Court gradually adopted the position that Stone laid out. As we have seen, civil liberties issues came to occupy the largest share of the agenda. Moreover, the Court generally has been quite favorable to civil liberties in judging conflicts between those liberties and other values.

Like the Court's opposition to government economic policy a half century earlier, the Court's commitment to civil liberties developed gradually after 1937. In the 1940s the Court gave unprecedented support to civil liberties, but it had not yet established a strong position in favor of these liberties generally. The 1950s were a period of transition, with the Court's position remaining somewhat mixed but its commitment growing. *Brown v. Board of Education* (1954) was perhaps the Court's most important decision in support of civil liberties up to that time.

The Court's liberalism on civil liberties issues peaked in the 1960s. Decisions of the Court expanded liberties in a wide array of fields, from black civil rights to the rights of criminal defendants to freedom of expression. In comparison with that extraordinary decade the record of the Court in the 1970s and 1980s has been labeled conservative, but the Burger Court stands second only to the later Warren Court in its general support for civil liberties.

The development of the Court's policies is illustrated by the pattern of decisions that declared laws unconstitutional. Figure 5-1 depicts the numbers of economic statutes and statutes limiting civil liberties that were overturned by the Court in successive decades. As the figure shows, the number of laws involving the economic system that the Court struck down declined precipitously between the 1920s and 1940s and has remained fairly stable since that time. Meanwhile, the numbers of statutes struck down on civil liberties grounds became significant in the 1940s and 1950s and then grew tremendously in the two decades that followed. That growth reflects the Court's increasing liberalism.

Constitutional Doctrines. The Court's liberalism on civil liberties also has been reflected in a set of constitutional doctrines. Perhaps the most important of these is the Court's broad interpretation of the due process clause of the Fourteenth Amendment to encompass a wide range of procedural rights. Nearly all the rights of criminal defendants that are protected against federal violation by the Bill of Rights have been applied to the states through the due process clause. These include among others the right to a public trial (*In re Oliver*, 1948), the right to a trial by jury (*Duncan v. Louisiana*, 1968), and the protection against compulsory self-incrimination (*Malloy v. Hogan*, 1964). The clause also has been interpreted as establishing procedural rights for groups other than criminal defendants, such as recipients of public welfare benefits.[25]

Two other doctrines are notable because they underline the Court's willingness to depart from conventional interpretations of the Constitu-

Figure 5-1   Numbers of economic and civil liberties laws (federal, state, and local) overturned by Court, by decade

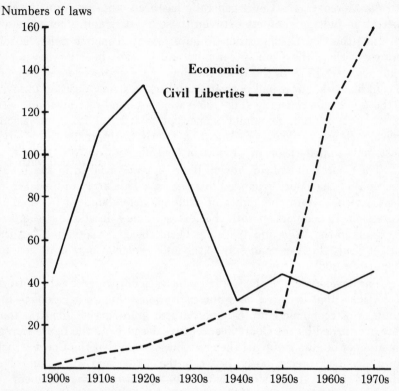

Numbers of laws

NOTE: Civil liberties category does not include laws supportive of civil liberties.

SOURCE: Congressional Research Service, *The Constitution of the United States of America: Analysis and Interpretation* (Washington, D.C.: Government Printing Office, 1973 and 1982).

tion to support civil liberties. The Constitution contains no protection against discrimination by the federal government, but in *Bolling v. Sharpe* (1954) the Court interpreted the due process clause of the Fifth Amendment to prohibit federal denial of equal protection of the laws. Like some interpretations of the Fourteenth Amendment due process in an earlier era, this interpretation seems to have little basis in the words of the Constitution itself. *Griswold v. Connecticut* (1965) created a new constitutional right to privacy. The opinions in the case based this right on several provisions of the Constitution, including the rather vague and previously dormant Ninth Amendment.[26]

In interpreting the equal protection clause of the Fourteenth Amendment, the Court gave greater emphasis to a doctrine that already existed in implicit form. Under this doctrine, some government policies would be given "strict scrutiny" when challenged as violations of equal protection, because of the identity of the groups who were treated differently or the significance of the rights that the policies affected. Increasingly government has been given a burden of proof to establish the legitimacy of its policies under the equal protection clause.

The Court's Beneficiaries. The groups that have benefited most from the Court's policies in the current era, of course, are those that bring civil liberties claims before the Court. These include socially and economically disadvantaged groups, criminal defendants, and people who take unpopular political stands. As long ago as 1950 a federal judge argued that the Court's conception of liberty was "concerned with the privileges of picketers, prisoners, proselyters, publicans . . . and pigmented portions of the population." [27] In 1967, during the Warren Court's most active period, an unsympathetic editorial cartoonist depicted the Court as a Santa Claus whose list of gift recipients included Communists, pornographers, extremists, drug pushers, criminals, and perverts.[28] Whatever one may think of these characterizations, they underline the change in the Court. An historian summarizes the change: "Whereas the beneficiaries of the Court before 1937 had been businessmen and other propertied interests, after 1937 they became the less advantaged groups in America." [29]

The sector of the population that the Court has aided most is black citizens. Since the 1940s the Court has given extraordinary support to black civil rights, particularly in the fields of education and voting rights. The Court also took great efforts to protect the civil rights movement when it was under attack in the late 1950s and 1960s. Southern statutes designed to cripple the NAACP were struck down. In addition, the Court overturned criminal convictions of civil rights activists in more than 50 cases arising from "sit-ins" and other demonstrations against segregation.

The Court's support for black civil rights has not been absolute, and that support declined somewhat in the 1970s. But the Court generally has been more favorable to civil rights than have the other branches of government. Congress did not adopt a major civil rights statute until 1964, and after 1968 it did relatively little to advance black rights. Some presidents such as Lyndon Johnson gave strong support to black civil rights, but others such as Dwight Eisenhower and Richard Nixon seemed indifferent. In a real sense, black citizens have been a special clientele of the Supreme Court during much of the current era.

The Court's support for some other groups has diverged even more from the positions of the other branches of government. Convicts have had few advocates in the executive and legislature. Leftist political groups such as the Communist Party have been subject to a good deal of congressional attack. As it did when it supported business interests, the Court has provided relief for groups that fare badly elsewhere in government.

The Burger Court and Beyond. In this section, as in previous chapters, I have emphasized the continuity between the Court of the 1970s and 1980s and its recent predecessors. The Court headed by Chief Justice Burger fits well into most of the generalizations about the Court's policy positions during the past half century. Only in comparison with the Court of the 1960s can the current Court seem conservative or anti-libertarian, and even in that comparison the picture is a bit complicated. In virtually every respect, the Burger Court resembles the Warren Court much more closely than it resembles the Court prior to 1937.

Yet the Burger Court has modified some patterns and trends in Court policy that were established earlier in the current era. Civil liberties has declined a bit as an agenda item. Although the Burger Court has continued the expansion of civil liberties in some areas, it has held the line or cut back in several others. The area in which the Court has cut back most clearly is criminal procedure, where the majority generally has been unsympathetic to claims by defendants. In some other areas, such as black civil rights, the Warren Court's strong liberal record has been replaced by a more mixed and complex one.

These shifts in the Court's direction and role have been only moderate so far, but they receive attention because they *are* shifts and because they may portend more massive changes in the future. Indeed, the Court's relatively conservative record in the 1983 term convinced many commentators that massive changes had begun. While future trends are impossible to predict confidently, the Court's history makes it clear that a major shift in its policy position is quite possible.

This point should be emphasized. Because the current era has lasted for several decades, some observers of the Court see its role as a supporter of civil liberties as both permanent and inevitable. Our examination of the Court's policies over an entire century makes it clear that this is not the case. Rather, the Court's support for civil liberties developed late in its history. For most of that history, the Court was devoted far more to the interests of business than it was to what we think of as civil liberties. In ideological terms the Court was generally a conservative institution until the era that began in the late 1930s. Certainly it might become a conservative institution once again at some time in the future, even the relatively near future.

This discussion raises questions of explanation for the Court's policy positions over time. What accounts for the patterns that I have described, and how can we understand changes in those patterns? The next section will examine the forces that have shaped the Court's policies.

Explaining the Court's Policies

The preceding sections of this chapter have examined several facets of the Supreme Court's policy outputs. A number of patterns have emerged. Some of these patterns are particularly important:

—During a particular historical period the Court may devote a large portion of its output to a particular policy goal, such as the protection of civil liberties.

—This goal may be quite different from the positions of other public policy makers on the set of issues in question.

—The Court's collective policy goal underwent a fundamental change rather rapidly in at least one instance, beginning in the late 1930s.

—Whatever its differences with the other branches of the national government, only during one limited period did the Court use judicial review to overturn a major element of congressional and presidential policy.

—The Court has been considerably more active in striking down significant policies of state and local governments.

In this section I will seek to provide a brief and partial explanation for these patterns. To do so, I will draw upon the discussion in Chapter 4 of the major factors that shape Supreme Court decisions. Two of these factors are particularly useful in understanding broad patterns of policy: the Court's environment and its members' policy preferences.

The Court's Environment

Freedom from External Pressures. Perhaps the most important characteristic of the Supreme Court's environment is its limited impact on the Court's decisions. Compared to policy makers such as legislators or trial judges, Supreme Court justices have unusual freedom to adopt the policies that they prefer.

This freedom explains a great deal about the Court's policies, because it allows justices to take positions that diverge from the local and national consensus of opinion. The Court's decisions on black civil rights in the 1950s and early 1960s illustrate the potential for divergence. During that period Southern policy makers in other institutions were prevented from supporting civil rights by the strong opposition of their constituents. Members of Congress from the Deep South were likely to be defeated for reelection if they voted for any civil rights legislation. For this reason, even the liberals among them, such as Senator Fulbright of Arkansas, generally felt compelled to oppose this legislation. The federal district judges of the South held lifetime terms, but they faced possible ostracism by their friends and violence from their neighbors if they favored the interests of blacks. In contrast, Southern members of the Supreme Court had both lifetime tenure and physical separation from the South. As a result, they were relatively free to support civil rights, and they frequently did so: the unanimous Court in *Brown v. Board of Education,* for instance, included members from Kentucky, Texas, and Alabama.

In the same way, justices' freedom from popular control allows them to take other relatively unpopular positions. The Court could resist the national tide of opinion that favored regulation of business in the early twentieth century. In the current era it can take policy positions that lack anything like majority support, such as protection of the rights of criminal defendants and prohibition of organized prayers in public schools.

Minimum Levels of Social Support. Yet there are some limits to the Court's divergence from public opinion. No matter how independent justices may feel, it would be difficult for them to take a strong position that had no support at all outside the Court. As a result, the Court is unlikely to adopt major policies that lack at least some significant social support.

External support is important in a more direct way as well. The Court acts on the litigation that is brought to it. Concerted litigation on a set of issues usually requires considerable group activity. If a policy position had very limited support, the Court might not receive the cases that would allow it to develop that position.

The Court has had the necessary external support for both of its distinctive policy positions during the twentieth century. Its opposition to government economic policy prior to 1937 was a minority position. But that position was supported actively by most of the business community and much of the legal profession. The Court received a good deal of praise for its economic decisions from respected individuals and groups. Moreover, through the efforts of corporations and their representatives to challenge government policy the Court received a steady flow of litigation on this subject and strong legal arguments against the legislation in question.

Similarly, the Court's current favor for civil liberties has considerable support. A great many legal commentators view the Court's position favorably. So does a significant minority of political and social leaders. The NAACP, the ACLU, and a variety of other groups bring civil liberties cases to the Court and present arguments in support of expanding liberties.

At the beginning of the twentieth century, little of this support for civil liberties existed. At that time it would have been difficult for the Court to take strong positions in favor of black civil rights or the rights of criminal defendants. For the same reason, the Court today would find it difficult to oppose government management of the economy even if most of its members wished to do so; there simply is too little support for that position. Societal opinion does create subtle boundaries on the range of policies that the Court might adopt.

Congressional Sanctions. A more concrete constraint on the Court is the array of potential sanctions that Congress possesses, such as the power to limit the Court's jurisdiction. Congress seldom employs these sanctions but frequently threatens to do so. The existence of this authority gives justices an incentive to minimize direct conflicts with Congress.

Occasionally congressional sanctions have a very clear impact on Supreme Court policy. This was the case with the Court's "retreats" on economic policy in 1937 and on civil liberties policy in the late 1950s. Even when there is no direct threat, however, the Court may be cautious about opposing the direction of national policy in order to avoid incurring congressional wrath.

This caution probably is reflected in the Court's limited use of judicial review at the national level. As we have seen, only in the 1920s and 1930s has the Court overturned a set of major congressional policies. In contrast, the Court has been far more active in striking down state and local laws. This difference stems from several factors. But one important factor is the power of Congress to injure the Court in significant ways and the more limited ability of state and local policy makers to do so.

Policy Preferences and the Appointment Power

The Importance of Preferences. Despite the significance of these constraints on the Court, it does possess considerable autonomy. As a result, the single most important influence on the Court's direction is the values held by its members—specifically, their preferences on the policy issues that the Court addresses.

From this perspective, a great deal about the Court's direction can be explained quite simply. During any given period in its history, the Court's policies have reflected the collective preferences of its membership. The justices who served during the half century from the 1880s to the 1930s were primarily political conservatives. As such, they supported government restrictions on civil liberties but were highly skeptical of economic policies that infringed upon the freedom of business enterprises. The justices who have served since that time are primarily liberals by historical standards—people who are favorable to civil liberties and to government management of the economy. The shift from the first of these eras to the second was fairly abrupt, reflecting a rapid change in the Court's membership.

This explanation is not entirely satisfying, because it does not tell why certain preferences predominated on the Court during particular eras. The patterns of preferences over time might be explained in a variety of ways. These include the dominant values during the periods in which justices developed their attitudes, their social class backgrounds, and the ideology of the organized bar. But the most direct explanation for the collective preferences of the Court is the decisions that presidents make in appointing justices. Chapter 2 examined these decisions in some detail. In this section we may look at the broad impact of these decisions on Supreme Court policy.

The Impact of Appointments. We have seen that the Court's policy direction is largely a function of the appointments that presidents make. If a series of appointees are political conservatives, the Court is likely to become a conservative body. Moreover, because vacancies occur on the Court with some frequency—on the average, once every two years—most presidents can have a significant impact on the Court's direction.

Thus, Robert Dahl has argued that "the policy views dominant on the Court are never for long out of line with the policy views dominant among the lawmaking majorities of the United States." [30] In Dahl's judgment, the president's power to make appointments has limited the number of major statutes overturned by the Court. For the most part, justices view policy in the same ways as do Congress and the president, so they seldom upset the policies of these branches.

I think that there is much to Dahl's argument. The Court's general willingness to accept national public policy can be traced in part to the selection process. Certainly this process helps to explain the Court's greater propensity to overturn state policies. State governors and legislators, unlike their federal counterparts, cannot shape the Court's collective views. Yet the process of control through appointments is imperfect, because of several complicating factors.

One of these is time lag. The average justice serves for several years after the departure of the appointing president, so that the Court nearly always reflects the views of past presidents and "lawmaking majorities" at least as much as those of the present time. Fred Rodell has suggested that the aphorism, "the Supreme Court follows the election returns" be amended to refer to the returns "of ten or twelve years before." [31]

The extent of the lag may vary, chiefly because presidents have differing opportunities to make appointments. President Nixon was able to select four justices during his first term in office, while Franklin Roosevelt and Jimmy Carter made none in that period. Roosevelt's bad luck in this respect helped to produce his conflict with the Court over its handling of the New Deal legislation. Had he been able to replace two conservative justices early in his tenure, the Court would not have served as a major roadblock to his program. Carter's luck was even worse; the absence of vacancies during his term, combined with his defeat for reelection in 1980, made him the first president in more than a century who made no appointments to the Court. As a result, he had no opportunity to strengthen the Court's liberalism. Of course, as the example of Roosevelt illustrates, a president's influence over the Court's direction depends only in part on the number of appointments to be made. It also depends on the ideological configuration of the Court and on the identity of the members who leave it.

Another factor is deviation of justices from presidential expectations. Presidents usually get what they want from their appointees, but this is not an absolute rule. Wilson's selection of the conservative McReynolds affected the Court's balance for two decades. The unprecedented liberalism of the Court in the 1960s resulted in part from Eisenhower's miscalculations in his nominations of Warren and Brennan.

Finally, appointments reflect not the views of a "lawmaking majority" so much as the views of the president. A conservative Republican who perseveres in selecting like-minded nominees to the Court, such as Richard Nixon, will obtain a more conservative Court even when Congress is Democratic and liberal. Nor do all appointments reflect a national consensus about policy. John Kennedy in 1960 and Richard Nixon in 1968 won the presidency by very small margins; their elections hardly represented general endorsements of their views. But the narrowness of their victories did not prevent either from reshaping the Court.

For these reasons, Dahl's argument is valid only as a statement of a general tendency. The process of appointment does limit the Court's disagreement with the policies of Congress and the president. But the lag that is inherent in the selection process weakens the relationship between the Court and current lawmaking majorities. Moreover, the element of chance in the timing of vacancies in the Court and in the performance of appointees makes the Court's reflection of even past majorities somewhat uneven. The two policy orientations that have prevailed on the Supreme Court over the last century reflected in part the existence of strong lawmaking majorities during particular time periods: the conservative Republican governments that dominated much of the period from the Civil War to the Great Depression, and the unprecedented 12-year tenure of Franklin D. Roosevelt. However, they also reflected patterns of resignations and deaths, unexpected behavior on the part of justices, and other factors that were a good deal less systematic. The forces that shape the Court's role as a policy maker, like so much about the Court, are highly complex.

Conclusions

This chapter has examined a wide range of subjects concerning the Supreme Court's policy outputs. Of the many conclusions that might be drawn from the chapter, three are most central.

First, there are fairly strong themes in the Court's policy-making activity during particular periods. In the current era, for instance, the dominant theme is a concern for civil liberties. The Supreme Court devotes a large proportion of its agenda to civil liberties issues. Moreover, it has been basically supportive of civil liberties in its decisions, though that support has varied over time and among issues. Similarly, an earlier Court was heavily devoted to scrutiny of government economic policy.

Second, these themes and other elements of the Court's work reflect both the justices' preferences and the influence of the Court's environment. In large part the Court's policies are what its members would like them to be. But a series of environmental constraints limits the divergence between Supreme Court decisions and the policies of the rest of the government. The president's appointment power also establishes an important link between the justices' preferences and their environment.

Finally, the Court's role as a policy maker is a limited one. The Court specializes in some fields of policy. It scarcely touches several major policy areas. Even in the areas of significant Supreme Court activity, the Court does not often disturb the basic elements of national policy.

The significance of the Supreme Court as a policy maker is ultimately dependent on the impact of its decisions. This impact will be the subject of the final chapter. After examining the effect of the Court's decisions, we can make a firmer assessment of the Supreme Court's role in the policy-making process.

Notes

1. Except where indicated, statistics for the 1978-1982 terms were calculated from data in the summaries of Supreme Court business in November issues of the *Harvard Law Review*.
2. This calculation is based on the categorization of cases in Richard Pacelle, "The Supreme Court Agenda Across Time: Dynamics and Determinants of Change" (Ph.D. dissertation, Ohio State University, forthcoming), ch. 3.
3. Calculated from data in Pacelle, "Supreme Court Agenda," ch. 3.
4. The discussion of agenda change that follows draws from Pacelle, "Supreme Court Agenda," ch. 3. Data on the 1973-1982 terms are taken from that source.
5. The primary case was *Miller v. California* (1973).

6. Arthur D. Hellman, "The Supreme Court, the National Law, and the Selection of Cases for the Plenary Docket," *University of Pittsburgh Law Review* 44 (Spring 1983): 557.

7. Data on the courts of appeals and state supreme courts come from the following sources: Lawrence Baum, Sheldon Goldman, and Austin Sarat, "The Evolution of Litigation in the Federal Courts of Appeals, 1895-1975," *Law & Society Review* 16 (1981-1982): 291-309; J. Woodford Howard, Jr., *Courts of Appeals in the Federal Judicial System: A Study of the Second, Fifth, and District of Columbia Circuits* (Princeton: Princeton University Press, 1981), chs. 2-3; Robert A. Kagan, Bliss Cartwright, Lawrence M. Friedman, and Stanton Wheeler, "The Business of State Supreme Courts, 1870-1970," *Stanford Law Review* 30 (November 1977): 121-156; and Burton M. Atkins and Henry R. Glick, "Environmental and Structural Variables as Determinants of Issues in State Courts of Last Resort," *American Journal of Political Science* 20 (February 1976): 97-115.

8. Atkins and Glick, "Environmental and Structural Variables," 100-101.

9. Data provided by John Kessel were helpful in the writing of this subsection.

10. This discussion is based in part on material in Aage R. Clausen, *How Congressmen Decide: A Policy Focus* (New York: St. Martin's Press, 1973); and Aage R. Clausen and Carl E. Van Horn, "How to Analyze Too Many Roll Calls and Related Issues in Dimensional Analysis," *Political Methodology* 4 (1977): 313-331.

11. Because some cases are ambiguous, and because "laws" can be counted in various ways, different observers reach different totals of laws overturned. This figure and later figures on numbers of federal and state laws struck down by the Court are based on data in Congressional Research Service, *The Constitution of the United States of America: Analysis and Interpretation* (Washington, D.C.: Government Printing Office, 1973 and 1982), updated by the author.

12. The distinctions made in the paragraphs that follow are drawn chiefly from Robert A. Dahl, "Decision-Making in a Democracy: The Supreme Court as a National Policy-Maker," *Journal of Public Law* 6 (Fall 1957): 279-295.

13. *Scott v. Sandford* (1857); *Hammer v. Dagenhart* (1918); *Bailey v. Drexel Furniture Co.* (1922). Among the 1935-1936 decisions were *United States v. Butler* (1936); *Carter v. Carter Coal Co.* (1936); and *Schechter Poultry Corp. v. United States* (1935).

14. Compiled from data in Congressional Quarterly, *The Supreme Court: Justice and the Law,* 3d ed. (Washington, D.C.: Congressional Quarterly Inc., 1983), 159-164.

15. Glendon A. Schubert, Jr., *The Presidency in the Courts* (Minneapolis: University of Minnesota Press, 1957), 354-365.

16. The decisions were, respectively, *Bob Jones University v. United States* (1983) and *Motor Vehicle Manufacturers Assn. v. State Farm Mutual* (1983).

17. The decisions were, respectively, *Cincinnati, New Orleans, and Texas Pacific Railway Co. v. Interstate Commerce Commission* (1896) and *United States v. E. C. Knight Co.* (1895).

18. To provide these figures and some others to be presented later in the chapter, I have categorized decisions that declared laws unconstitutional as involving economics, civil liberties, or other subjects. The criteria that I used necessarily were arbitrary; other criteria would have resulted in some laws being categorized differently.

19. *Newton v. Consolidated Gas Co.* (1922); *Ottinger v. Brooklyn Union Co.* (1926).

20. Benjamin Twiss, *Lawyers and the Constitution* (Princeton: Princeton University Press, 1942).

21. *Gitlow v. New York* (1925); *Fiske v. Kansas* (1927); *Stromberg v. California* (1931); *Near v. Minnesota* (1931).

22. Henry Steele Commager, "Judicial Review and Democracy," *Virginia Quarterly Review* 19 (Summer 1943): 428.

23. Robert H. Jackson, *The Struggle for Judicial Supremacy* (New York: Alfred A. Knopf, 1941), 187.

24. *United States v. Cardiff* (1952); *National League of Cities v. Usery* (1976); *Marshall v. Barlow's, Inc.* (1978); *Railway Labor Executives' Association v. Gibbons* (1982); *Northern Pipeline Construction Co. v. Marathon Pipe Line Co.* (1982); *Process Gas Consumers Group v. Consumer Energy Council* (1983); *United States Senate v. Federal Trade Commission* (1983).

25. *Goldberg v. Kelly* (1970).

26. The Ninth Amendment reads as follows: "The enumeration in the Constitution, of certain rights, shall not be construed to deny or disparage others retained by the people."

27. Edward Dumbauld, "Judicial Review and Popular Sovereignty," *University of Pennsylvania Law Review* 99 (November 1950): 201.

28. *San Francisco Examiner,* December 14, 1967, 42.

29. William E. Leuchtenburg, "Franklin D. Roosevelt's Supreme Court 'Packing' Plan," in *Essays on the New Deal,* ed. Harold M. Hollingsworth and William F. Holmes (Austin: University of Texas Press, 1969), 108.

30. Dahl, "Decision-Making in a Democracy," 285.

31. Fred Rodell, *Nine Men* (New York: Random House, 1955), 9. The original aphorism was coined by Finley Peter Dunne and put in the mouth of his character Mr. Dooley in 1901. See Finley Peter Dunne, *Mr. Dooley on Ivrything and Ivrybody,* selected by Robert Hutchinson (New York: Dover Publications, 1963), 160.

The Court's Impact 6

Decisions of the Supreme Court are important for a variety of reasons, both practical and symbolic. In practical terms the significance of decisions rests primarily on their effects elsewhere in government and in American society. These effects are the subject of this final chapter.

The Court's impact requires careful examination because it is not always easy to predict. We might assume that a Court prohibition of some government practice will eliminate that practice, but some policy makers may refuse to comply. A decision that overturns state capital punishment laws may not bring about the end of the death penalty because it is superseded by the adoption of new, modified laws. The long-term effects of the Court's policies on such subjects as the status of women and relations between labor and management are particularly difficult to predict. For all these reasons the impact of Supreme Court policies must be investigated rather than taken for granted.

There are so many levels and types of impact for Supreme Court policies that it would be impossible to deal with all of them. The chapter will focus on three sorts of impact that are particularly important. The first section will discuss the implementation of Supreme Court decisions by lower courts and administrative agencies. The second section will examine the responses of legislatures and chief executives to the Court's policies. The final section will deal with the societal impact of the Court's decisions.

Implementation of Decisions

An Overview

After the Supreme Court makes a decision, that decision must be carried out by other public policy makers. Most commonly, the Court's decisions are to be put into effect by lower court judges and by administrators. The tasks of these policy makers take two different forms: the implementation of a decision as it concerns the litigants in the

193

case, and the implementation of a general policy established in the decision. I will begin by looking broadly at both forms. The remainder of the section will focus on implementation of general policies, the more important part of the implementation process.

Treatment of the Litigants. When the Court affirms a lower court decision, that decision becomes final. If the Court vacates (makes void), reverses, or modifies a decision, the case may be handled in either of two ways. The Court may simply return the case to the lower court to reach a new decision dictated by the Court's ruling. For instance, in *Lynch v. Donnelly* (1984) the Court ruled that a city-sponsored nativity scene did not violate the Constitution, and its decision required that the lower courts rule against the parties who had challenged the nativity scene. More frequently, the Court "remands" the case to the lower court for reexamination. In doing so it will direct that the case be given "further proceedings consistent with this opinion," or the like.

In remanded cases the Court's opinion often leaves a great deal of leeway to the lower courts in determining the final result of the case, because it does not settle all the issues in the case. As a result, the party who won in the Supreme Court often loses when the lower courts reexamine the case after the Court's remand. Criminal cases illustrate how this can happen. The Supreme Court frequently reverses a state criminal conviction on the ground that some of the evidence used against the defendant was obtained in violation of Fourteenth Amendment due process rights. When such a case is remanded to a state supreme court, that court is likely to send it back to the original trial court for retrial without the offending evidence. Even without this evidence, the defendant may be convicted once again and go to prison. This was the result for Ernesto Miranda, in whose case the Court made its famous 1966 decision on police interrogation of criminal suspects.

A result like the one in the *Miranda* case is not necessarily illegitimate. The Court, after all, had said not that Miranda was innocent but that certain evidence used against him was tainted. In such a case it may be quite appropriate for the party who won in the Supreme Court to lose afterward in the lower courts.

Yet occasionally it appears that lower court judges are behaving in an evasive manner, using the leeway that the Supreme Court provided to reach a result contrary to the Court's intent. Sometimes the picture is ambiguous. In *Sumner v. Mata* (1981, 1982) the Supreme Court twice vacated decisions of the Ninth Circuit Court of Appeals after that court had overturned a murder conviction, but the court of appeals reinstated its earlier decision even after the second Supreme Court remand. The majority on the court of appeals panel sought to show that its reinstating decisions were consistent with the Supreme Court mandate, but a dissenter was more dubious; in one of the decisions he declared that "I cannot join in this disregard of the Supreme Court's authority." [1]

Sometimes there is no ambiguity about the lower court's disobedience. In *Sullivan v. Little Hunting Park, Inc.* (1968), the Court directed the Virginia Supreme Court to reexamine the case in light of a Supreme Court decision in another case. On remand, the Virginia court simply refused on jurisdictional grounds to consider the case further, thereby failing to follow the Court's instructions.

This kind of subversion of Supreme Court decisions might seem to be pointless. The party who was a victim of lower court subversion could go back to the Supreme Court for a decision with more specific instructions to the lower court, perhaps accompanied by criticism of that court's behavior. This was the course of events in the *Sullivan* case. The Court might even direct that the case be assigned on remand to a different judge, as it did in a 1967 antitrust case.[2] If the lower court remained recalcitrant, the Court then could exercise its power to render a final judgment in the case rather than remanding it. Alternatively, the Court could issue a writ of mandamus to the lower court, requiring it to take specified action. If that writ was disobeyed, the judges could be cited for contempt of the Supreme Court.

In practice, lower courts may be successful in subverting a decision on remand. Perhaps the major reason is the extreme reluctance of the Court to do more than reverse and criticize the judges involved. For instance, the Court never has held a judge in contempt, though it nearly did so in a 1969 case (*In re Herndon*). Judges who are strongly opposed to the Court's position in a case can refuse to comply with the terms of a mandate, knowing that they will have ample warning if the Court contemplates use of strong measures to attack the lower court's resistance. In the face of continued resistance, either the Supreme Court or the litigant it seeks to benefit may give up, leaving the lower court triumphant.

An extreme but illustrative case of successful lower court resistance was the futile effort of Virgil Hawkins to enter the University of Florida. Hawkins, a black man, sued in 1949 for admission to the law school of the all-white university. In 1952 the Florida Supreme Court dismissed his suit. Two years later the U.S. Supreme Court remanded the case back to the Florida Supreme Court for reconsideration in light of *Brown v. Board of Education*. On rehearing, the Florida court said that Hawkins was entitled to admission, but it allowed that admission to be delayed indefinitely. Hawkins returned to the Supreme Court, which held in 1956 that he was "entitled to prompt admission." Nonetheless, the Florida court ruled in the following year that the Supreme Court could not have meant to limit the prerogatives of a state supreme court in such a way, and it refused to order Hawkins's admission. The Supreme Court then refused to hear the case a third time, suggesting in a brief note that

Hawkins might try his luck in federal district court—which he did without success, as the district court in 1958 also prevented his admission. Thus, after nine years of litigation and two favorable Supreme Court decisions, Virgil Hawkins was unable to enter the University of Florida law school.[3]

It should be emphasized that this kind of resistance is not typical. In the great majority of cases lower courts respond to a remanded case in general compliance with the Supreme Court's instructions. But an extreme case such as that of Virgil Hawkins illustrates the capacity of lower courts to subvert a Supreme Court policy even in its application to the litigants who won in the Court.

Implementation of General Policies. The proclamation of binding general rules creates an implementation process with two important aspects. One is interpretation by lower court judges. Judges must apply Supreme Court rules of law to cases in which those rules are relevant. When the Court adopts a certain interpretation of an antitrust statute, federal district judges who hear other cases under the statute are obliged to interpret it in the same way.

A second aspect is action by government officials whose practices are impinged upon by Supreme Court decisions. Such officials may include legislators, trial judges, or—most important—administrators. (I will use the term *administrators* broadly, to refer to officials such as teachers and police officers as well as members of administrative agencies.) If the Court prohibits a practice, officials who engage in the practice are under some obligation to eliminate it. Thus, when the Court forbids a police search procedure, any department that uses the procedure needs to change it. Of course, a great many Supreme Court decisions are "permissive," in that they uphold some government practice rather than declaring it illegal. In recent years the Court generally has approved police procedures that it considers; such approving decisions may influence police behavior, but they require no action from officers.

As the discussion so far suggests, the responses of judges and administrators to rules of law can be examined in terms of compliance and noncompliance with the Supreme Court. But the Court's decisions can evoke responses that range from complete rejection to enthusiastic acceptance and extension, and the concept of compliance does not capture all the possible variation. The discussion that follows will examine the range of responses to the Court's general policies by judges and administrators, as well as the factors that explain those responses.

Implementation Successes and Failures

Implementation as a General Process. The Supreme Court is not unique in its dependence on other policy makers to carry out its policies.

Congress, the president, and other appellate courts all require action by administrators and judges to put their decisions into effect. Implementation is a basic process of government.

Wherever it is found, however, implementation is an imperfect process. Observers of politics sometimes assume that when Congress adopts a statute or the Supreme Court makes a decision, other policy makers automatically do what the statute or decision requires to make it effective. Increasingly we are becoming aware that this assumption is faulty. Effective implementation is not automatic. Indeed, policies frequently fail to achieve their objectives because they are carried out poorly, as a result of intentional resistance or problems that implementors cannot overcome. Speaking of the ambitious "Great Society" legislation of the 1960s, for instance, one commentator argued that "implementation was the Achilles heel of the Johnson Administration's social policy." [4] Similar problems of implementation have been discovered in a variety of other public policies, large and small.

This does not mean that implementation always works badly. Rather, any policy maker is likely to have a mixed record in getting its policies put into effect. This certainly is true of the Supreme Court. The Court's situation can be illustrated with a look at three areas of policy in which it has suffered from serious implementation problems but achieved some successes as well. After these illustrations, I will discuss the Court's record more generally.

School Desegregation. Prior to the Supreme Court's 1954 decision in *Brown v. Board of Education,* separate sets of schools for black and white students existed throughout the Deep South and in most Border state districts. The Court's decision required that these dual systems be eliminated. In the Border states considerable compliance with the Court's ruling came within a few years. In contrast, policies in the Deep South changed extremely slowly. As late as the 1964-1965 school year, there was no Deep South state in which as many as 10 percent of the black students went to school with any white students—a rather minimal definition of desegregation. [5] This resistance demands a closer look.

Judges and school officials responded to the *Brown* decision in an atmosphere hostile to desegregation. Visible white opinion was strongly opposed to desegregation, and black opinion was largely irrelevant because a high proportion of black citizens was prevented from voting. Southern public officials encouraged resistance to the Supreme Court. In 1956, 96 Southern members of Congress signed a "Southern Manifesto" that attacked the *Brown* decision. Governors and legislatures throughout the South expressed a distaste for desegregation and took official action to prevent it. Governor Orval Faubus of Arkansas, for instance, interceded to prevent desegregation in Little Rock in 1957.

In this atmosphere school officials generally sought to maintain the status quo. Most administrators personally favored segregation and did everything possible to preserve it. Administrators who were willing to adopt the Court's policy were deterred from doing so by pressure from state officials and local citizens.

In the absence of voluntary compliance by school administrators, black citizens could bring suits to the federal district courts to challenge the continuation of segregated systems. In many districts no suits ever were brought. One reason was black parents' fear of retaliation if they actively supported integration in their communities.

Even where suits were brought, they were not always successful. In its second decision in the *Brown* case in 1955, the Supreme Court gave great freedom to district judges to determine the appropriate timing for desegregation in their areas. Many judges themselves disagreed with the *Brown* decision, and all felt some local pressure to proceed slowly if at all. As a result, few demanded speedy desegregation of the schools, and many abetted school officials in resisting change. Judges William Atwell and T. Whitfield Davidson of Dallas, for instance, struggled mightily to maintain segregation.

Some judges did support the Court wholeheartedly. But they had some difficulty in overcoming dilatory tactics by school administrators and elected officials. In New Orleans Judge J. Skelly Wright worked hard to bring about desegregation, but his efforts were fought by the governor and legislature with considerable success.

This multileveled opposition to the Court's decision helps to explain the absence of desegregation in the Deep South until the mid-1960s. After that time, the Southern states began to comply. In the second decade after *Brown* the dual school systems of the South finally were dismantled. Although school segregation was not eliminated altogether, the proportion of black students attending school with whites rose tremendously. That growth is illustrated in Table 6-1.

This change occurred in part because the Court made a series of decisions between 1969 and 1971 that demanded effective desegregation without further delay. However, earlier congressional action was more important. The Civil Rights Act of 1964 allowed federal funds to be withheld from institutions that practiced racial discrimination. In carrying out that provision, the Department of Health, Education, and Welfare required a "good-faith start" toward desegregation if schools were to receive federal aid. Faced with a threat to important financial interests, school officials felt some compulsion to go along. The 1964 act also allowed the Justice Department to bring desegregation suits where local residents were unable to do so. In an indirect way the Voting Rights Act of 1965 also played a significant role, because it increased the numbers of black voters in the South and thus made it

Table 6-1. Percentages of black elementary and secondary students going to school with any whites, in 11 Southern states[a]

School year	Percentage
1954-55	0.001
1956-57	0.14
1958-59	0.13
1960-61	0.16
1962-63	0.45
1964-65	2.25
1966-67	15.9
1968-69	32.0
1970-71	85.6
1972-73	91.3

[a] States are Alabama, Arkansas, Florida, Georgia, Louisiana, Mississippi, North Carolina, South Carolina, Tennessee, Texas, Virginia.

SOURCES: Southern Education Reporting Service, *A Statistical Summary, State by State, of School Segregation-Desegregation in the Southern and Border Area from 1954 to the Present* (Nashville: Southern Education Reporting Service, 1967) (for 1954-1967); U.S. Bureau of the Census, *Statistical Abstract of the United States* (Washington, D.C.: Government Printing Office, 1971 and 1975) (for 1968-1973).

more risky for officials to attack civil rights as vehemently as they had in the past.

In the 1970s the Court turned its attention to the North. In many Northern cities a combination of housing patterns and school board policies had created a situation in which white and nonwhite students tended to go to different schools. In a Denver case, *Keyes v. School District No. 1* (1973), the Court held that government-induced segregation in such cities violated the Fourteenth Amendment and required a remedy. In a series of decisions over the next decade, the Court spelled out rules with which to identify constitutional problems and to fashion remedies for Northern-style segregation.

On the whole, federal district judges in the North have been more supportive of the Court than their Southern counterparts were. Indeed, some judges had acted against segregated districts even before the *Keyes* decision. Others adopted remedies for segregation that the Court found too sweeping, as in Detroit and Pasadena,[6] or that it accepted with some reluctance. While some foot dragging occurred in the lower courts, it has been much less extensive than in the South.

Keyes and later Supreme Court decisions left a great deal of ambiguity in the law, especially as to appropriate remedies for Northern segregation. The Court's rulings, however, indicated that the existing arrangements in many school districts were unconstitutional. In response, some districts changed their practices voluntarily. But strong public opposition to remedies for segregation, especially busing, meant that local governments generally have not taken strong action until faced with a court order or pressure from federal administrators. As a result, change in Northern districts has come slowly and unevenly. For the most part, however, school districts faced with desegregation orders have complied grudgingly rather than resisting. Compliance has been increased by the willingness of district judges such as W. Arthur Garrity in Boston to supervise school action directly.

When the courts began to attack Northern school segregation, Congress became less supportive of their efforts. Several pieces of legislation in the 1970s and 1980s contained antibusing provisions, provisions that were largely symbolic. More important has been the unwillingness of some presidents to support desegregation through litigation and financial pressure, thereby slowing the process.

Overall, the record of implementation in school desegregation is a mixed one. In the Deep South the Court's decisions ultimately were implemented, but only with major help from the other branches. In the Border states the Court secured substantial change even before receiving outside aid. In the North the Court has helped to bring about major changes in school practices, and the degree of change is striking in light of the Court's mixed and ambiguous position on the scope of remedies.

Police Investigation. The Warren Court imposed heavy procedural requirements on the police in two areas of criminal investigation, with a landmark decision in each area. In search and seizure cases, *Mapp v. Ohio* (1961) applied to the states the "exclusionary rule," under which evidence illegally seized by the police could not be used against a defendant in court. The *Mapp* decision thereby provided a possible incentive for police to follow rules for legal searches that were established in other decisions. In the area of interrogation *Miranda v. Arizona* (1966) required that suspects be given a series of warnings prior to police questioning if their statements were to be used as evidence.

The Burger Court subsequently weakened the *Mapp* and *Miranda* decisions in some respects, and some commentators viewed its 1984 decisions on the exclusionary rule as negating much of the rule's force. But the basic rules of both decisions remained standing at least until 1984. How have judges and police officers responded to those rules?

Lower court responses to *Mapp* and *Miranda* have been mixed. Some state supreme courts criticized the decisions and interpreted them narrowly. Others were more supportive; indeed, supreme courts in states such as Hawaii, Pennsylvania, and California have evaded the Burger Court's narrowing of *Mapp* and *Miranda* through broad interpretations of provisions in state constitutions.[7] At the trial level, where judges frequently deal with challenges to searches and confessions, the record also varies. Clearly many judges who are sympathetic toward the police have been reluctant to order the exclusion of evidence from trials.

The evidence on police response to the Court's requirements is not as extensive as we might like, but we know a good deal about that response. Most police officers seek maximum freedom for their investigative activities and resent the Court's efforts to impose constraints on those activities. At the same time, they want their evidence to stand up in court. The result has been a complex pattern of police behavior.

In the case of *Miranda,* studies in New Haven and Washington, D.C., shortly after the decision found that police officers usually failed to give suspects all the warnings required by the Court.[8] Since that time the level of literal compliance with the *Miranda* rules apparently has become rather high. But officers often make it difficult for suspects to make effective use of the rights contained in the warnings. For instance, as a study in Denver found, officers sometimes put great pressure on suspects to waive their rights and to answer questions.[9] Even without such pressure, most suspects disregard the *Miranda* warnings and talk to the police. As a result, officers have found that they can live with the decision; as a public defender has noted, they even gain an advantage from it.

> Police *love* the *Miranda* decision. They speed-read the suspect his rights and tell him to fill in and sign a printed waiver form. He's frightened; he doesn't understand what was read to him; he's afraid he'll look guilty if he doesn't sign; he signs, and school's out. The signed waiver is almost impossible for the defense to overcome.[10]

In search and seizure, there is disagreement about the extent of police compliance with rules established by the Court. This disagreement reflects an ambiguous picture. There is some evidence that *Mapp* produced changes in police behavior, including a major increase in the use of search warrants in some departments.[11] But it appears that the Court has faced more noncompliance in this area than in interrogations, because the Court's search requirements are more difficult to reconcile with police needs: compliance with rules for searches sometimes makes it impractical to obtain needed evidence. After *Mapp,* observers of police activities in cities such as Oakland and New York City reported that illegal searches were common.[12] Studies indicate that in a relatively small but significant number of cases, prosecutors drop charges because of illegally seized evidence or judges grant motions to suppress illegal evidence; such actions occur most often for "search-intensive" crimes such as drug offenses.[13]

The imperfect adherence of police to court-mandated rules for searches may be puzzling, given that noncompliance jeopardizes the use of evidence in court. One reason for rule violations is that officers do not always concern themselves with obtaining convictions, particularly in minor cases. In addition, illegal searches may not prevent convictions. A great many defendants plead guilty, thereby waiving their right to challenge the legality of evidence against them. Sympathetic trial judges may give the benefit of the doubt to police officers on borderline evidentiary questions. All these factors reduce the risks in departing from judicial rules.

School Religion. In *Engel v. Vitale* (1962) and *Abington School District v. Schempp* (1963), the Supreme Court ruled that public schools could not hold prayer and Bible-reading exercises for their students. At that time both practices were quite widespread. After these decisions a great many schools eliminated religious exercises. According to one survey the proportion of classrooms with prayers declined from 60 percent to 28 percent; for Bible reading, the decline was from 48 percent to 22 percent.[14]

The decline, of course, still left a large number of schools in noncompliance with the Court's rulings. Such noncompliance is not difficult to explain. Prayer and Bible reading were deeply rooted in many schools, with a good deal of strong support from school personnel and people in the community. In many school districts there was no open opposition to the religious observances, in part because few people disagreed with them and in part because potential opponents were afraid to come forward. Under these conditions it was easiest for school officials simply to maintain the observances. Some reconciled that policy with the Supreme Court's decisions through reinterpretation of the decisions—as allowing prayers where participation was voluntary, for instance.

In the late 1970s and early 1980s there seemed to be something of a resurgence in school religious observances, perhaps because of a more conservative political climate and because of the increasing age of the relevant Supreme Court decisions. School officials in some districts established new observances or proclaimed existing ones more openly. Legislatures in several states, including Louisiana, Massachusetts, and Oklahoma, adopted laws providing for school prayers in some form.

When legal challenges are brought against school religion, judges generally have supported the Supreme Court. Lower courts have acted quickly to strike down state laws mandating prayer and religious observances in local schools. One exception was an Alabama federal judge who upheld both a state prayer law and local observances in 1983, declaring that "the United States Supreme Court has erred" in its interpretation of the Constitution; that judge was overruled on appeal.[15]

The Broader Picture. School desegregation, police investigation, and school religion all illustrate the imperfections of the implementation process for Supreme Court decisions. In each area the Court's rulings have suffered from some slippage in the lower courts and even more slippage in the administrative arena.

These examples of implementation problems are not unique in recent history. Several Warren Court decisions on criminal trial procedures were given narrow interpretations in state appellate courts and applied only in part at the trial level. For instance, *In re Gault* (1967) held that juvenile defendants must be given basic procedural rights, thereby requiring fundamental changes in the procedures of many juvenile courts, but some judges failed to make these changes. Law enforcement agencies and movie censorship boards have not always followed the Court's definitions of obscenity and rules for its control. The federal Patent Office essentially ignored the Court's long effort to establish a higher standard for the assessment of patent applications.

Yet we should not conclude from this record that the implementation of Supreme Court policies invariably is poor. First of all, even in the areas that I have discussed, the Court has had significant successes as well as failures. Desegregation of schools in the Border states, widespread modification of police practices, and elimination of prayers in thousands of classrooms are all substantial policy changes that the Court secured. Under difficult circumstances the Court has had a considerable impact on judicial and administrative behavior.

Second, the Court has been more successful with major policy initiatives in some other areas. One particularly clear example is legislative apportionment. In 1964 the Court ordered that state legislatures be apportioned according to population, and at that time nearly every state legislature was in violation of that principle. Compliance with the Court's ruling required fundamental restructuring of the rules for apportionment in most states, and it would lead inevitably to many legislators' losing their jobs. Nonetheless, through action by courts and legislatures the states moved toward compliance. Some states complied rather quickly, and eventually all the states fell into line.

Thus the pattern of implementation for Supreme Court decisions is complex. It is difficult to generalize about the relative frequency of successes and failures; all we can say confidently is that the picture is mixed. Given the traditional expectation that Supreme Court decisions are carried out faithfully, it is understandable that the negative side of the record has received more attention. Certainly both the imperfections of implementation and the variation in its success require explanation.

Explaining the Implementation Process

The effectiveness with which public policies are implemented depends upon a variety of factors. My discussions of three policy areas may have suggested the complexity of these factors for Supreme Court decisions. Five general factors seem to be particularly important in explaining the responses of judges and administrators to the Court's decisions. Each of these factors may be viewed as a potential source of difficulties and as a basis for differences in the ways that decisions are carried out.

Clarity and Ambiguity. The opinions that proclaim Supreme Court policies frequently are unclear as to what they require of judges and administrators. This ambiguity arises for several reasons. One is that opinions must speak in general terms, and their application to specific situations may be uncertain. In laying down rules for police searches, for instance, the Court cannot indicate what is required in every search situation that arises. The same problem exists for the Court's general definition of obscenity in *Miller v. California* (1973).

Another source of ambiguity is the Court's group decision process. The justice who writes a majority opinion often needs to compromise on language to obtain agreement from other justices. The result may be an opinion that fails to address important questions clearly or one that makes inconsistent statements on an issue. The existence of multiple opinions also can create confusion, particularly where a justice who joins in the Court's opinion writes separately to "interpret" that opinion. Thus Justice Stewart's opinion for the Court in *Gannett v. De Pasquale* (1979) seemed to say that criminal trials could be closed to the public, but Chief Justice Burger's concurring opinion indicated otherwise. Of course, ambiguity is almost guaranteed when the Court fails to produce a majority opinion at all.

Finally, decisions that are inconsistent with each other in spirit create ambiguity. Such inconsistency is almost inevitable when the Court deals with issues over a long period of time. This is true of the Court's decisions on police procedure, in part because liberal Warren Court rulings and conservative Burger Court rulings exist side by side in some areas.

Ambiguity is likely to produce problems for two reasons. First, it leaves officials uncertain as to what the Court wants. After the *Gannett* decision, judges could not rule with confidence on requests to close trials, until the Court clarified its position a year later.[16]

Second, ambiguity provides officials who seek to avoid implementing the Court's policies with some leeway with which to do so. Conservative state supreme courts were able to evade the Court's liberal rulings on internal security legislation because of the Court's inconsistencies and ambiguity in the application of decisions to specific statutes.[17] A more striking example is the implementation of *Brown v. Board of Education.* It will be recalled that the Court gave district judges a free hand to determine the timing for desegregation rather than setting a firm timetable itself. As a result, those judges were under great pressure to allow delay by school districts. Had the Court taken the responsibility for timing on itself, this pressure might have been removed. "If the Supreme Court had issued unequivocal mandates insisting that the district judge promptly order recalcitrant boards to act, the board could blame the district judge and he could blame the Supreme Court." [18] As a result, desegregation might have come about more quickly.

In some other areas the Court has profited from its clarity. In *Roe v. Wade* (1973) Justice Blackmun's opinion laid down fairly specific rules as to what regulation of abortion was allowable, and this specificity undoubtedly helped to improve implementation of the decision. The Court also has decided a series of other cases on abortion to reduce the remaining ambiguities. In legislative apportionment the Court established a somewhat vague principle of equality in district population, but it then decided a large number of additional cases to clarify the application of that principle. As a result, lower court judges learned what was expected of them and could follow through. These two areas underline the capacity of a determined Court to reduce the ambiguity of its policies and thereby improve their implementation.

Communication of Decisions. We tend to assume that officials who are affected by Supreme Court decisions automatically become aware of those decisions. But communication of decisions is not at all automatic. Few officials monitor the Supreme Court's output systematically to identify relevant decisions; even federal judges generally are too busy to do so. Instead, decisions must come to people's attention in other ways. Decisions are transmitted to judges and administrators through several channels, channels that may be only partially effective in informing them of Supreme Court policies.

One of these channels is the mass media. A few major Supreme Court decisions are heavily publicized by newspapers, magazines, and television. As a result of media attention, most policy makers quickly become aware of such decisions as the *Bakke* decision of 1978 on reverse discrimination and the Court's 1984 ruling on home videotaping (*Sony Corporation v. Universal City Studios*). But most decisions do not receive this kind of publicity. Moreover, what the mass media report about a decision may be misleading or simply incorrect. In 1956 most newspapers reported that the Supreme Court had banned racial segregation on intrastate bus lines when the Court actually had refused to hear a case on that question. Before the mistake was discovered, 11 Southern cities had desegregated their bus lines in what they thought was compliance with the Court's ruling.[19]

Attorneys serve an important communication function for some officials. Through their arguments in court proceedings and administrative hearings they bring favorable precedents to the attention of judges and administrators. Lawyers on the staffs of administrative agencies often inform agency personnel of relevant decisions. Through these roles attorneys help to ensure that communication of Supreme Court policies to some policy makers, especially appellate judges, generally is effective.

But where attorneys do not come into direct contact with policy makers or where their role is somewhat informal, their impact necessarily will be more limited. Even when a school system employs an attorney, for instance, that attorney is likely to provide little information on court decisions to teachers. The atmosphere of some trial courts is sufficiently "nonlegal" to limit the role of lawyers as communicators there as well. A study of juvenile justice in rural Kentucky found that many judges simply were unaware of the Supreme Court's landmark ruling on procedures in juvenile cases. In part this was because juveniles seldom were represented by counsel in some areas.[20]

For judges and administrators at low levels in their professional hierarchies, officials at higher levels often play an important role in providing information about Supreme Court decisions. State trial judges become aware of those decisions largely as they are cited by state appellate courts. Police officers often learn of decisions from departmental superiors. There is an inevitable loss of information in this process; those who communicate a Supreme Court policy generally will give a partial and distorted picture of that policy. The distortion will be particularly great where the communicator disapproves of a decision. Many state supreme courts and most police officials offered negative views of liberal criminal justice decisions by the Warren Court as they informed their subordinates of those decisions.

Effective communication of decisions depends on the receivers as well as the channels of transmission. Legally trained officials are best able to understand decisions and their implications. Nonlawyers who work regularly with the law, such as police officers, have the same advantage to a lesser degree. Teachers and other people who work outside the legal system are likely to have the greatest difficulties in interpreting what they learn of Supreme Court rulings.

Because the communication of decisions is imperfect, they frequently are misunderstood by the policy makers who must respond to them. In the mid-1970s, for instance, only 17 percent of a sample of Florida school teachers knew that the Court had prohibited the recitation of the Lord's Prayer in public schools. The same survey found higher levels of knowledge for judges and law enforcement officers. But even the judges showed limitations in their understanding of some of these policies.[21]

The impact of these problems, of course, may be tremendous. Policy makers who do not know of a decision, such as the rural Kentucky judges, cannot implement it. Teachers who believe that the Supreme Court has allowed the recitation of voluntary prayers will continue their recitation. Police officers whose superiors portrayed *Mapp* and *Miranda* in a negative light as they communicated these decisions thereby developed a bias against compliance. Certainly weaknesses in the communication process help to explain inadequate implementation of the Court's decisions.

Incentives to Disobey. Once policy makers become aware of a relevant Supreme Court decision, they must choose a response to it. In large part, their response will be determined by their agreement or disagreement with the policy and by their assessment of its effect on their self-interest. Where these factors are favorable, as they often are, officials are likely to carry out a policy faithfully. It will be useful, however, to focus on situations in which the policy preferences or interests of officials provide incentives to resist Supreme Court policies.

Disagreement with a Supreme Court policy is probably the most common reason for appellate court refusals to implement Court decisions faithfully. Particularly when the Court adopts a controversial new policy, many lower court judges may conclude that the Court has made a serious mistake. Sometimes this belief is expressed rather clearly in opinions. Members of several state supreme courts attacked the values expressed in the Warren Court's criminal procedure decisions. The New Jersey Supreme Court, for instance, said, "It is idle to suppose" that decisions such as *Mapp* "have no impact upon law enforcement or at the worst only a minimal one." [22] More recently, the chief justice of the Utah Supreme Court wrote of the U.S. Supreme Court's position on obscenity that "it would appear that such an argument ought only to be advanced by depraved, mentally deficient, mind-warped queers." [23]

Of course, trial judges and administrators also disagree with some Supreme Court decisions. A great many teachers, for instance, disapproved of the Court's decisions limiting school religious observances. Similarly, most police officers regard decisions that limit their investigative powers as bad policy. In three of four Wisconsin cities surveyed, more than 80 percent of the officers who were questioned disagreed with *Miranda*.[24] This level of disagreement ensured that implementation would be imperfect in both areas.

Administrators and trial judges are especially likely to find that a Supreme Court decision conflicts with their self-interest because it threatens existing practices that serve important purposes. Law enforcement officers feel that decisions which constrain their investigations of crime will make their jobs more difficult. Detectives, for instance, could expect to have more difficulty in achieving a satisfactory "clearance rate" of crimes solved by arrests. Members of some administrative agencies may feel that compliance with Supreme Court rulings would damage important relationships with private interest groups. State trial judges who need to dispose of criminal cases rapidly may resist implementing due process decisions that would slow the rate of dispositions. This factor helps to account for noncompliance with such decisions as *Argersinger v. Hamlin* (1970), which extended the right to counsel for indigent defendants to some misdemeanor cases, and *Tate v. Short* (1972), which held that defendants cannot be jailed because of their inability to pay fines. Elected officials often shy away from supporting unpopular Supreme Court decisions, and the recent campaigns of "law and order" groups may make state judges wary of vigorously applying decisions that expand the rights of criminal defendants. In administrative agencies and even in trial courts, organizational inertia gives officials an incentive to maintain existing practices, and decisions that require massive changes may be resisted for that reason alone.

Federal judges might seem to be immune from these kinds of concerns. They are appointed for life and are relatively free from administrative problems. But under some circumstances even their self-interest may be affected by a Supreme Court decision. Full adherence to *Brown v. Board of Education* would have made district judges' lives less pleasant because of the reaction of their friends and neighbors. J. Skelly Wright, who did adhere to *Brown,* found that his life was affected a great deal: "I never have been a gregarious type, and I've become much less so in the past few years. You never know whether people really want to talk with you and I don't see a lot of people any more." [25]

That was not all that happened to Wright, as one newspaper reported after he refused to allow the state legislature to take over the New Orleans school system.

> Parents and children from integrated New Orleans schools bore a miniature black coffin, containing a blackened effigy of U.S. Judge J. Skelly Wright, into the Louisiana Capitol. . . .
>
> The House stood up and with a long roll of applause, saluted the parents. The legislature last week by resolution urged white parents to boycott the two integrated New Orleans schools.
>
> As the demonstrators moved into the legislative chambers, one woman shouted, "the judge is dead, we have slaughtered him."
>
> Some of the group feigned weeping and mourning, others laughed. [26]

Judge Wright was willing to accept the costs of supporting the Supreme Court, and Northern federal judges such as W. Arthur Garrity in Boston have ordered school desegregation despite the likelihood of severe public criticism. But these are exceptions to the rule. Where the perceived impact of carrying out a decision is highly negative, a person is unlikely to offer total obedience to the Court. Few Southern officials could be expected to support desegregation in the face of strong public disapproval. Police officers naturally sought to limit the effects of *Mapp* and *Miranda* on their work.

As this discussion suggests, variation in response to Supreme Court decisions can be traced primarily to differences in the policy preferences and self-interest of implementors. Police departments tend to resist decisions that limit their powers but follow with alacrity those that expand police powers. The difference between the responses of the Deep South and the Border states to the *Brown* decision was primarily a function of different attitudes toward race.

Acceptance of the Court's Authority. Policy makers may implement the Supreme Court's decisions even when they have incentives not to do so. One important reason is the Court's authority as interpreter of the law. Most people believe that the Court's decisions are authoritative judgments about the law and that there is an obligation to comply with those decisions. Because of this belief, even officials who are disposed to disobey the Court's decisions may choose not to do so. Certainly a policy maker who is indifferent toward a policy issued by the Supreme Court will be inclined to go along because of the Court's authority.

The Court's authority is strongest for judges, primarily because they have been socialized to accept the leadership of higher courts. The attitude of most judges is reflected in the statement of one member of a federal court of appeals: "Our job is to follow the Supreme Court whether we like the decisions or not." [27] Judicial acceptance of the Court's authority goes far toward explaining why judges generally respond positively to the Court's rulings in their decisions.[28]

But the loyalty of judges to the Court is seldom absolute. Judges often criticize the Court, and some express a resentment of the Court that is similar to the feelings of subordinates in other organizations toward their superiors. Because of this degree of psychic independence, judges who dislike a particular Supreme Court policy may not feel compelled to implement it fully. Rather, they can take a middle course, following the Court where the language of its opinions leaves no choice but using the ambiguity in the Court's decisions to limit their impact. One member of a somewhat rebellious lower court put the matter flatly: "We follow Supreme Court decisions when we can't get around them." [29] Occasionally, as we have seen, a judge will go further and fail altogether to follow the Court's lead on an issue. Several recent members of the Utah

Supreme Court seemed to go even further, rejecting the Supreme Court's authority altogether. One Utah justice said of the Court and the Constitution, "They're destroying it, and we're upholding it." [30]

The Court holds authority for administrators as well as judges. Studies of the school prayer decisions found that some school officials were willing to eliminate religious observances that they would have preferred to maintain, because they accepted a duty to follow Supreme Court rulings.[31] But the Court's authority for administrators as a group is weaker than it is for judges. Administrative agencies are somewhat removed from the judicial system and its norm of obedience to higher courts. Moreover, administrators such as police officers and school personnel usually have not received law school socialization in this norm. As a result, administrative officials find it somewhat easier to justify deviation from Supreme Court policies than do judges. Certainly the most blatant noncompliance with the Court's decisions comes primarily from the administrative sector.

The weight of the Court's authority tends to decline as organizational distance from the Court increases. Officials at the grassroots level, far removed from direct contact with the Court, may feel little need to adjust their policies to the Court's decisions. This feeling is typified by the experience of a legal scholar who was caught in a speed trap in Pennsylvania and was brought before the local justice of the peace. The scholar pointed out that the J.P.'s practice of taking part of each fine as a personal fee was unconstitutional. " 'Who said that?' he was asked. Upon learning that it was the United States Supreme Court, the J.P. shrugged and said, 'Oh well, I didn't think it was any Pennsylvania court.' " [32]

The Court's authority, then, is an important force for acceptance of its policies, but not an overwhelming one. Particularly for judges, the authority attached to Supreme Court decisions reduces noncompliance with those decisions. But the Court's authority is not so strong as to prevent all subversion of the Court's policies where other motivations incline judges and administrators toward subversion.

Sanctions for Disobedience. More tangible than the Court's authority as a force for compliance is the potential application of sanctions for noncompliance. Judges and administrators might follow the Court's lead despite negative inclinations because they wish to avoid those sanctions.

For judges, the primary sanction is reversal. If a judge fails to follow an applicable Supreme Court policy, the losing litigant may appeal the case and secure a reversal of the decision. This sanction is significant, in part because the ability to avoid reversals is one major criterion by which the performance of judges is measured. G. Harrold Carswell's high reversal rate helped to bring about the 1970 defeat of his nomination to the Supreme Court in the Senate because it suggested that he was not competent. Judges express a variety of attitudes toward reversal, but because of professional pride few are indifferent toward it. One judge on a federal court of appeals said of reversals, "Everybody minds it. Don't believe that business about 'I don't mind a bit'—at least from any judge who is any good." [33]

But reversal is not an overwhelming sanction. A judge who feels strongly about an issue such as abortion may be willing to accept a few reversals on that issue as the price of following personal convictions. Nor does reversal follow inevitably from a failure to accept the Supreme Court's policies, particularly where that failure is somewhat ambiguous. The losing litigant may not appeal. Moreover, the great majority of judges are reviewed by a court other than the Supreme Court, and the reviewing court may share their opposition to the Court's policies. After several state supreme courts expressed their lack of sympathy for the Burger Court's conservative positions on criminal procedure, lower court judges in those states could feel fairly safe in deviating from the Court's positions.

For administrators, the most common sanction is a court order that directs compliance with a decision. If a public welfare agency fails to follow an applicable Supreme Court policy, a person who is injured by its failure may bring a lawsuit to compel compliance with the Court. Such a suit in itself is undesirable, because of the trouble and expense that it entails. A successful suit is even worse, because an order to comply with a Supreme Court rule is something of an embarrassment and puts an agency under judicial scrutiny that officials would prefer to avoid.

But this sanction suffers from the weaknesses of reversal in even stronger form. First, it depends on people's willingness to bring litigation challenging agency behavior. Frequently noncompliant policies will continue unchallenged. This was the case with school religious and racial policies in many communities. Where a lawsuit appears to be unlikely, officials may see no reason to change their practices. Moreover, a potential court order is not a tremendously powerful sanction. Officials can live with the possibility of such an order if they have reason to oppose a Supreme Court policy.

Administrators who are directly dependent upon the courts have a stronger incentive to follow Supreme Court decisions. Police officers who wish to secure convictions of defendants may jeopardize those convictions with illegal searches. A federal regulatory agency whose decisions are enforced by the courts is in a similar position. As the discussion of the police indicated, however, even these administrators may feel some freedom to depart from the Court's rules.

If an agency does receive a direct order to comply with Supreme Court policies its resistance is likely to end, because officials do not want to risk citations for contempt of court. Such citations are rare but possible. In a 1909 case the Court did hold some law enforcement officers in contempt and jailed them for allowing the lynching of a prisoner whose execution the Court had stayed.[34] But if agencies are not brought to court, or if lower court judges do not support Supreme Court policies, these agencies will not become subject to direct orders.

This discussion suggests two conditions that affect the enforcement process. First, enforcement of a Supreme Court decision is enhanced when groups act to challenge noncompliance. The NAACP Legal Defense Fund and the American Civil Liberties Union are important not only because they bring cases to the Supreme Court but also because they bring legal actions against policy makers who disobey the Court. We might suspect that schools are most likely to follow Supreme Court decisions on such issues as religious observances and procedures for suspension of students in cities where the ACLU plays an active role.

Second, the Court's decisions are easiest to enforce when the affected policy makers are small in number and highly visible. It was relatively simple for the Court to oversee the 50 state legislatures that ultimately were responsible for carrying out the first wave of reapportionment decisions. Interested groups easily could bring actions against any legislature that refused to reapportion, and the Court itself could hear all the necessary cases. It is a far more difficult matter to oversee the day-to-day activities of thousands of police officers involved in the investigation of crime.

In general, the sanctions available to the Court are fairly weak. Faced with resistance to its policies, the Court can do relatively little to overcome that resistance. Thus the willingness of Congress and the president to offer their help can make a great deal of difference when the Court faces widespread noncompliance. Ultimately it was federal legislation and its enforcement by the executive branch that brought about the beginning of real school desegregation in the Deep South.

Conclusions. A great deal about the success and failure of implementation can be explained in terms of the factors that have been examined. Ineffective implementation results in part from ambiguity in decisions and weaknesses in their communication. More important, however, is the existence of incentives for administrators and judges to oppose the Court's policies.

Implementation is likely to be rather successful when these problems are absent. This is particularly true of the incentives to disobey. When policy makers like a decision, they can be expected to carry it out. The Court's authority and its stock of sanctions provide an additional impetus for positive response to its decisions, but their force is limited.

Because of the ways in which the implementation process works, we can expect judges generally to carry out Supreme Court policies more effectively than do administrators. Communication of decisions to judges is relatively good, they tend to accept the Court's authority, and their self-interest is less likely to conflict with implementation of decisions. For some of the same reasons, federal judges and administrators tend to be better implementors than their state counterparts: they are "closer" to the Supreme Court and more directly affected by its authority and sanctions.

Inevitably, Supreme Court policies as a whole are implemented with only partial success. The gap between the rules that the Court hands down and the actions that judges and administrators take is often considerable. In this respect, as I have noted, the Court is not unique. Congress and the president also suffer from problems of implementation. But the Court's problems are particularly great, because it has little ability to control the implementation process. Most notably, the sanctions that it can apply to disobedient officials are much weaker than those available to policy makers such as the president. As a result, the Court may have special difficulty in obtaining effective implementation of its policies.

Responses by Legislatures and Chief Executives

After Supreme Court decisions are handed down, Congress, the president, and their state counterparts may play a variety of roles in responding to those decisions. They may help or hinder the implementation of decisions, they may act to change the Court's interpretations of the law, and they can attack the Court or its members. In addition, they may themselves be required to comply with the Court's decisions. In this section I will examine these various roles, both for their own significance and for what they tell about the Court's relationships with the other branches of government.

Congress

Responding to Decisions: Statutory Interpretation. In the interpretation of federal statutes, the Supreme Court's legal position is inferior to that of Congress. If an effective majority in Congress disagrees with the Court's interpretation of a provision, that provision simply can be changed in new legislation to overcome the Court's interpretation.

As we might expect, the great majority of the Court's statutory decisions are left standing by Congress. Many of its interpretations are relatively uncontroversial. Because of the difficulty of adopting statutes, Congress often will fail to act even when most of its members disagree with the Court.

But Congress occasionally does act to change the statutory interpretations established by the Court. A study by Beth Henschen found that Congress overturned nine of the Supreme Court's 222 decisions in labor and antitrust law between 1950 and 1972, and bills to modify or reverse 17 other decisions were considered seriously. Another study, which looked at all policy areas, found 21 instances of congressional reversals of the Court between 1945 and 1957.[35]

In recent years bills have been introduced in Congress to overturn Supreme Court decisions in several areas of statutory law, and Congress has enacted some of these bills. Three of the enactments came in 1982. In *McCarty v. McCarty* (1981), the Court held that under federal law state courts could not order military retirement pay to be shared with a spouse as part of a divorce settlement; the next year Congress adopted legislation directly overturning that decision. In 1982 Congress also overturned a 1978 decision by limiting the damages that foreign governments could collect in antitrust suits.[36] And after a long and heated battle, Congress in 1982 amended the Voting Rights Act to overrule *City of Mobile v. Bolden* (1980), in which the Court held somewhat indirectly that voting systems which had the result of reducing black representation in office violated the act only if they were adopted with the intent to discriminate. More recently, in 1984 Congress took only four months to overturn *National Labor Relations Board v. Bildisco and Bildisco* (1984), in which the Court ruled that federal law allowed a company to alter the terms of its labor contracts unilaterally after it filed a bankruptcy petition.

Some element of institutional conflict is always present when Congress overturns a Supreme Court decision. Members of Congress generally are explicit about their intent to attack the Court's interpretation, and often they criticize the Court for what they see as a misguided view of the law. Sometimes, especially on civil liberties issues, the attack on the Court is rather heated. This was true of the efforts to overturn several decisions concerning subversive activities and the rights of criminal defendants in the late 1950s.

But this element of conflict should not be exaggerated. Frictions between branches of government in the making of policy are common, and they do not always indicate deep hostility between policy makers. Moreover, members of the Court are well aware that Congress has the final word in this area, and they do not necessarily resent that fact. As Justice Minton wrote after his retirement:

> I don't see why the liberal press gets in a tizzy when Congress tries to change a rule of law, not Constitutional, that the Court has laid down. I was never conscious of the feeling while I was there that the Court felt that was an attack on it. . . .[37]

Indeed, the Court sometimes encourages Congress to overturn a decision. We would expect dissenters to do so when they are distressed by a decision. This was the course taken by Justice Clark, for instance, in *Jencks v. United States* (1957), which concerned disclosure of information provided by government informers. By decrying the potential effects of the decision, Clark sought to secure congressional action to overturn it. He did succeed in arousing concern in Congress, but the ironic result was a law that essentially ratified *Jencks*.

Even the Court majority in a case may invite reversal. Opinions in statutory cases sometimes note that Congress can rewrite the statute if it disagrees with the Court. Occasionally the Court even seems to encourage congressional action. In *McCarty v. McCarty,* the military retirement pay case, Justice Blackmun's opinion for the Court alluded to the negative effects of the decision: "We recognize that the plight of an ex-spouse of a retired service member is often a serious one." Then he reminded Congress of its ultimate responsibility: ". . . Congress may well decide . . . that more protection should be afforded a former spouse of a retired service member. This decision, however, is for Congress alone." [38] Blackmun probably was not unhappy when Congress did act to negate the Court's interpretation of the law.

This focus on congressional overturning of a ruling by the Court may give a misleading picture of the relationship between the two institutions in statutory law. Perhaps more important is the fact that both Congress and the Court make contributions to the development of the law in any field, and each institution helps to reshape public policy. This complex interaction is readily apparent in a field such as antitrust, in which Congress and the Court each have taken a number of significant actions since the basic statutes were adopted. Conflict between the Court and Congress is only a small part of their work in such fields; far more often, they implicitly or explicitly accept each other's initiatives.

Responding to Decisions: Constitutional Interpretation. When the Court makes a decision on constitutional grounds, that decision generally is more difficult to overturn than a statutory decision. Nonetheless, Congress does have two avenues with which to reverse a constitutional decision or at least to reduce its effects.

One of these avenues is statutory. If the Court has nullified a statute on constitutional grounds, Congress can write a second statute to try to meet the Court's objections. For instance, in 1916 Congress used its power over interstate commerce to limit the employment of child labor. In *Hammer v. Dagenhart* (1918) the Court held that the commerce power was inadequate for this purpose. In response, Congress adopted a new child labor statute in 1919 based on the taxing power. The Court rejected this line as well in *Bailey v. Drexel Furniture Co.* (1922), and the effort to prohibit child labor failed for the time being. After the Supreme Court struck down six major New Deal statutes in 1935 and 1936, Congress rewrote five of the laws. Four of the five were upheld by the Court after its collective change of heart in 1937, and the fifth was not challenged.

Statutes also may be used to limit the impact of a constitutional decision. After the Supreme Court struck down government prohibitions on abortion in 1973, Congress adopted a series of provisions restricting the use of federal funds to pay for abortions. In *Maher v. Roe* (1977) and *Harris v. McRae* (1980) the Court indicated that these provisions were constitutionally acceptable.

When the Supreme Court rules that a right is not protected by the Constitution, Congress ordinarily is free to establish such a protection through statute. Congress seldom takes such action. It did so, however, after *Zurcher v. Stanford Daily* (1978), in which the Court held that newsrooms could be searched on the basis of warrants even if no news personnel were suspected of crimes. In 1980 Congress overturned *Zurcher* by requiring that most such searches operate through subpoenas, a procedure providing greater protection for news organizations in that a subpoena can be challenged in court before a search takes place.

Constitutional decisions, of course, may be overturned directly by constitutional amendment. Congress formally has proposed and sent to the states amendments to reverse Supreme Court decisions at least five times. The Eleventh Amendment, which broadened state immunity from lawsuits, overturned *Chisholm v. Georgia* (1793). The Fourteenth Amendment's provision upholding the right of citizenship for black persons nullified part of the *Dred Scott* decision of 1857. The Sixteenth Amendment, allowing a federal income tax, reversed *Pollock v. Farmers' Loan and Trust Co.* (1895). Congress proposed the Child Labor Amendment in 1924 to overcome the Court's rulings that Congress lacked the power to regulate child labor. This amendment, however, was not ratified by the states. The Twenty-sixth Amendment nullified the Court's limitation on congressional power to reduce the legal voting age in *Oregon v. Mitchell* (1970). A few other amendments also can be interpreted in part as attacks on the Court's positions.

The constitutional decisions that Congress has acted to overturn are only a small proportion of those that aroused congressional displeasure. This small proportion reflects the difficulty of the amendment process. Members of Congress are hesitant to tamper with the Constitution, especially to limit the protections of civil liberties in the Bill of Rights, and the requirement of a two-thirds majority in each house presents a formidable obstacle to action.

It is especially striking that Supreme Court decisions expanding civil liberties in the past quarter century have not led to formal amendment proposals. Conservative members of Congress frequently have been distressed by decisions supporting civil liberties during this period. In several instances they have urged the adoption of constitutional amendments to overturn these decisions. This was the case with the school prayer decisions of 1962 and 1963, the reapportionment decisions of 1962 and 1964, the abortion decision of 1973, and the decisions that allowed busing of public school students for purposes of racial integration.

Because most of these decisions were highly unpopular in Congress, favorable congressional action on amendment efforts would seem likely. But in no instance has either house provided the necessary two-thirds majority for an amendment resolution. In 1979 an antibusing amendment failed even to obtain a majority in the House, despite overwhelming congressional opposition to busing. The election of President Reagan and of a more conservative Congress in 1980 seemed to ease the way for amendments on abortion and school prayer. But in 1983 the Senate defeated an amendment to allow Congress and the states to prohibit abortion, and in 1984 it defeated an amendment to allow school prayer exercises.

Attacks on the Court and Individual Justices. When members of Congress are dissatisfied with the Supreme Court's behavior, they may attack the Court as an institution or individual justices as well as the Court's policies. The simplest and easiest form of such attacks is verbal, and members of Congress frequently express their disapproval of the Court by denouncing it. Unhappy with a 1956 decision on state regulation of subversive activities, for instance, one member of the House announced that the Court was "a greater threat to this Union than the entire confines of Soviet Russia. If some way is not found to stop them, God help us." [39]

This kind of verbal attack may injure the Court by reducing public esteem for it, but its impact is uncertain. Congress can have a more direct impact by taking legislative action against the Court or its members. This action may take several forms.

One very important but disputed power of Congress over the Court as an institution is its capacity to limit the Court's appellate jurisdiction. The Constitution gives Congress control over the appellate jurisdiction through simple legislation, though there is some question as to whether Congress could limit the Court's jurisdiction to prevent it from protecting constitutional rights. Congress has used its power over the Court's jurisdiction to control the Court only once, in a rather unusual situation; in 1869 it withdrew the Court's right to hear appeals in habeas corpus actions in order to prevent it from deciding a pending challenge to the post-Civil War Reconstruction legislation. In the case, *Ex parte McCardle* (1869), the Court ruled that the congressional action was proper.

In recent years Congress has considered several bills that would have limited the Court's jurisdiction in areas of civil liberties activism. In 1964 the House actually passed a bill to remove the jurisdiction of all federal courts over state reapportionment, and in 1979 the Senate adopted a provision that would eliminate the federal courts' jurisdiction over cases involving school prayer. Both the 1964 and 1979 bills died in the other house. In 1981 a variety of bills were introduced to limit Supreme Court jurisdiction in the areas of abortion, school busing, and prayer, but even in a newly conservative Congress none passed either house.

Another kind of proposal that was popular in the past would have required extraordinary majorities of justices to declare acts of Congress unconstitutional. A 1923 proposal set the required number at seven, a 1936 proposal at six. No bill of this kind has been adopted.

The device of adding members to the Court in order to change its policies was made famous by President Roosevelt's Court-packing plan in 1937, which would have increased the Supreme Court at least temporarily to 15 members. The size of the Court was altered several times in the nineteenth century, and a desire to affect its policies played a part in some of the changes. However, the Court's size has not changed since 1869, and by now it seems rather firmly set at nine.

Along with these means to affect the Court as an institution, Congress also may attack its members. The most extreme method of individual attack is impeachment. As noted in Chapter 2, one justice was impeached by the House—though not convicted by the Senate—in the early nineteenth century, and impeachment has been threatened in several other instances.

Congress holds power over the Court and its justices through its control over the Court budget, limited only by the constitutional prohibition against reducing the justices' salaries. With a few exceptions, Congress has refrained from attacking the Court openly through its budget.[40] But in 1964 Congress singled out the justices when it increased their salaries by $4,500, $3,000 less than the raises given to other federal judges. That action was motivated by displeasure with the Court's civil liberties policies. A year later Representative Robert Dole of Kansas expressed that displeasure in speaking against a bill to eliminate the $3,000 gap.

> ...whenever thinking about the Supreme Court, I think of last June 15, 1964, and the reapportionment decisions handed down in *Reynolds against Simms* and the related cases. It has been suggested that perhaps Section 2 of this bill might be amended whereby the effective date of the pay increase, if adopted by this House, would be the date the Supreme Court reverses the decision in *Reynolds against Simms*.[41]

For whatever reasons, the bill to restore the gap was defeated by 26 votes.

That attack on the justices' salaries was perhaps the most serious concrete action that Congress has taken against the Court in this century; Congress has made rather little use of its enormous powers over the Court. Why has it been so hesitant to employ these powers even during those times when most members were unhappy about the Court's direction?

The answer seems to have several parts. To begin with, there always are a good many members of Congress who agree with the Court's policies and lead its defense. Further, serious forms of attack against the Court such as impeachment and reduction of jurisdiction seem illegitimate in many people's minds. In part this is because most members of Congress believe that the Court should have some independence from the other branches of government. This widespread perception of illegitimacy is a powerful weapon with which to defend the Court. Finally, when threatened with serious measures the Court sometimes has retreated to reduce the impetus for action.

All of these factors can be seen at work in the failures of the most serious attacks on the Court in this century. Both the Court's economic conservatism during the 1930s and its support of civil liberties since the 1950s accorded with the views of many members of Congress, who worked hard to defeat anti-Court legislation. Even some legislators who disagreed with the Court were troubled by the extreme character of bills to "pack" the Court or to limit its jurisdiction. In both the 1930s and the late 1950s, the Court abandoned some of the policies that were under attack, though in more recent years it has maintained highly unpopular policies and still avoided the imposition of limits on its jurisdiction.

Affecting the Implementation of Decisions. Through legislation Congress can influence the implementation of Supreme Court decisions. Its most important tool is budgetary. Congress can provide or fail to provide funds to carry out a decision. Furthermore, Congress can help the Court by withholding federal funds from state and local governments that refuse to comply with the Court's decisions.

This latter power has played an important role in the process of school desegregation. As noted earlier, the 1964 Civil Rights Act gave to the Department of Health, Education, and Welfare (HEW) the power to withhold funds from school districts that refused to desegregate. HEW's fairly enthusiastic implementation of this provision under the Johnson administration was crucial in bringing about the first meaningful compliance with *Brown v. Board of Education* in the Deep South. Later, after the federal courts began to require desegregation of Northern school systems, Congress reversed its role. Beginning in 1975 appropriations bills for HEW were adopted with provisions that forbade the department from using its financial powers in support of school busing. In 1980 the appropriations bill for the Justice Department prohibited government lawsuits that might bring about busing; President Carter vetoed the bill because of that provision.

Occasionally a Supreme Court decision requires implementation by Congress itself. *Powell v. McCormack* (1969), for instance, required the House of Representatives to admit Representative Adam Clayton Powell, who earlier had been excluded from membership for misconduct and misuse of public funds. In these situations Congress generally has accepted its obligation with little resistance. However, after the Court held in *United States v. Lovett* (1946) that Congress could not withhold salaries from three federal employees who were accused of subversive affiliations, the House agreed to appropriate the required money by only a single vote.

An Overview. Two themes in congressional response to the Court should be emphasized. The first is that this response is "political," in that members of Congress react to Court decisions largely in partisan and ideological terms. During any controversy the major defenders of the Court are those who agree with its policies, while the major opponents are those who find its policies unpalatable. As the Court's policies change, former supporters may become opponents and vice versa. Conservatives who supported the Court when Roosevelt offered his Court-packing plan later denounced the liberal Court that developed from Roosevelt's appointments.

Second, despite frequent disagreement between Congress and the Court, congressional attacks on the Supreme Court generally are limited in severity and scope. While Congress acts to limit or overturn some decisions, it makes surprisingly little use of its powers to propose constitutional amendments and to attack the Court as an institution. The record of Congress in 1981-1982, highlighted in Table 6-2, is fairly typical. In those years Congress overturned at least three statutory decisions and sought to reduce the impact of *Roe v. Wade* with restrictions on the use of federal funds for abortion. But efforts to overturn decisions with constitutional amendments and to cut back the Court's jurisdiction failed. As this two-year period suggests, on the whole the congressional bark at the Supreme Court has been a good deal worse than its bite.

The President

Influencing Congressional Response. The president may influence congressional action concerning the Supreme Court by taking a position on proposals for action. However, presidents often remain aloof from debates over the Court. For example, in 1957 President Eisenhower refused to express a clear position on legislation to attack the Warren Court. One reason for this lack of involvement is a reluctance to take

Table 6-2. Selected "anti-Court" activity in the 97th Congress, 1981-1982

Action taken by Congress

Adopted legislation to overturn Supreme Court statutory decisions on spouses' rights to military retirement pay, on damages that foreign governments can recover in antitrust cases, and on standards for proving racial discrimination in voting systems.

Maintained and adopted severe limits on funding of abortion under Medicaid and other federal programs.

Action considered but not taken

Bill prohibiting nearly all school busing orders by federal courts and barring the Justice Department from bringing legal actions that could lead to busing was adopted by Senate, died in House.

Proposal to eliminate federal court jurisdiction over voluntary school prayer cases was killed after Senate filibuster.

Constitutional amendment to allow organized voluntary prayer in public schools died in Senate committee.

Constitutional amendment to allow Congress and the states to prohibit abortion was approved by Senate Judiciary Committee but got no further.

---

sides in a conflict that may have little relevance to the president's own goals.

Sometimes, however, the president actually proposes anti-Court action by Congress. Thomas Jefferson attempted to curb the Federalist judiciary through Congress. Acting largely behind the scenes, he helped to engineer the removal of a lower court judge as well as the impeachment of Justice Chase. Jefferson sought ultimately to remove other justices, including Chief Justice Marshall. This effort was unsuccessful, in part because of Marshall's deft maneuvering. Jefferson also considered other anti-Court measures, such as a constitutional amendment to allow the removal of judges by the president, but none of these were adopted.

Franklin Roosevelt's Court-packing plan is by far the most dramatic presidential intervention in this century. It is striking that the plan received considerable support in Congress despite the radical impact that it would have had on the Court. This support reflected the power of a very strong president in Congress.

Ronald Reagan came into office with a record of opposition to many of the Court's decisions expanding civil liberties. As president he encouraged congressional efforts to limit or overturn the school prayer and abortion decisions. Some critics of those decisions, however, complained that Reagan had not given these issues a high priority on his agenda. These complaints reflect the reality that only decisions which impinge on foreign policy, economic management, and presidential power are likely to be of central importance to presidents in the current era.

Shaping the Implementation Process. The president also can seek to influence the responses of judges and administrators to Supreme Court decisions. Most directly, the president must choose whether to support the Court with the power of the federal government when its decisions meet with open resistance. The president's legal duty in cases of resistance is somewhat uncertain. Practically speaking, the president has pretty much a free hand.

The most coercive form of federal power is the military. In the famous aftermath of *Worcester v. Georgia* (1832), where the Court ruled that a state lacked power to pass laws affecting Indians living on Indian territory within that state, President Jackson refused to provide military force to overcome Georgia's noncompliance with the Supreme Court mandate. Legally and practically, the situation was highly ambiguous. It became famous because Jackson is purported to have said, "John Marshall has made his decision; now let him enforce it." Real or apochryphal, that statement expresses the Court's dependence on other institutions for help in enforcing its decisions.

When Southern defiance of *Brown v. Board of Education* began, President Eisenhower indicated that he would not use troops to enforce the decision. By doing so he may have encouraged efforts to prevent desegregation. In 1957 a combination of state interference and mob action prevented court-ordered desegregation of the schools in Little Rock, Arkansas. At that point Eisenhower abandoned his earlier position and brought in troops. In 1962 President Kennedy used federal troops to enforce desegregation at the University of Mississippi.

Federal funds and litigation have become important instruments of national power, as demonstrated by their use in the desegregation controversy. Heavy use of these mechanisms under President Johnson was very important in attacking school segregation. When President Nixon came into office in 1969 he brought about a much more limited use of these mechanisms. Indeed, his administration intervened in some court cases to support requests for delay by some Southern districts. These actions reduced the momentum behind the desegregation process.

The president may seek to influence implementation indirectly by shaping public opinion. President Eisenhower seemed to be personally unsympathetic with the *Brown* decision, and he refused to encourage compliance with it. Rather, he made ambiguous statements that indicated some support for white Southerners who opposed the decision. This position undoubtedly hurt the Court; given Eisenhower's enormous popularity, wholehearted support of the Court might have quieted some opposition to desegregation. "If Mr. Eisenhower had come through,"

Justice Tom Clark later said, "it would have changed things a lot." [42] Several other justices expressed resentment at Eisenhower's failure to support the *Brown* decision.[43]

President Kennedy played a very different role in the controversy over *Engel v. Vitale* (1962), the first of the decisions that declared school prayer exercises to be unconstitutional. Asked about the decision, Kennedy responded:

> The Supreme Court has made its judgment. Some will disagree and others will agree. In the efforts we're making to maintain our Constitutional principles, we will have to abide by what the Supreme Court says. We have a very easy remedy here, and that is to pray ourselves.[44]

While Kennedy's statement certainly did not produce perfect compliance with the Court's decision, it may have increased the level of compliance marginally.

Presidential Compliance. Occasionally a Supreme Court decision requires compliance by the president, either as a party in the case or—more often—as the person who controls action by a federal agency involved in litigation. Some presidents and commentators have argued that the president need not accede to an order of the Supreme Court, which is only a coequal body rather than a legal superior. Indeed, in a few instances presidents have indicated that they would not obey an adverse decision in a pending case. Franklin Roosevelt did so twice, in a 1935 challenge to New Deal legislation that limited gold backing for the dollar and in a 1942 challenge to his establishment of a military tribunal to try eight alleged German saboteurs.[45] In both of these cases a confrontation was avoided when the Court ruled in favor of the president.

In terms of physical power, the president would seem to be in a position to disobey the Court with impunity. In reality, the president's position is not quite that strong. The political power of the president is rather amorphous, based largely on the capacity to obtain support from other policy makers. This capacity in turn is dependent in part on perceptions of the president's legitimacy. Disobedience of the Court would threaten this legitimacy. For this reason, Samuel Krislov has argued that presidents "cannot afford to defy the Court." [46]

That statement is supported by the presidential response to the two most visible Court orders in this century. In *Youngstown Sheet and Tube Co. v. Sawyer* (1952) the Court ruled that President Truman had acted illegally in seizing steel mills to keep them operating during a wartime strike and ordered that they be released. The president immediately complied.

The case of President Nixon's tape recordings, *United States v. Nixon,* is even more striking. During congressional and judicial investigation of the Watergate episode in 1973, the existence of recordings of the president's conversations in his offices was made public. Nixon released edited transcripts of selections from the recordings in April 1974. But Leon Jaworski, the special prosecutor in the Watergate cases, sought access to the recordings that were being withheld.

Jaworski won this point in federal district court, and the case went to the Supreme Court on an expedited appeal in July 1974. During oral argument James St. Clair, the president's counsel, indicated that Nixon might not comply with an adverse decision. Shortly afterward, the Court ruled against Nixon by a unanimous vote.

Apparently, Nixon briefly considered noncompliance with the decision. Then it was announced that the president would comply. The administration sent the recordings to the district court as required, and in early August it released transcripts of the tapes to the public. Information in the transcripts provided strong evidence of presidential misdeeds, especially an effort by Nixon to halt the investigation of the Watergate break-in primarily for political reasons. Support for Nixon against impeachment evaporated, and three days after the transcripts became public he announced his resignation.

Why did President Nixon comply with the Court when the result was to assure his removal from office? He apparently did not realize how damning the evidence in the tapes actually was. Just as important, however, noncompliance would have damaged his remaining legitimacy fatally. For many members of Congress noncompliance in itself would have constituted an impeachable offense, one on which there would be no dispute about the evidence. Under the circumstances it was not necessarily irrational for the president to comply with the Court's order to yield the tapes.

This episode suggests that even an official as powerful as the president cannot disobey a direct order from the Court with impunity. Indeed, the president probably is in a particularly weak position to do so because of the need for public legitimacy. In any case, the compliance by President Nixon creates a powerful precedent for similar compliance by future presidents.

State Legislatures and Governors

State governments have no direct powers over the Supreme Court as an institution. They interact with the Court primarily through their responses to decisions that strike down statutes or other government policies at the state level. These responses help to determine how decisions are implemented and their ultimate impact on state policy.

Since the 1950s the most visible responses of legislatures and governors to the Supreme Court have been efforts to overturn or limit the impact of major decisions. State governments have responded positively to some decisions; for instance, legislatures allocated a good deal of money to help fund legal services for indigent criminal defendants after *Gideon v. Wainwright* (1963) required that such services be available. But negative responses, including many that were legally questionable, have been prominent.

Like Congress, state legislatures can rewrite statutes to try to meet the Court's constitutional objections. An important recent example involves capital punishment. In *Furman v. Georgia* (1972), the Court held that the death penalty statutes which existed in 39 states violated the constitutional prohibition against cruel and unusual punishment. The decision was confusing because each member of the 5-4 majority wrote a separate opinion. But the Court's primary objection to the statutes seemed to be the arbitrary and capricious manner in which some defendants were singled out to receive the death penalty.

After the *Furman* decision, 35 states adopted new capital punishment laws that were designed to avoid the problem of arbitrary sentencing. The new statutes took various forms. In *Gregg v. Georgia* (1976) and four other 1976 decisions, the Court upheld some of the new statutes and overturned others. Its opinions in those cases also provided guidelines under which the new laws that it had found unacceptable could be further revised to establish capital punishment once again. As a result, the impact of *Furman* has largely been blunted.

The states' responses to *Furman* were legitimate efforts to reestablish a policy under Supreme Court rules. But state legislatures also have been willing to adopt laws of dubious constitutionality in order to limit the Court's impact. A striking example is the body of Southern statutes designed to prevent school desegregation in the decade after *Brown v. Board of Education*. During one period of several weeks at the end of 1960, the Louisiana legislature passed more than 40 laws to maintain segregation in New Orleans, all of which were overturned by the federal courts. Another example is state statutes that simply reinstated school religious observances which the Supreme Court had declared unconstitutional.

On abortion, state legislative action has been quite diverse. After the Court struck down state prohibitions of abortion in 1973, most states adopted laws to regulate abortion. Many of these laws were neutral regulations of a sort clearly acceptable to the Court, such as a requirement that abortions be performed by licensed physicians. But other laws were motivated by disagreement with the Court's ruling and a desire to limit its impact by making abortions more difficult to obtain. Rhode Island sought to nullify the Court's decision altogether with a new statute. Ultimately, lower federal courts and the Court itself overturned much of this restrictive legislation. However, the Court did allow states as well as Congress to limit government funding of abortions.

Governors, like presidents, help to determine legislative responses to the Court and the general atmosphere in which decisions are carried out. Southern governors such as Orval Faubus of Arkansas and George Wallace of Alabama helped to block school desegregation in the 1950s and 1960s through their efforts to stir up resistance. Governors also have been prominent in state controversies over the school prayer and abortion decisions, most often in opposition to the Court.

When Congress proposes constitutional amendments to overturn Supreme Court decisions, the states are responsible for ratifying the amendments. State legislatures also can play a role in the proposal stage. Article V of the Constitution allows amendments to be proposed by a convention, called into being by Congress on the application of two-thirds of the state legislatures. This procedure has never been used. But in the last quarter century large numbers of state legislatures have adopted various resolutions asking for conventions to consider limiting or over-turning controversial Supreme Court decisions. Thirty-two states, two fewer than the required number, proposed a convention to override the decisions of the 1960s on state legislative apportionment. Several legislatures have adopted resolutions calling for a convention to deal with the issue of abortion or with busing to achieve school integration. (In addition, a great many states have asked for a convention to consider a balanced budget amendment, unrelated to Supreme Court decisions.) A number of questions concerning the procedures for a convention remain unresolved.

It is difficult to compare the responses of state legislatures and governors to Supreme Court decisions with congressional and presidential responses. Perhaps the clearest difference is that state governments engage in more direct defiance of Court decisions. This difference may result from the sheer number of states rather than from differences between state and federal officials in their attitudes toward the Court. Even so, it suggests that the Court may face special difficulties when it seeks to bring about fundamental changes in state policies.

Impact on Society

A General View

The Importance of Societal Impact. Supreme Court decisions are directed at other public policy makers, establishing legal rules to govern policy decisions within government. But the ultimate importance of the Court's decisions rests primarily on their impact outside government, on American society as a whole. For example, the Court's rulings in antitrust law are important chiefly because of their potential effects on the structure of industries; its decisions on sex discrimination, because of their impact on the status of women. The responses of other policy makers to Supreme Court decisions can be considered a kind of intermediate step, albeit a crucial one.

One way to assess the impact of the Court on society is in terms of the goals that seem to underlie the Court's policies. The Supreme Court generally does not proclaim long-term goals in its opinions. However, the intent of the justices often is fairly clear from what the Court does. *Brown v. Board of Education* certainly was intended to improve the quality of education for black children and eventually to improve the status of blacks in American life. Some of the Court's antitrust decisions have been efforts to increase competition in particular sectors of the economy. Beginning with these implicit goals, we may examine the Court's success in advancing them.

Yet the Court's effects are not limited to those intended by its members. Critics of decisions often charge that the Court's efforts to serve one goal damage the achievement of another. Decisions that support the rights of criminal defendants, for instance, may be seen as leading to increases in crime rates. On another level, a Supreme Court policy can influence the course of action by political and social groups. The Court's decision in *Roe v. Wade,* for instance, helped to bring about a mass antiabortion movement in the United States. As these examples suggest, it is important to look widely in order to gauge the Court's full effects on American society.

Assessing the Court's Impact. Observers of the Supreme Court often ascribe tremendous impact to its decisions. This is especially true of people who disapprove of the Court's policies. Thus two conservative commentators who reviewed the work of Justice William Brennan reached a striking conclusion: "To the extent that the America of 1984 is different from the America of 1956," Brennan "is in significant part responsible." [47] George Wallace in 1972 painted a bleak picture of what had happened as a result of the Court's school prayer decisions:

> Public school prayer has been nearly nonexistent for the past eight years. What has happened in those eight years? Crime, especially juvenile crime, has risen at a most alarming rate. Eight years ago, drug abuse in schools was almost unheard of; today it is an epidemic. Our nation's moral fabric has been rotting away—as evidenced by the hard-core pornographic filth that now flourishes on our newsstands and in our theaters. This may be coincidence, but I don't think so. [48]

Such statements deserve a degree of skepticism, for they seem to ignore limits on the Court's impact. In reality, the effects of Supreme

Court decisions on society are constrained a great deal by the context in which those policies operate.

Part of that context is governmental. As we have seen, the impact of decisions is often narrowed by other policy makers who fail to implement them fully or who take other action to limit them. George Wallace's complaints about the consequences of the school prayer decisions lose some force in light of the reality that school religious observances were *not* "nearly nonexistent" after the Court prohibited them.

More generally, the Court seldom is the only government agency that deals with a particular set of issues. Rather, in most areas the Court is one policy maker among many that make decisions and undertake initiatives. In the regulation of labor-management relations, for instance, Congress sets the basic rules, administrative agencies elaborate on these rules and apply them to specific cases, and lower courts resolve most disagreements over agency decisions. The Court's participation is limited to the resolution of a few legal questions that arise in the lower courts. Under these circumstances, the Court hardly could determine the character of labor relations by itself.

The Court's policies also operate within a context of nongovernment action. Even the direct impact of most decisions depends largely on the responses of people outside government.[49] Decisions often have beneficiaries such as businesses that gain favorable tax rules or hospitals that become free to provide abortions. These beneficiaries may or may not take full advantage of the opportunities that the Court provides them. By the same token, people who are affected negatively by a Court policy may fail to comply or may take other action to minimize its effects. For instance, parents who oppose school busing can react to a busing order by moving to a different school district or enrolling their children in private schools.

Nongovernment forces also are important in determining the broad impact of Supreme Court decisions on society. Phenomena such as crime and sex discrimination are affected by family socialization, the mass media, and the economy. These kinds of forces are likely to exert a more fundamental impact on the propensity to commit crimes or to discriminate than does a Supreme Court policy. The effects that the Court does have will occur within the context of more basic and more powerful influences.

This limitation is one common to all public policies, whatever their sources. The effects of government, good or bad, are constrained by other social forces. We have learned in recent years that government policies have only a limited capacity to reduce crime or to strengthen the economy. But the Supreme Court is in an especially weak position to shape American society, because it has little direct control over behavior in the private sector and because it seldom makes comprehensive policy in a particular area.

All this does not mean that Supreme Court decisions have no impact on society. Frequently their direct impact is considerable, and they may play a part in shaping important social phenomena. It does mean, however, that we should not expect the Court generally to have an overwhelming effect. Nor should we declare that the Court's policies have failed because their impact is limited.

Problems in Determining Impact. The forces that limit and channel the Court's impact also make it difficult to ascertain that impact. Social changes that appear to result from Supreme Court decisions may have been caused, at least in part, by other policy makers or by events outside government. For this reason the effects of the Court's policies must be investigated carefully rather than assumed.

A good example is the tremendous growth in the number of legal abortions since 1970. The Supreme Court struck down state prohibitions on abortion in 1973, so we might assume that the Court was responsible for the change in the abortion rate. But the picture is not that simple.[50] Changing social attitudes led a large minority of states to ease restrictions on abortion prior to 1973, and the sharpest increase in legal abortions occurred in the pre-1973 period. If the Supreme Court had not acted, the process of legal change would have continued. Indeed, the Court's decision helped to mobilize opposition to abortion that in turn led to new limits on access to abortion in some states. Although the Court has affected the abortion rate, then, its effect has been more limited than we might have predicted in 1973 and less extensive than the increase in legal abortions suggests.

Thus the task of determining the Court's impact is not easy. But it is possible to reach some tentative conclusions about the effects of Supreme Court policies in particular areas. Two important areas that illustrate some aspects of the Court's impact are black civil rights and freedom of expression.

Black Civil Rights

Chapter 5 discussed the high level of support that the Supreme Court has given to the civil rights of blacks since the 1940s. This support has not been total, and it has declined markedly from its peak in the 1960s. But the general thrust of the Court's policies has been quite favorable by most measures. The Court has supported civil rights in substantive areas such as education and voting. It also did much to protect the civil rights movement when the movement came under attack in the South in the 1950s and 1960s.

The implicit goal that underlies the Court's work in this area has been improvement of the status of blacks in American society. To what extent have the Court's policies actually furthered that goal? Although that question cannot be answered with certainty, we can get some sense of the Court's contribution.

Change in the Status of Blacks. The process of change in the situation of black Americans has been complex and ambiguous. Understandably, commentators disagree as to how much blacks have gained since the 1940s. Perhaps the best generalization is that progress has varied among the major areas of black disadvantage.

The clearest change has been political. Black political power has grown tremendously in the past three decades. One important reason is the increased ability of Southern blacks to vote. In 11 Southern states, 29 percent of the nonwhite adults were registered to vote in 1960; by 1982, 57 percent of the black adults were registered.[51] Another is the development of a vastly strengthened civil rights movement. The growth in political power is reflected in the increase in black elected officials from about 100 in 1964 to 5,100 in 1982.[52] Another reflection is a growing willingness of white officials to respond to black concerns. Some former advocates of white supremacy, such as Senator Strom Thurmond of South Carolina, now feel compelled to seek black votes.

Socially, the segregation of American life has broken down to some degree. Dual school systems no longer exist in the Deep South and Border states. Black access to accommodations in hotels and restaurants has improved tremendously throughout the country. But education in practice remains largely segregated in much of the United States, including many large Northern cities. Nationally, 18 percent of all nonwhite public school students attended schools whose enrollments were less than 1 percent white in 1980.[53] This segregation in turn results in part from continuing segregation of housing. It is in the area of housing that discrimination has been most unyielding.

Economic status may be the most important issue of all, because of its own significance and its implications for social and political gains. Here the picture is confused and a matter of heated debate. By some measures, there has been an improvement in economic equality. But the average income of blacks remains a good deal lower than that of whites; in 1982 the median income for black families was about $13,600, compared with $24,600 for white families.[54] As these figures suggest, a disproportionate number of blacks live in poverty. On the basis of this continuing disparity and other measures, some observers argue that the change in black economic status has been minimal.

The Court's Role. To some degree, at least, the position of blacks has improved. How much of this improvement can be ascribed to the

Supreme Court? Certainly the Court has worked alongside other important sources of change. Particularly during the 1960s, Congress and the federal executive branch made some significant contributions to equal rights. So did state and local governments in much of the country. Nongovernment forces for change include the mass media and, more important, the civil rights movement itself.

The limits of the Court's impact are clear in the two substantive areas in which it has been most active, education and voting. Despite *Brown v. Board of Education,* school segregation in the Deep South did not break down until the Civil Rights Act of 1964 provided financial inducements for desegregation. The Court's decisions eliminated some barriers to black voting, but those decisions did not bring about full access to the ballot box in the South. That access came after the Voting Rights Act of 1965 created administrative mechanisms for effective enforcement of the right to vote.

The Court has played a more limited role in some other areas, including employment and housing. In both of these areas the major government initiatives in support of black rights came from the legislative and executive branches. Because constitutional protections do not apply directly to private discrimination, the Court's activity has been limited chiefly to interpretations of federal legislation. If government has contributed to an improvement in black economic status, it is primarily Congress that is responsible.

But it would be a mistake to dismiss the Court's impact on black Americans as unimportant. Indeed, it can be argued that the Court's decisions in this field were of central importance in bringing about federal legislation on civil rights and strengthening the civil rights movement itself. This is particularly true of the *Brown* decision, which was a tremendously important symbol despite its problems of implementation.

The development of the mass civil rights movement in the South probably was inevitable. But the Court speeded that development. Its decisions in education and other areas created hope for change and established rights to be vindicated by political action. Its protection for the movement itself did not eliminate harassment of civil rights groups in the South or violence against their members, but the Court did help to ensure that the movement was able to withstand the pressures against it.

The series of civil rights laws that were adopted from 1957 on also owes much to the Court. In the areas of education and voting the Court initiated government action against discrimination and helped to create expectations that Congress and the executive branch were pressed to fulfill. It is true that congressional action was most directly responsible for bringing about school desegregation in the Deep South. But if the Court had not made the *Brown* decision, Congress might have had no impetus to act against segregation at all. After civil rights legislation was adopted, the Court affirmed the validity of laws that were challenged and increased their effectiveness through a general pattern of broad interpretations, at least until recently.

General Assessment. The example of black civil rights illustrates both the strengths and limitations of government in society. Public policy has helped to bring about significant reductions in the disadvantages of blacks. Yet these disadvantages hardly have been wiped out, and even a stronger government commitment to equality could not have eliminated them altogether.

For the Supreme Court specifically, the assessment also is mixed. The Court has had little direct impact on discrimination in the private sector. Even in the public sector it has been weak in the enforcement of rights. But it has played a major role in initiating and supporting processes of change, and its members certainly can take some credit for improvements in the status of black Americans. If the Court's effects have been more limited than many observers had hoped, still the Court has demonstrated a capacity to contribute to significant social change.

Freedom of Expression

The Supreme Court's policies on freedom of expression issues have been less consistent than its policies on black civil rights. But since the 1940s the Court has done much to expand legal protection for speech and writing. Certainly the Court has been far more supportive of First Amendment rights than the other branches of government, whose policies frequently have been antagonistic to these rights. How much impact has this line of policy had on the effective state of freedom in the United States? [55]

The Court's Policies. To answer this question, it is necessary first of all to examine briefly the Court's work in this field. There are several areas in which the Court has been active in providing legal protection for expression. One is the area of conflict between freedom of expression and national security. During the cold war era, the Court gave mixed support to the constitutional rights of persons who were accused of subversive activities and associations. Later, during the war in Vietnam, the Court was more consistent in protecting freedom of expression for opponents of the war.

A second area might be called "public speech." It involves efforts by local authorities to restrict picketing, demonstrations, speeches, and other forms of expression in public places. The Court has acted against arbitrary prohibitions of these activities that authorities justify by the need to maintain public order.

A third area is that of "commercial speech." In 1976 the Court overturned a long-standing doctrine and held that expression which is commercial in nature enjoys broad constitutional protection.[56] Since that time the Court has loosened government restraints on such commercial expression as advertising by attorneys.

Two other areas affect primarily the print media. Beginning with its decision in *New York Times Co. v. Sullivan* (1964), the Court established rules that limited the ability of public officials and public figures to bring libel suits. In doing so it broadened the freedom of newspapers and magazines to comment on public issues.

In the area of obscenity, the Court has taken a series of complicated and contradictory positions, but since the late 1950s it has been consistent in giving government only limited power to censor materials or to prosecute on grounds of obscenity. The Burger Court has been more favorable to regulation of obscenity than was the Warren Court. But its guidelines for the definition of obscenity, though less protective of expression than those of the Warren Court, indicated that only the most offensive and least serious material may be held obscene.[57]

The Court's Effects. It is not possible to speak precisely about the impact of these policies, but it is possible to reach some general conclusions. To begin with, it appears that the Court has expanded freedom in practice as well as legal rights in each of the five areas that I discussed.

For instance, the Court's protection of people who opposed the war in Vietnam probably encouraged the open expression of dissent. This was particularly true of its decisions which disallowed retaliation by the Selective Service System against antiwar protesters.[58] By increasing the safety of opposition to American policy, the Court may have contributed subtly to the growth of the antiwar movement.

In obscenity cases the Court has contributed to a general trend toward freer publication and distribution of materials containing sexual matter. The Court's decisions have been only one element in a general process of social change. But by reducing the risk of successful prosecution for obscenity the Court has had an impact on the practices of groups such as booksellers.

Yet the Court's policies on freedom of expression have not eliminated all constraints on speech and writing. Efforts by public and private authorities to suppress or punish expression remain common. The press and the American Civil Liberties Union regularly report actions such as the following:[59]

—The Customs Bureau and the Federal Bureau of Investigation seized 11 books on U.S. involvement in Iran that journalists brought back with them from that country.

—Residents of an Oklahoma town who challenged school religious activities were subjected to harassment from townspeople, including death threats and a physical assault.

—The Texas Rangers, a major-league baseball team, fired its leading ballpark peanut vendor after he wrote a letter to the editor about the team's cutting of commissions for vendors.

While these examples are not "typical," they remind us that the Court's impact on the state of freedom has not been overwhelming.

Explaining the Court's Limited Impact. Why has the Supreme Court not had a greater effect in this area? There appear to be several reasons. First, the Court's support for freedom of expression has been limited both in degree and in scope. By no means has the Court invalidated all governmental restrictions on expression. For instance, it has limited prosecutions for obscenity but has not prohibited them altogether. Some important government policies that limit freedom of expression, such as surveillance of political dissenters, have hardly been restricted at all by the Court.

Second, implementation of the Court's decisions frequently has been quite imperfect. On some issues such as libel of public figures the Court's own vagueness and vacillation have made implementation difficult. Even where the Court is clear, strong-minded officials sometimes choose to ignore its rulings. Some movie censorship boards have operated in violation of the Court's guidelines. And local officials occasionally restrict demonstrations in ways that the Court has prohibited.

For these reasons people cannot feel entirely safe from punishment for what they speak or write. Despite the Court's decisions, a person who protested against the war in Vietnam still might suffer government harassment or even prosecution. Similarly, the producer of a motion picture can take only limited comfort in the Court's liberal guidelines on obscenity. In the early 1970s a prosecutor, trial jury, and state supreme court in Georgia all agreed that the movie *Carnal Knowledge* was obscene, despite the fact that the film—a Hollywood product of recognized merit—clearly was not obscene according to the criteria established by the Court.[60]

But the most important limitation on the Court's impact concerns restrictions on freedom of expression from nongovernment sources. People may refrain from expressing themselves because they fear that their friends and neighbors will ostracize them, community groups will attack them, or employers will fire them. Economic pressures may be the most significant, especially when an employer wishes to restrict an employee's expression. As one employer said, "Freedom of speech isn't carte blanche when you're taking someone's money."[61]

The courts have little control over these private restrictions on freedom. With a few exceptions, primarily in the area of labor-management relations, there are no legal protections for expression against action by private authorities. Certainly, the courts can do nothing directly to keep unpopular expressions from making people unpopular. The Court's pronouncements on freedom of expression might have an indirect impact on the private sector by building public support for free expression, but there is little evidence of such an effect.

General Assessment. The Supreme Court has had a real impact on freedom of expression. At least some groups in society—booksellers, critics of public officials, dissenters against American foreign policy— have had more freedom because of the Court's decisions. But Supreme Court support for First Amendment rights has not brought about total protection for speaking and writing. Indeed, the constraints that remain seem much more important than those that the Court has eliminated.

In some respects this picture parallels what has happened in the field of black civil rights. There is at least one important difference, however. In civil rights the Court's policies have been reinforced by other institutions working in the same direction, including Congress and a major social movement to achieve racial equality. In freedom of expression the Court has lacked that kind of reinforcement. The private forces that support free expression, such as the ACLU, are hardly comparable in strength with the civil rights movement. The other branches of government tend to restrict freedom of expression rather than working for it. In this situation, the Court's impact necessarily has been a modest one.

The Court, Public Policy, and Society

It is now possible to reach some general conclusions about the role of the Supreme Court as a public policy maker. As the material in these last two chapters suggests, that role is fundamentally limited in some respects but nonetheless quite important.

The most obvious limitation on the Court's role lies in the small number of issues that it addresses. In a great many policy areas, including some of the most important, the Court rarely makes decisions. The Court is at most a minor participant in the making of foreign policy, to use the most notable example. Moreover, it takes only a small part in a good many areas of "legal" policy, such as contract law and family relations.

Even in the areas in which the Court specializes, its intervention into the policy-making process is limited. It addresses only a small sample of the issues that arise concerning the rights of criminal defendants or freedom of expression. Its intervention also is limited in the sense that it has been cautious about substituting its judgment for that of Congress and the president.

Where the Court does intervene, its impact may be minimized by the actions of other institutions and individuals. A ruling that schools must eliminate prayer exercises does not guarantee that those exercises will disappear. Efforts to broaden freedom of expression may be stymied by conditions in government and society that the Court cannot reach.

These limitations must be balanced against the Court's strengths. At a specific level, a great many Supreme Court decisions have significant effects. The Court's school desegregation decisions in cities such as Dayton and Detroit have determined whether or not thousands of students are enrolled in schools outside their neighborhoods. The Court's 1976 decision on federal regulation of campaign financing has affected the course of each presidential election campaign since that time. Many more examples could be cited.

The Court also plays a large part in major processes of change in society. While the impact of *Roe v. Wade* (1973) often is exaggerated, that decision nonetheless has been the centerpiece of a national struggle over a major issue. The Court's opposition to government control over private business ultimately was unsuccessful, but it succeeded in delaying a fundamental change in the role of government. The Court's decisions have not brought about equality for black citizens, even in conjunction with other forces, but they have effected real improvement in the status of blacks.

The Court is perhaps most important in creating the conditions for action by others. Its decisions put issues on the national agenda so that other policy makers and the general public consider them. The Court generally does not do well in enforcing rights, but it often legitimates efforts to achieve them and thus provides the impetus for legal and political action. The Court's decisions affect the positions of interest groups and social movements, strengthening some and weakening others.

The Supreme Court, then, is neither all-powerful nor insignificant. It is one of many public and private institutions that shape American society in significant ways. That is a smaller role than some have claimed for the Court. But the role that the Court does play is an extraordinary one for a single small body that holds little concrete power. In this sense, perhaps more than any other, the Supreme Court is a remarkable institution.

Notes

1. *Mata v. Sumner,* 649 F.2d 713, 718 (9th Cir. 1981).
2. *Cascade Natural Gas Corp. v. El Paso Natural Gas Co.* (1967).

3. Much of the history is laid out in the final Florida Supreme Court decision, *State ex rel. Hawkins v. Board of Control* (Fla. Sup. Ct. 1957). The U.S. Supreme Court decisions are under the title *Florida ex rel. Hawkins v. Board of Control* (1954, 1956, 1957).

4. Walter Williams, *Social Policy Research and Analysis* (New York: American Elsevier Publishers, 1971), 11.

5. Harrell R. Rodgers, Jr., and Charles S. Bullock III, *Law and Social Change: Civil Rights Laws and Their Consequences* (New York: McGraw-Hill Book Co., 1972), 75.

6. *Milliken v. Bradley* (1974); *Pasadena Board of Education v. Spangler* (1976).

7. Note, "Stepping into the Breach: Basing Defendants' Rights on State Rather Than Federal Law," *American Criminal Law Review* 15 (Spring 1978): 339-381.

8. Michael Wald et al., "Interrogations in New Haven: The Impact of *Miranda*," *Yale Law Journal* 76 (July 1967): 1519-1648; Richard J. Medalie, Leonard Zeitz, and Paul Alexander, "Custodial Police Interrogation in Our Nation's Capital: The Attempt to Implement *Miranda*," *Michigan Law Review* 66 (May 1968): 1347-1422.

9. Lawrence S. Leiken, "Police Interrogation in Colorado: The Implementation of *Miranda*," *Denver Law Journal* 47 (1970): 1-53.

10. James S. Kunen, *"How Can You Defend Those People?": The Making of a Criminal Lawyer* (New York: Random House, 1983), 132.

11. Bradley C. Canon, "Is the Exclusionary Rule in Failing Health? Some New Data and a Plea Against a Precipitous Conclusion," *Kentucky Law Journal* 62 (1974): 702-725.

12. Jerome H. Skolnick, *Justice Without Trial: Law Enforcement in Democratic Society* (New York: John Wiley & Sons, 1966), 164-181; Comment, "Effect of *Mapp v. Ohio* on Police Search-and-Seizure Practices in Narcotics Cases," *Columbia Journal of Law and Social Problems* 4 (1968): 87-104.

13. Thomas Y. Davies, "A Hard Look at What We Know (and Still Need to Learn) About the 'Costs' of the Exclusionary Rule: The NIJ Study and Other Studies of 'Lost' Arrests," *American Bar Foundation Research Journal* (Summer 1983): 611-690.

14. H. Frank Way, Jr., "Survey Research on Judicial Decisions: The Prayer and Bible Reading Cases," *Western Political Quarterly* 21 (June 1968): 191.

15. The quotation is from *Jaffree v. Board of School Commissioners,* 554 F. Supp. 1104, 1128 (S.D. Alab. 1983). The decision on appeal was *Jaffree v. Wallace* (11th Cir. 1983).

16. *Richmond Newspapers, Inc. v. Virginia* (1980).

17. Carol E. Jenson, *The Network of Control: State Supreme Courts and State Security Statutes, 1920-1970* (Westport, Conn.: Greenwood Press, 1982).

18. J. W. Peltason, *Fifty-Eight Lonely Men: Southern Federal Judges and School Desegregation,* 2d ed. (Urbana: University of Illinois Press, 1971), 246.

19. Stephen L. Wasby, *The Impact of the United States Supreme Court: Some Perspectives* (Homewood, Ill.: Dorsey Press, 1970), 94-95.

20. Bradley C. Canon and Kenneth Kolson, "Rural Compliance with Gault: Kentucky, a Case Study," *Journal of Family Law* 10 (1971): 300-326.

21. Larry C. Berkson, *The Supreme Court and Its Publics* (Lexington, Mass: Lexington Books, 1978), 79-86.
22. *State v. Gerardo,* 250 A.2d 130, 131 (N.J. Sup. Ct. 1969).
23. *Salt Lake City v. Piepenburg,* 571 P.2d 1299 (Utah Sup. Ct. 1977).
24. Neal Milner, "Comparative Analysis of Patterns of Compliance with Supreme Court Decisions: *Miranda* and the Police in Four Communities," *Law & Society Review* 5 (August 1970): 126.
25. Peltason, *Fifty-Eight Lonely Men,* 9.
26. "Parents Stage Demonstration," *New Orleans Times Picayune,* November 24, 1960, quoted in Robert Coles, *Children of Crisis: A Study of Courage and Fear* (Boston: Little, Brown, 1967), 385, n. 2. Used by permission of Associated Press.
27. Sheldon Goldman, "Conflict and Consensus in the United States Courts of Appeals," *Wisconsin Law Review* (1968): 477.
28. See Charles A. Johnson, "Follow-Up Decisions by Lower Federal Courts" (Paper delivered at annual meeting of the Law and Society Association, Denver, June 1983).
29. Interview by the author with a federal appellate judge.
30. Grace Lichtenstein, "Utah's Conservative Court Center of Dispute over Rulings," *New York Times,* November 30, 1975, 63.
31. William K. Muir, Jr., *Prayer in the Public Schools: Law and Attitude Change* (Chicago: University of Chicago Press, 1967); Richard Johnson, *The Dynamics of Compliance* (Evanston, Ill.: Northwestern University Press, 1967).
32. George D. Braden, "Legal Research: A Variation on an Old Lament," *Journal of Legal Education* 5 (1952): 41, n. 1.
33. J. Woodford Howard, Jr., *Courts of Appeals in the Federal Judicial System: A Study of the Second, Fifth, and District of Columbia Circuits* (Princeton: Princeton University Press, 1981), 140, n. j.
34. *United States v. Shipp* (1909).
35. Beth Henschen, "Statutory Interpretations of the Supreme Court: Congressional Response," *American Politics Quarterly* 11 (October 1983): 444-446; Note, "Congressional Reversal of Supreme Court Decisions: 1945-1957," *Harvard Law Review* 71 (May 1958): 1324-1337.
36. *Pfizer, Inc. v. Government of India* (1978).
37. David N. Atkinson, "Justice Sherman Minton and Behavior Patterns Inside the Supreme Court," *Northwestern University Law Review* 69 (November-December 1974): 733.
38. *McCarty v. McCarty,* 453 U.S. 210, 235-236 (1981).
39. U.S. Congress, House, *Congressional Record,* 84th Cong., 2d sess., 1956, 102, pt. 5:6385.
40. Dean L. Yarwood and Bradley C. Canon, "On the Supreme Court's Annual Trek to the Capitol," *Judicature* 63 (February 1980): 324.
41. U.S. Congress, House, *Congressional Record,* 89th Cong., 1st sess., 1965, 111, pt. 4:5275. The misspelling of "Sims" was in the *Record.*
42. Richard Kluger, *Simple Justice: The History of Brown v. Board of Education and Black America's Struggle for Equality* (New York: Alfred A. Knopf, 1976), 753.

43. Bernard Schwartz, *Super Chief: Earl Warren and His Supreme Court—A Judicial Biography* (New York: New York University Press, 1983), 175.
44. "Transcript of President's News Conference on Foreign and Domestic Affairs," *New York Times,* June 28, 1962, 12.
45. *Norman v. Baltimore and Ohio Railroad Co.* (1935); *Ex parte Quirin* (1942).
46. Samuel Krislov, *The Supreme Court in the Political Process* (New York: Macmillan, 1965), 140.
47. Stephen J. Markman and Alfred S. Regnery, "The Mind of Justice Brennan: A 25-Year Tribute," *National Review,* May 18, 1984, 31.
48. Jack Bass and Walter De Vries, *The Transformation of Southern Politics* (New York: Basic Books, 1976), 67.
49. Charles A. Johnson and Bradley C. Canon, *Judicial Policies: Implementation and Impact* (Washington, D.C.: CQ Press, 1984), ch. 4.
50. Susan B. Hansen, "State Implementation of Supreme Court Decisions: Abortion Rates Since *Roe v. Wade,*" *Journal of Politics* 42 (May 1980): 372-395; Michael Barone, "The Court's Politics Backfired," *Washington Post,* September 1, 1983, A23.
51. U.S. Bureau of the Census, *Statistical Abstract of the United States: 1984* (Washington, D.C.: Government Printing Office, 1983), 261.
52. Charles S. Bullock III and Harrell R. Rodgers, Jr., *Racial Equality in America* (Pacific Palisades, Calif.: Goodyear Publishing Co., 1975), 172; Bureau of the Census, *Statistical Abstract of the United States: 1984,* 261.
53. Bureau of the Census, *Statistical Abstract of the United States: 1984,* 149.
54. U.S. Bureau of the Census, Current Population Reports, Series P-60, No. 142, *Money Income of Households, Families, and Persons in the United States: 1982* (Washington, D.C.: Government Printing Office, 1984), 35-36.
55. The discussion that follows draws in part from Samuel Krislov, *The Supreme Court and Political Freedom* (New York: Free Press, 1968), 165-200.
56. *Virginia State Board of Pharmacy v. Virginia Citizens Consumer Council* (1976).
57. *Miller v. California* (1973).
58. *Oestereich v. Selective Service System* (1968); *Gutknecht v. United States* (1970).
59. The incidents described below were reported in, respectively, *Civil Liberties,* the American Civil Liberties Union newsletter, February 1982, 2; *Civil Liberties,* June 1983, 10-11; and *The Sporting News,* May 14, 1984, 22.
60. *Jenkins v. Georgia* (1974).
61. Red Smith, "Grass on Buckwheat," *New York Times,* September 24, 1979, C-3.

Glossary

Legal Terms Related to the Supreme Court

Affirm. In an appellate court, to reach a decision that agrees with the result reached in the case by the lower court.

Amicus curiae. "Friend of the court." A person, private group or institution, or government agency, not a party to a case, that participates in the case (usually through submission of a brief) at the invitation of the court or at its own initiative.

Appeal. In general, a case brought to a higher court for review. In the Supreme Court, certain cases are designated as appeals under federal law; formally, these must be heard by the Court.

Appellant. The party that appeals a lower court decision to a higher court.

Appellee. A party to an appeal who wishes to have the lower court decision upheld and who responds when the case is appealed.

Brief. A document submitted by counsel to a court, setting out the facts of the case and the legal arguments in support of the party represented by the counsel.

Certiorari, Writ of. A writ issued by the Supreme Court, at its discretion, to order a lower court to prepare the record of a case and send it to the Supreme Court for review. Most cases come to the Court as petitions for writs of certiorari.

Civil cases. All legal cases other than criminal cases.

Class action. A lawsuit brought by one person or group on behalf of all persons in similar situations.

Concurring opinion. An opinion by a member of a court that agrees with the result reached by the court in the case but disagrees with or departs from the court's rationale for the decision.

Dicta. See Obiter dictum.

Discretionary jurisdiction. Jurisdiction that a court may accept or reject in particular cases. The Supreme Court has discretionary jurisdiction over most cases that come to it.

Dissenting opinion. An opinion by a member of a court that disagrees with the result reached by the court in the case.

Habeas corpus. "You have the body." A writ issued by a court to inquire whether a person is lawfully imprisoned or detained. The writ demands that the persons holding the prisoner justify the detention or release the prisoner.

In forma pauperis. "In the manner of a pauper." In the Supreme Court, cases brought in forma pauperis by indigent persons are exempt from the Court's usual fees and from some formal requirements.

Judicial review. Review of legislation or other governmental action to determine its consistency with the federal or state constitution, with the power to strike down policies that are inconsistent with the Constitution. The Supreme Court reviews governmental action only under the federal constitution.

Jurisdiction. The power of a court to hear a case in question.

Litigants. The parties to a court case.

Majority opinion. An opinion in a case that is subscribed to by a majority of the judges who participated in the decision. Also known as the opinion of the court.

Mandamus. "We command." An order issued by a court that directs a lower court or other authority to perform a particular act.

Mandatory jurisdiction. Jurisdiction that a court must accept. Cases falling under a court's mandatory jurisdiction must be decided officially on their merits, though a court may avoid giving them full consideration.

Modify. In an appellate court, to reach a decision that disagrees in part with the result reached in the case by the lower court.

Moot. A moot case is one which has become hypothetical, so that a court need not decide it.

Obiter dictum. (Also called dictum or dicta.) A statement in a court opinion that is not necessary to resolve the case before the court. Dicta are not binding in future cases.

Original jurisdiction. Jurisdiction as a trial court.

Per curiam. "By the court." An unsigned opinion of the court, often quite brief.

Petitioner. One who files a petition with a court seeking action or relief, such as a writ of certiorari.

Ratio decidendi. Statements in a court opinion that are necessary to resolve the case before the court. Such statements are binding in future cases.

Remand. To send back. When a case is remanded, it is sent back by a higher court to the court from which it came for further action.

Respondent. The party in opposition to a petitioner or appellant, who answers the claims of that party.

Reverse. In an appellate court, to reach a decision that disagrees with the result reached in the case by the lower court.

Standing. A requirement that the party who files a lawsuit have a legal stake in the outcome.

Stare decisis. "Let the decision stand." The doctrine that principles of law established in earlier judicial decisions should be accepted as authoritative in similar subsequent cases.

Statute. A written law enacted by a legislature.

Stay. To halt or suspend further judicial proceedings. The Supreme Court sometimes issues a stay to suspend action in a lower court while the Supreme Court considers the case.

Vacate. To make void or annul. The Supreme Court sometimes vacates a lower court decision, requiring the lower court to reconsider the case.

Writ. A written court order commanding the designated recipient to perform or not perform acts specified in the order.

Supreme Court Nominations, 1789-1983

Name	Nominated by	Service
John Jay	Washington	1789-1795
John Rutledge	Washington	1789-1791
William Cushing	Washington	1789-1810
Robert H. Harrison	Washington	(D, 1790)
James Wilson	Washington	1789-1798
John Blair	Washington	1789-1796
James Iredell	Washington	1790-1799
Thomas Johnson	Washington	1791-1793
William Paterson	Washington	(W, 1793)
William Paterson[a]	Washington	1793-1806
John Rutledge[b]	Washington	(R, 1795)
William Cushing[b]	Washington	(D, 1796)
Samuel Chase	Washington	1796-1811
Oliver Ellsworth	Washington	1796-1800
Bushrod Washington	J. Adams	1798-1829
Alfred Moore	J. Adams	1799-1804
John Jay[b]	J. Adams	(D, 1801)
John Marshall	J. Adams	1801-1835
William Johnson	Jefferson	1804-1834
H. Brockholst Livingston	Jefferson	1806-1823
Thomas Todd	Jefferson	1807-1826
Levi Lincoln	Madison	(D, 1811)
Alexander Wolcott	Madison	(R, 1811)
John Quincy Adams	Madison	(D, 1811)
Joseph Story	Madison	1811-1845
Gabriel Duval	Madison	1811-1835
Smith Thompson	Monroe	1823-1843

Name	*Nominated by*	*Service*
Robert Trimble	J. Q. Adams	1826-1828
John J. Crittenden	J. Q. Adams	(P, 1829)
John McLean	Jackson	1829-1861
Henry Baldwin	Jackson	1830-1844
James M. Wayne	Jackson	1835-1867
Roger B. Taney	Jackson	(P, 1835)
Roger B. Taney[a]	Jackson	1836-1864
Philip P. Barbour	Jackson	1836-1841
William Smith	Jackson	(D, 1837)
John Catron	Jackson	1837-1865
John McKinley	Van Buren	1837-1852
Peter V. Daniel	Van Buren	1841-1860
John C. Spencer	Tyler	(R, 1844)
Reuben H. Walworth	Tyler	(W, 1844)
Edward King	Tyler	(P, 1844)
Edward King[a]	Tyler	(W, 1845)
Samuel Nelson	Tyler	1845-1872
John M. Read	Tyler	No action
George W. Woodward	Polk	(R, 1846)
Levi Woodbury	Polk	1846-1851
Robert C. Grier	Polk	1846-1870
Benjamin R. Curtis	Fillmore	1851-1857
Edward A. Bradford	Fillmore	No action
George E. Badger	Fillmore	(P, 1853)
William C. Micou	Fillmore	No action
John A. Campbell	Pierce	1853-1861
Nathan Clifford	Buchanan	1858-1881
Jeremiah S. Black	Buchanan	(R, 1861)
Noah H. Swayne	Lincoln	1862-1881
Samuel F. Miller	Lincoln	1862-1890
David Davis	Lincoln	1862-1877
Stephen J. Field	Lincoln	1863-1897
Salmon P. Chase	Lincoln	1864-1873
Henry Stanbery	Johnson	No action
Ebenezer R. Hoar	Grant	(R, 1870)
Edwin M. Stanton[c]	Grant	1869
William Strong	Grant	1870-1880

Name	*Nominated by*	*Service*
Joseph P. Bradley	Grant	1870-1892
Ward Hunt	Grant	1872-1882
George H. Williams	Grant	(W, 1874)
Caleb Cushing	Grant	(W, 1874)
Morrison R. Waite	Grant	1874-1888
John M. Harlan	Hayes	1877-1911
William B. Woods	Hayes	1880-1887
Stanley Matthews	Hayes	No action
Stanley Matthews[a]	Garfield	1881-1889
Horace Gray	Arthur	1881-1902
Roscoe Conkling	Arthur	(D, 1882)
Samuel Blatchford	Arthur	1882-1893
Lucius Q. C. Lamar	Cleveland	1888-1893
Melville W. Fuller	Cleveland	1888-1910
David J. Brewer	Harrison	1889-1910
Henry B. Brown	Harrison	1890-1906
George Shiras Jr.	Harrison	1892-1903
Howell E. Jackson	Harrison	1893-1895
William B. Hornblower	Cleveland	(R, 1894)
Wheeler H. Peckham	Cleveland	(R, 1894)
Edward D. White	Cleveland	1894-1921
Rufus W. Peckham	Cleveland	1895-1909
Joseph McKenna	McKinley	1898-1925
Oliver W. Holmes	T. Roosevelt	1902-1932
William R. Day	T. Roosevelt	1903-1922
William H. Moody	T. Roosevelt	1906-1910
Horace H. Lurton	Taft	1909-1914
Edward D. White[b]	Taft	1910-1921
Charles E. Hughes	Taft	1910-1916
Willis Van Devanter	Taft	1910-1937
Joseph R. Lamar	Taft	1910-1916
Mahlon Pitney	Taft	1912-1922
James C. McReynolds	Wilson	1914-1941
Louis D. Brandeis	Wilson	1916-1939
John H. Clarke	Wilson	1916-1922
William H. Taft	Harding	1921-1930

Name	*Nominated by*	*Service*
George Sutherland	Harding	1922-1938
Pierce Butler	Harding	1922-1939
Edward T. Sanford	Harding	1923-1930
Harlan F. Stone	Coolidge	1925-1946
Charles E. Hughesb	Hoover	1930-1941
John J. Parker	Hoover	(R, 1930)
Owen J. Roberts	Hoover	1930-1945
Benjamin N. Cardozo	Hoover	1932-1938
Hugo L. Black	F. Roosevelt	1937-1971
Stanley F. Reed	F. Roosevelt	1938-1957
Felix Frankfurter	F. Roosevelt	1939-1962
William O. Douglas	F. Roosevelt	1939-1975
Frank Murphy	F. Roosevelt	1940-1949
Harlan F. Stoneb	F. Roosevelt	1941-1946
James F. Byrnes	F. Roosevelt	1941-1942
Robert H. Jackson	F. Roosevelt	1941-1954
Wiley B. Rutledge	F. Roosevelt	1943-1949
Harold H. Burton	Truman	1945-1958
Fred M. Vinson	Truman	1946-1953
Tom C. Clark	Truman	1949-1967
Sherman Minton	Truman	1949-1956
Earl Warren	Eisenhower	1953-1969
John M. Harlan	Eisenhower	1955-1971
William J. Brennan Jr.	Eisenhower	1956-
Charles E. Whittaker	Eisenhower	1957-1962
Potter Stewart	Eisenhower	1958-1981
Byron R. White	Kennedy	1962-
Arthur J. Goldberg	Kennedy	1962-1965
Abe Fortas	Johnson	1965-1969
Thurgood Marshall	Johnson	1967-
Abe Fortasb	Johnson	(W, 1968)
Homer Thornberry	Johnson	No action
Warren E. Burger	Nixon	1969-
Clement Haynsworth Jr.	Nixon	(R, 1969)
G. Harrold Carswell	Nixon	(R, 1970)
Harry A. Blackmun	Nixon	1970-
Lewis F. Powell Jr.	Nixon	1971-
William H. Rehnquist	Nixon	1971-

Name	*Nominated by*	*Service*
John Paul Stevens	Ford	1975-
Sandra Day O'Connor	Reagan	1981-

[a] Earlier nomination not confirmed.
[b] Earlier Court service.
[c] Died four days after confirmation.
Boldface type indicates nomination as chief justice.
(D) Declined
(P) Postponed
(R) Rejected
(W) Withdrawn

SOURCES: Leon Friedman and Fred L. Israel, eds., *The Justices of the United States Supreme Court, 1789-1969* (New York: R. R. Bowker Co., 1969); Executive Journal of the U.S. Senate, 1789-1975; *Guide to the U.S. Supreme Court* (Washington, D.C.: Congressional Quarterly Inc., 1979); updated by author.

Selected Bibliography

The books listed below may be useful to readers who would like to explore further the subjects discussed in this book. Books that are general in their subject matter are listed first, followed by books that are especially relevant to specific chapters.

General

Congressional Quarterly. *Guide to the U.S. Supreme Court.* Washington, D.C.: Congressional Quarterly Inc., 1979.

Douglas, William O. *The Court Years 1939-1975: The Autobiography of William O. Douglas.* New York: Random House, 1980.

Glick, Henry R. *Courts, Politics, and Justice.* New York: McGraw-Hill, 1983.

Goldman, Sheldon, and Jahnige, Thomas P. *The Federal Courts as a Political System,* 2d ed. New York: Harper & Row, 1976.

Goldman, Sheldon, and Sarat, Austin, eds. *American Court Systems: Readings in Judicial Process and Behavior.* San Francisco: W. H. Freeman & Co., 1978.

Jacob, Herbert. *Justice in America: Courts, Lawyers, and the Judicial Process,* 4th ed. Boston: Little, Brown & Co., 1984.

Krislov, Samuel. *The Supreme Court and Political Freedom.* New York: Free Press, 1968.

Lewis, Anthony. *Gideon's Trumpet.* New York: Random House, 1964.

Murphy, Bruce Allen. *The Brandeis/Frankfurter Connection: The Secret Political Activities of Two Supreme Court Justices.* New York: Oxford University Press, 1982.

Schmidhauser, John R., and Berg, Larry L. *The Supreme Court and Congress: Conflict and Interaction, 1945-1968.* New York: Free Press, 1972.

Scigliano, Robert. *The Supreme Court and the Presidency.* New York: Free Press, 1971.

Shapiro, Martin. *The Supreme Court and Administrative Agencies.* New York: Free Press, 1968.

Simon, James F. *Independent Journey: The Life of William O. Douglas.* New York: Harper & Row, 1980.

Ulmer, S. Sydney, ed. *Courts, Law, and Judicial Processes.* New York: Free Press, 1981.

Wilkinson, J. Harvie III. *Serving Justice: A Supreme Court Clerk's View.* New York: Charterhouse, 1974.

Chapter 2: The Justices

Abraham, Henry J. *Justices and Presidents: A Political History of Appointments to the Supreme Court.* New York: Oxford University Press, 1974.

Danelski, David J. *A Supreme Court Justice is Appointed.* New York: Random House, 1964.

Friedman, Leon, and Israel, Fred L., eds. *The Justices of the United States Supreme Court 1789-1969: Their Lives and Major Opinions.* New York: R. R. Bowker Co., 1969. (Updated with an additional volume in 1978.)

Schmidhauser, John R. *Judges and Justices: The Federal Appellate Judiciary.* Boston: Little, Brown & Co., 1979.

Shogan, Robert. *A Question of Judgment: The Fortas Case and the Struggle for the Supreme Court.* Indianapolis: Bobbs-Merrill Co., 1972.

Simon, James F. *In His Own Image: The Supreme Court in Richard Nixon's America.* New York: David McKay Co., 1973.

Chapter 3: The Cases

Casper, Gerhard, and Posner, Richard A. *The Workload of the Supreme Court.* Chicago: American Bar Foundation, 1976.

Casper, Jonathan D. *Lawyers Before the Warren Court: Civil Liberties and Civil Rights, 1957-66.* Urbana: University of Illinois Press, 1972.

Kluger, Richard. *Simple Justice: The History of Brown v. Board of Education and Black America's Struggle for Equality.* New York: Alfred A. Knopf, 1976.

Meltsner, Michael. *Cruel and Unusual: The Supreme Court and Capital Punishment.* New York: Random House, 1973.

O'Connor, Karen. *Women's Organizations' Use of the Courts.* Lexington, Mass.: Lexington Books, 1980.

Provine, Doris Marie. *Case Selection in the United States Supreme Court.* Chicago: University of Chicago Press, 1980.

Sorauf, Frank J. *The Wall of Separation: The Constitutional Politics of Church and State.* Princeton: Princeton University Press, 1976.

Vose, Clement E. *Constitutional Change*. Lexington, Mass.: D. C. Heath & Co., 1972.

Chapter 4: Decision Making

Hirsch, H. N. *The Enigma of Felix Frankfurter*. New York: Basic Books, 1981.

Howard, J. Woodford, Jr. *Mr. Justice Murphy: A Political Biography*. Princeton: Princeton University Press, 1968.

Murphy, Walter F. *Elements of Judicial Strategy*. Chicago: University of Chicago Press, 1964.

Rohde, David W., and Spaeth, Harold J. *Supreme Court Decision Making*. San Francisco: W. H. Freeman & Co., 1976.

Schwartz, Bernard. *Super Chief: Earl Warren and His Supreme Court— A Judicial Biography*. New York: New York University Press, 1983.

Wasby, Stephen L. *Continuity and Change: From the Warren Court to the Burger Court*. Pacific Palisades, Calif.: Goodyear Publishing Co., 1976.

Woodward, Bob, and Armstrong, Scott. *The Brethren: Inside the Supreme Court*. New York: Simon & Schuster, 1979.

Chapter 5: Policy Outputs

Blasi, Vincent, ed. *The Burger Court: The Counter-Revolution That Wasn't*. New Haven: Yale University Press, 1982.

Casper, Jonathan D. *The Politics of Civil Liberties*. New York: Harper & Row, 1972.

Halpern, Stephen C., and Lamb, Charles M., eds. *Supreme Court Activism and Restraint*. Lexington, Mass.: Lexington Books, 1982.

Horowitz, Donald L. *The Courts and Social Policy*. Washington, D.C.: Brookings Institution, 1977.

Mason, Alpheus Thomas. *The Supreme Court from Taft to Burger,* 3rd ed. Baton Rouge: Louisiana State University Press, 1979.

McCloskey, Robert G. *The American Supreme Court*. Chicago: University of Chicago Press, 1960.

Miller, Arthur Selwyn. *The Supreme Court and American Capitalism*. New York: Free Press, 1968.

Schubert, Glendon. *The Constitutional Polity*. Boston: Boston University Press, 1970.

Shapiro, Martin. *Law and Politics in the Supreme Court*. New York: Free Press, 1964.

Chapter 6: The Court's Impact

Becker, Theodore L., and Feeley, Malcolm M., eds. *The Impact of Supreme Court Decisions,* 2d ed. New York: Oxford University Press, 1973.

Bullock, Charles S. III, and Lamb, Charles M., eds. *Implementation of Civil Rights Policy.* Monterey, Calif.: Brooks/Cole Publishing Co., 1984.

Dolbeare, Kenneth M., and Hammond, Phillip E. *The School Prayer Decisions: From Court Policy to Local Practice.* Chicago: University of Chicago Press, 1971.

Jenson, Carol E. *The Network of Control: State Supreme Courts and State Security Statutes, 1920-1970.* Westport, Conn.: Greenwood Press, 1982.

Johnson, Charles A., and Canon, Bradley C. *Judicial Policies: Implementation and Impact.* Washington, D.C.: CQ Press, 1984.

Milner, Neal A. *The Court and Local Law Enforcement: The Impact of Miranda.* Beverly Hills: Sage Publications, 1971.

Muir, William K., Jr. *Prayer in the Public Schools: Law and Attitude Change.* Chicago: University of Chicago Press, 1967.

Murphy, Walter F. *Congress and the Court.* Chicago: University of Chicago Press, 1962.

Peltason, J. W. *Fifty-Eight Lonely Men: Southern Federal Judges and School Desegregation,* 2d ed. Urbana: University of Illinois Press, 1971.

Tarr, George Alan. *Judicial Impact and State Supreme Courts.* Lexington, Mass.: Lexington Books, 1977.

Wasby, Stephen L. *The Impact of the United States Supreme Court: Some Perspectives.* Homewood, Ill.: Dorsey Press, 1970.

Index of Cases

In this index the titles of cases are followed by citations to the legal reports in which they are contained. The abbreviation for the title of the set of reports is preceded by the volume number and followed by the page on which the case begins. The citations for nearly all Supreme Court decisions are to *U.S. Reports* (U.S.), the official report of Court decisions. Until 1875, a citation to a volume of official reports was to the name of the Court's reporter at the time. Citations for 1983 and 1984 cases that are not yet published in *U.S. Reports* are to the "Lawyer's Edition" (L. Ed. 2d), another set of reports of Supreme Court decisions. Lower court decisions have citations to the most commonly available set of reports for the courts involved.

Index